AMERICA'S CHILDREN

OPPOSING VIEWPOINTS®

Other Books of Related Interest in the Opposing Viewpoints Series:

American Values
Chemical Dependency
Civil Liberties
Criminal Justice
Economics in America
The Elderly
Health Crisis
The Homeless
Immigration
Male/Female Roles
Poverty
Social Justice
Teenage Sexuality
Violence in America
War on Drugs

AMERICA'S CHILDREN

OPPOSING VIEWPOINTS ®

David L. Bender & Bruno Leone, *Series Editors*

Carol Wekesser, *Book Editor*

OPPOSING VIEWPOINTS SERIES ®

Greenhaven Press, Inc.   PO Box 289009   San Diego, CA 92198-0009

Library of Congress Cataloging-in-Publication Data

America's children : opposing viewpoints / Carol Wekesser,
book editor.
    p.   cm. — (Opposing viewpoints series)
    Includes bibliographical references and index.
    Summary: Experts debate what school policies would help
children, how to protect children from abuse, the effects of
working parents on children, and if children are
disproportionately poor in the United States. Includes critical
thinking skills activities.
    ISBN 0-89908-461-3 (paper). — ISBN 0-89908-486-9 (library)
    1. Child welfare—United States—Juvenile literature.
2. Children—United States—Social conditions—Juvenile
literature.   3. Education—United States—Juvenile literature.
[1. Child welfare.   2. United States—Social conditions—1980-
3. Education.   4. Critical thinking.]   I. Wekesser, Carol, 1963-   .
II. Series: Opposing viewpoints series (Unnumbered)
HV741.A733   1991
362.7'0973—dc20   90-24085

"Congress shall make no law . . . abridging the freedom of speech, or of the press."

First Amendment to the U.S. Constitution

The basic foundation of our democracy is the first amendment guarantee of freedom of expression. The Opposing Viewpoints Series is dedicated to the concept of this basic freedom and the idea that it is more important to practice it than to enshrine it.

Contents

Chapter 3: What Government Policies Would Help America's Poor Children?

Chapter 4: How Can the Health of America's Children Be Improved?

Why Consider Opposing Viewpoints?

The Importance of Examining Opposing Viewpoints

The purpose of the Opposing Viewpoints Series, and this book in particular, is to present balanced, and often difficult to find, opposing points of view on complex and sensitive issues.

Probably the best way to become informed is to analyze the positions of those who are regarded as experts and well studied on issues. It is important to consider every variety of opinion in an attempt to determine the truth. Opinions from the mainstream of society should be examined. But also important are opinions that are considered radical, reactionary, or minority as well as those stigmatized by some other uncomplimentary label. An important lesson of history is the eventual acceptance of many unpopular and even despised opinions. The ideas of Socrates, Jesus, and Galileo are good examples of this.

Readers will approach this book with their own opinions on the issues debated within it. However, to have a good grasp of one's own viewpoint, it is necessary to understand the arguments of those with whom one disagrees. It can be said that those who do not completely understand their adversary's point of view do not fully understand their own.

A persuasive case for considering opposing viewpoints has been presented by John Stuart Mill in his work *On Liberty*. When examining controversial issues it may be helpful to reflect on this suggestion:

9

The only way in which a human being can make some approach to knowing the whole of a subject, is by hearing what can be said about it by persons of every variety of opinion, and studying all modes in which it can be looked at by every character of mind. No wise man ever acquired his wisdom in any mode but this.

Analyzing Sources of Information

The Opposing Viewpoints Series includes diverse materials taken from magazines, journals, books, and newspapers, as well as statements and position papers from a wide range of individuals, organizations, and governments. This broad spectrum of sources helps to develop patterns of thinking which are open to the consideration of a variety of opinions.

Pitfalls to Avoid

A pitfall to avoid in considering opposing points of view is that of regarding one's own opinion as being common sense and the most rational stance, and the point of view of others as being only opinion and naturally wrong. It may be that another's opinion is correct and one's own is in error.

Another pitfall to avoid is that of closing one's mind to the opinions of those with whom one disagrees. The best way to approach a dialogue is to make one's primary purpose that of understanding the mind and arguments of the other person and not that of enlightening him or her with one's own solutions. More can be learned by listening than speaking.

It is my hope that after reading this book the reader will have a deeper understanding of the issues debated and will appreciate the complexity of even seemingly simple issues on which good and honest people disagree. This awareness is particularly important in a democratic society such as ours where people enter into public debate to determine the common good. Those with whom one disagrees should not necessarily be regarded as enemies, but perhaps simply as people who suggest different paths to a common goal.

Developing Basic Reading and Thinking Skills

In this book, carefully edited opposing viewpoints are purposely placed back to back to create a running debate; each viewpoint is preceded by a short quotation that best expresses the author's main argument. This format instantly plunges the reader into the midst of a controversial issue and greatly aids that reader in mastering the basic skill of recognizing an author's point of view.

A number of basic skills for critical thinking are practiced in the activities that appear throughout the books in the series. Some of the skills are:

Evaluating Sources of Information. The ability to choose from among alternative sources the most reliable and accurate source in relation to a given subject.

Separating Fact from Opinion. The ability to make the basic distinction between factual statements (those that can be demonstrated or verified empirically) and statements of opinion (those that are beliefs or attitudes that cannot be proved).

Identifying Stereotypes. The ability to identify oversimplified, exaggerated descriptions (favorable or unfavorable) about people and insulting statements about racial, religious, or national groups, based upon misinformation or lack of information.

Recognizing Ethnocentrism. The ability to recognize attitudes or opinions that express the view that one's own race, culture, or group is inherently superior, or those attitudes that judge another culture or group in terms of one's own.

It is important to consider opposing viewpoints and equally important to be able to critically analyze those viewpoints. The activities in this book are designed to help the reader master these thinking skills. Statements are taken from the book's viewpoints and the reader is asked to analyze them. This technique aids the reader in developing skills that not only can be applied to the viewpoints in this book, but also to situations where opinionated spokespersons comment on controversial issues. Although the activities are helpful to the solitary reader, they are most useful when the reader can benefit from the interaction of group discussion.

Using this book and others in the series should help readers develop basic reading and thinking skills. These skills should improve the reader's ability to understand what is read. Readers should be better able to separate fact from opinion, substance from rhetoric, and become better consumers of information in our media-centered culture.

This volume of the Opposing Viewpoints Series does not advocate a particular point of view. Quite the contrary! The very nature of the book leaves it to the reader to formulate the opinions he or she finds most suitable. My purpose as publisher is to see that this is made possible by offering a wide range of viewpoints that are fairly presented.

David L. Bender
Publisher

Introduction

"The test of a civilization is in the way that it cares for its helpless members."

Pearl S. Buck

Most of America's children are fortunate. They are healthy, well-fed, safe from abuse, and educated. Yet the lives of a significant minority of children are marred by poverty, neglect, or abuse. According to a 1990 *Time* magazine cover story, nearly one in four children under the age of six lives in poverty, and every forty-seven seconds a child is abused or neglected. Child advocate Bob Keeshan states, "The children of America are at a greater risk today than at any time in recent memory."

The implications of society's neglect go far beyond a single child or a single generation. "The inattention to children by our society poses a greater threat to our safety, harmony, and productivity than any external enemy," asserts Marian Wright Edelman, founder of the Children's Defense Fund. Experts on both sides of the political fence agree that children who are abused and neglected are likely to present serious problems to society when they become adults. Child abuse expert Andrew Vachss states that abused children "are the recruits for an ever-growing army of predatory criminals. Today's victim is tomorrow's predator."

Most of these neglected, troubled children live in homes torn apart by social problems such as poverty and substance abuse. For example, one-quarter of America's children live with parents struggling to survive on less than $12,675 a year, the official poverty line. Two-thirds of abused and neglected children live in households where drugs are used. And many troubled children have had their lives disrupted by divorce and separation. Parents burdened with drug and alcohol problems, poverty, divorce, or homelessness often cannot adequately care for children. Single parents are overwhelmed with responsibilities, chemically dependent parents are unable to conquer their addictions, and impoverished parents find it hard to afford food, clothing, and health care. Consequently, helping troubled children is complicated by finding ways to help their troubled parents.

While society must focus on the needs of this suffering minority, it also needs to address other widespread problems, such as inadequate child care and education, that affect a majority of

America's families. How society will deal with these problems, and whether children will continue to be a neglected minority in America, remain to be seen. *America's Children: Opposing Viewpoints* presents debates concerning the welfare of children and asks the following questions: What Education Policies Would Help Children? How Can Children Be Protected from Abuse? What Government Policies Would Help America's Poor Children? How Can the Health of America's Children Be Improved? Are Working Parents Harming America's Children? The welfare of a nation's children is of utmost importance to all its citizens. In the words of New York governor Mario Cuomo, "If compassion were not enough to encourage our attention to the plight of our children, self-interest should be."

What Education Policies Would Help Children?

AMERICA'S CHILDREN

Chapter Preface

Joel Pett/*Lexington Herald-Leader*. Reprinted with permission.

America's educational system is ineffective, in the opinion of many parents and professionals. In 1990, the SAT (Scholastic Aptitude Test) scores of high school seniors fell for the fourth year in a row. In a 1990 study by the National Endowment for the Humanities, more than 40 percent of college seniors did not know when the Civil War was fought. And in a comparison with other industrialized nations, American high-school seniors finished last in a National Science Foundation test.

Blame for the schools' failures is not easy to pinpoint, as the above cartoon illustrates. Parents blame teachers for a lack of real interest and understanding of children, teachers blame society for its unwillingness to support schools with increased taxes, and society blames parents for being inattentive to and unconcerned about their own children. Meanwhile, America's children continue to graduate with less knowledge and fewer skills than children in nearly all other developed nations.

The problems of America's schools are of concern to many Americans, for the uneducated children of today will be the uneducated—and unproductive—adults of the future. The authors in the following chapter discuss the problems America's schools face and offer possible solutions.

"Either America pays now for educational excellence, or it pays more, much more, later."

Increased Spending on Education Would Help Children

Ann Reilly Dowd

Many experts maintain that America's educational system needs to be reformed. In the following viewpoint, Ann Reilly Dowd argues that these reforms cost money. Government spending on education must increase, she contends, if America's children are going to have better teachers, textbooks, and educational programs. Dowd is an associate editor for *Fortune* magazine.

As you read, consider the following questions:

1. Why must the states, rather than the federal government, bear most of the burden of improving America's schools, according to Dowd?
2. What does the author believe is the most important thing the president can do for education?
3. What are some states doing to attract better teachers, according to the author?

By the year 2000, every child must start school ready to learn.
The United States must increase the high school graduation rate to
no less than 90%.
In critical subjects, at the fourth, eighth, and 12th grades, we must
assess our students' performance.
U.S. students must be the first in the world in math and science
achievement.
Every American adult must be a skilled, literate worker and citi-
zen.
Every school must offer the kind of disciplined environment that
makes it possible for our kids to learn.
And every school must be drug free.

—President George Bush
"The State of the Union," January 31, 1990

Great goals, Mr. President. Now it's time for you and the
governors to get to work. By most measures the nation's education system is badly broken. Despite a doubling of spending in
the 1980s, standardized test scores remain low, below those of
our leading competitors. "We can't fix the system," says
American Federation of Teachers President Albert Shanker with
painful honesty. "We need radical change."

Nearly everyone agrees that states must take the lead. The
Constitution omits any reference to education among federal
powers, so the responsibility lies by implication with them.
Along with local governments, states pay 86% of America's education bill. Moreover, the statehouse is closer to the problems—
and the solutions. Says South Carolina Governor Carroll Campbell
Jr., co-chairman of the National Governors' Association Education Task Force: "Communities need flexibility in dealing with
their particular areas. Parents don't want the federal government running education."

Evaluating Bush

Still, the President can focus public attention on the need for
educational reform. George Bush already has earned an A for
rhetoric by proclaiming goals, convening the first government-
sponsored education summit, and honoring a teacher of the
year. But to be worthy of the title Education President, he also
needs to muster the resources of the executive branch to
achieve results. On that score, he gets an Incomplete.

A President wise in the ways of Washington and committed to
education reform would appoint a more dynamic Education
Secretary than Lauro Cavazos, the first Hispanic president of
Texas Tech University, who seems to have been picked more for
ethnic balance than for his reformist zeal. Such a President

would create a new Cabinet Council on Human Resource Development that pulled together the Secretaries of Education, Labor, Health and Human Services, Agriculture, and Treasury, plus the Budget Director, for an all-out drive toward educational excellence. He would also appoint a high-level adviser in the White House to push important initiatives through political roadblocks. But Bush has done none of these things. Says former Labor Secretary Ann McLaughlin: "Managing U.S.-Soviet relations alone won't keep America strong. We need a national commitment to lifelong learning."

Though Bush has shown no interest in major increases in federal spending to improve education, he should. An epidemic of social ills from drug abuse to homelessness continues to distract youngsters from the business of learning. Washington must attack these problems more aggressively and improve the delivery of social services to the needy. One way is to tie federal aid to states to the development of so-called one-stop service centers in or near schools where poor people can get food stamps, housing, job training, and other kinds of help all in one place.

Joel Pett/*Lexington Herald-Leader.* Reprinted with permission.

The single most important thing President Bush can do is push for more money for existing federal programs that prepare poor children for school. The highly effective Head Start preschool program, for instance, reaches about a fifth of the poor children eligible for it. But the Head Start budget should plan for higher teacher salaries and better quality control—not just more students.

Nutrition and Health Care

Washington should also spend more on programs that provide nutrition and health care for needy children. A good example is federal legislation financing comprehensive social service centers along the lines of Chicago's innovative Beethoven Project. Funded from public and private sources, Beethoven trains older women in public housing developments to visit expectant mothers and tell them about available prenatal care, family counseling, and other social services. The program also provides health care, nutrition, and preschool classes for neighborhood children.

The payoffs from such investments are enormous both for individuals and for society. The House Select Committee on Children, Youth, and Families reports that a dollar invested in prenatal care saves up to $3 in hospital costs alone. A dollar invested in preschool education saves as much as $6 in special education, welfare, crime, and lost productivity. Says Ernest Boyer, president of the Carnegie Foundation for the Advancement of Teaching: "Early intervention is powerfully in America's self-interest."

The Administration can use its regulatory muscle as an instrument of change. Federal aid to education is so narrowly structured that it can penalize performance. For instance, computers bought with "Chapter 1" money for educationally disadvantaged children cannot be used at night to teach adults to read. And if a school succeeds in keeping more students from dropping out or failing, aid is reduced. The National Center on Education and the Economy, chaired by Apple Computer CEO [Chief Executive Officer] John Sculley, has a sensible alternative: Allow states greater flexibility in the use of federal funds in exchange for adopting—and living by—ambitious student performance goals. Legislation along those lines introduced by Vermont Congressman Peter Smith deserves serious attention by Congress.

The federal government should play a more extensive role in educational research and development. While the Department of Education has established some measures of student achievement nationally, it lacks the budget and in many cases the legal authority to gather information needed to compare countries, states, school districts, schools, or individual students. Education administrators, testing companies, and the Parent-Teacher Association—representing mostly teachers—have objected vehemently to some of the small steps Congress has taken to increase federal oversight. Educators object on grounds that accurate measures are not possible. But critics think they're mainly worried that comparisons will show how badly they're doing.

Some states are developing their own new measurements, but a coordinated approach demands federal leadership. A good beginning is New Mexico Senator Jeff Bingaman's national report card bill, which would set up a commission of experts to assess progress toward national goals, identify gaps in existing data, and make recommendations for improved testing.

Pilot Projects

Finally, Washington can spur innovation through well-designed pilot projects. The President has focused on the worthy goal of better teaching. His proposals include merit pay for excellent teachers and grants to states to improve math and science teaching and to develop alternative certification procedures.

The Proof Is in the Pocketbook

If the nation and its political leadership are serious about the need to improve the public schools for the sake of our economic well-being and civic health, then we have to prove it in the way this society proclaims its loyalties in every other field—through the pocketbook.

And what we spend for education has to be targeted to those areas and people who need it the most. Ignoring or, even worse, reinforcing educational inequity is a surefire prescription for educational failure. As Lyndon Johnson said years ago: "Progress in education won't solve all our problems. But without progress in education, we can't solve any of our problems."

Hodding Carter III, *The Wall Street Journal*, October 5, 1989.

But he has missed one enormous opportunity: the chance to lead the way to the classroom of the future by underwriting the development of interactive video software and training teachers in its use. Says California school superintendent Bill Honig, who has developed a new history video program with Lucasfilm, Apple Computer, and National Geographic: "Such investments can pay huge dividends."

Many governors have been pushing reform long enough to understand what works and what doesn't. Strategies are beginning to change. Most early efforts focused on tough rules: tighter course requirements, higher teacher certification standards, and the like. But performance did not improve markedly. Now many states are concentrating on results. Says Chester Finn, assistant secretary of education in the Reagan Administration: "The shift from regulating means to regulating ends represents a historic change."

The first state to move wholeheartedly in that direction was

California. In 1983 the state's Democratic leaders launched a major drive to prepare youngsters for the new information-age job market and to function as citizens of a democracy. The goal-setting process involved educators, parents, community leaders, business, and labor. The state-financed program involved heavy investment in new technology and teacher development, and resulted in major changes in curriculum, textbooks, teaching methods, and testing. Schools were encouraged to seek waivers from any state regulations they felt got in the way of specific programs. The result: Despite a surge in enrollments—including many poor and bilingual children—eighth-graders' performance improved 25% in three years.

South Carolina followed a similar course with equally impressive results. In six years the state raised average scores on the Scholastic Aptitude Test 40 points, more than any other state. Fifteen other states have enacted such reforms, including Kentucky, which was forced to do so by the Kentucky Supreme Court. Because of the way Kentucky's schools were funded, among other problems, the court ruled that the whole system violated the state's constitution. Starting from scratch, the state has opted for a performance-based system that gives unprecedented freedom and responsibility to individual schools.

What lessons can be drawn from these pioneering efforts? First, successful reform requires cooperation among traditionally combative power centers. Responsibility must flow from the statehouse to the schoolhouse without loss of accountability. Business must get involved. School administrators and union leaders must share control with teachers, parents, and students.

Accountability Is the Key

It isn't easy. Says New Mexico Governor Garrey E. Carruthers, a Republican who maneuvered a sweeping reform package through his Democratic legislature: "Make no mistake, it takes political leverage, good old-fashioned horse trading, and more money." To win support, Carruthers had to raise teachers' and administrators' salaries, fund after-school programs, and offer extra money to schools that restructured. The cost: $50 million a year more in revenues, raised through a 0.25% increase in gross-receipts taxes. His fellow Republicans howled, but the governor finally persuaded them with stiff accountability standards embedded in a report card bill. All 88 school districts must now report annually on how well their students do. Says Carruthers: "The key was accountability."

Many reform governors have found that accountability demands new measures of performance. Across America, most public schools rely on multiple-choice tests that measure a student's retention of facts but not the analytical skills that will be needed in the future. Critics say standardized tests discriminate

22

against minorities and distort classroom instruction by putting too much emphasis on memorization.

To refocus students and teachers on creative thinking and teamwork, several states are experimenting with new forms of testing. Vermont plans to test fourth- and eighth-graders in writing and math using three methods: a uniform test, a portfolio of work developed over the course of the year, and a single piece chosen by the student.

Improvement Requires Money

It is almost. . .impossible to obtain across-the-board educational improvement without money. To put it another way, the vast majority of school districts with the highest test scores and the highest public retention rates are those that spend the most money on their students.

Hodding Carter III, *The Wall Street Journal*, October 5, 1989.

In 1991, Connecticut will launch a new math and science assessment of high school students involving tasks that may take student teams as long as a semester to complete. A sample assignment: design, carry out, and report on an experiment to determine which food store in your community would save a family of four the most money over the course of a year.

Making the Grade

Once standards are set, schools must be held to them. Minnesota, Nebraska, Iowa, Arkansas, and Ohio rely on consumers to provide discipline. In the most radical change in the history of U.S. public school education, these states allow parental choice—students can attend any public school in the state.

Eight other states intervene directly when schools don't make the grade. In the best systems the state first offers financial and managerial assistance. If that fails, the state takes over the school or shuts it down. One South Carolina elementary school was turned around when state officials introduced IBM's innovative Writing to Read computer program. In Jersey City, school administrators stuck with their methods even when the dropout rate topped 30%. Thomas Kean, who was then New Jersey's governor, threw out the recalcitrants and installed a new management team.

A way to win teachers' support is to free them of the regulatory strings that bind them like Gulliver lying on the beach. State boards of education often dictate what teachers teach and from what texts. States also control pay. Excellence is rarely rewarded: Pay is generally based on years served—or in some cases endured. Many teachers lack career ladders: a 30-year veteran does the same work as a new recruit.

Connecticut put teacher excellence at the center of its restructuring plan. The state has raised pay almost 40% since 1986 to an average $37,339, and increased standards. New teachers serve under experienced mentors. Veterans have to take 90 hours of professional development every five years, at state expense.

Finding Quality Teachers

New Jersey eliminated its shortage of quality teachers through an alternative certification process launched by Kean. Applicants without traditional education degrees have to pass a test and agree to a year of supervision and after-hours training. Says Kean: "It means engineers from Bell Labs can teach computer science, jazz musicians can teach music, and former private-school teachers can work in the public schools. The profession is revitalized, and there's a great big teacher surplus." Twenty-seven states are following New Jersey's lead. . . .

Another key is higher student expectations and opportunities. That's what Minnesota Governor Rudy Perpich learned from his pioneering program that gives 11th- and 12th-graders a state stipend to attend classes at state colleges and universities. Says Perpich, who also started the nation's first statewide choice program: "A number of students drop out because they are bored. Of all our reforms, this one is doing the most for education."

Louisiana Governor Buddy Roemer learned the same lesson from a generous oilman. Two years ago Patrick F. Taylor offered to pay college tuition for 180 poor seventh- and eighth-graders—most of whom had repeated two or more grades—if they stayed out of trouble and graduated from high school with a B average. Today 150 are still in high school (19 moved, 11 were dismissed). On the precollege ACT test, half the tenth-graders scored at least 18, close to the national average. Inspired by Taylor's kids, Roemer pushed a bill through the legislature that puts state money behind a similar statewide program. . . .

Who will pay for such promising reforms? Ideally, all levels of government. But given Bush's no-new-taxes posture, the reality is that state and local governments will have to pick up the check for most of them. That's not necessarily bad. Many governors, like Carruthers, have had the courage to raise taxes. And if New Mexico is a bellwether, voters have grasped a truth that still escapes many politicians: Either America pays now for educational excellence, or it pays more, much more, later.

VIEWPOINT

"More money will not improve our schools. "

Increased Spending on Education Would Not Help Children

John Hood

John Hood, a contributing editor for the conservative magazine *Reason*, completed a study on education for the Cato Institute, a conservative think tank. In the following viewpoint, excerpted from that study, Hood argues that while educational reforms are necessary, increased spending is not. Several studies have shown that the amount of money a school spends is not related to the performance of the school's students, he maintains. Hood suggests that market influences—such as allowing parents to choose the schools their children will attend—are necessary to reform America's educational system.

As you read, consider the following questions:

1. What examples does the author give to show that school expenditures are not related to student performance?
2. Why does Hood believe that teachers' pay should not be increased?
3. Why does Hood believe that the results of several Gallup polls show that Americans are confused about school reform?

John Hood, "Education: Is America Spending Too Much?" *Cato Institute Policy Analysis,* January 18, 1990. Reprinted with permission.

When *A Nation at Risk* made its spectacular appearance in 1983, chronicling the deterioration of American schooling and the ignorance of graduates, the educational reform debate featured a cacophony of voices. Vastly different schools of thought were competing for center stage. Advocates of progressive education, who wanted to dissolve structured curricula and competitive grading, battled it out with tradition-minded conservatives seeking a return to school prayer, paddling, and the pledge of allegiance. Fad schools based on the ideas of John Dewey, Maria Montessori, and Jean Piaget were still in vogue. Political interest groups fought to introduce their pet causes, such as the nuclear freeze and sexual abstinence, into the school day. Busing, city-county mergers, and other forms of integration were still causing dissension. People debated the wisdom of lengthening the school year, teaching foreign languages in elementary schools, tracking skills, and other substantive proposals.

Today, after years of nonstop reform talk, cacophony has become chorus. Among politicians, teachers' groups, the prestige press, and educational bureaucrats, the great questions of American schooling have degenerated into a single message: the United States is not "investing in human capital"—in other words, we are not spending enough on education. . . .

Media Demand for More Spending

The media now banter about financing with exuberant ease. President Bush, who wants to be known as the Education President, won't put his money where his mouth is, network anchors confide with knowing smiles. In the realm of international business competition, write crusty *Washington Post* business reporters, America doesn't have the will to make tough investment choices. And compassionate commentators remark on the poor rural school district that spends only half as much per pupil as does the nearby city district—as if that means rural students receive half the education their urban peers do.

For most Washington politicians and the national media, how education should be structured and directed has become simply a question of dollars and cents; they assume that each increment of funding creates an increment of learning. Their fixation is completely divorced from reality. In the past three decades, spending on education has risen steadily to a level unsurpassed in U.S. history and, indeed, to one of the highest in the world. Meanwhile, academic researchers have conducted study after study, trying to find evidence for the spending-equals-learning theory. They haven't. And all the while, experiments in the trenches—from inner-city schools in Harlem to suburban schools in Minnesota—have been demonstrating that local control and parental choice, structural changes that are money neutral, hold the key to real educational reform.

26

Somehow such major news events have escaped the notice of the reform chorus, whose members continue, undaunted, to peddle their flawed vision of our educational woes. Theirs is a bill of goods that Americans, frustrated with inferior schools, will certainly buy—unless they get better consumer information.

Bill Garner. Reprinted with permission.

There has never been a time in recent U.S. history when government (federal, state, and local) has stopped "investing" in education. From the 1929-30 school year, the first on which comprehensive data are available, to the 1986-87 school year, total real expenditures per pupil in American public schools rose by 500 percent. More recently, total real expenditures shot up from $2,229 per pupil in 1965-66 to $4,206 per pupil 20 years later, an 89 percent hike. Keep in mind that this increase was *after inflation*, meaning that actual buying power available to schools almost doubled during that period. Real spending in the 1980s, during all the Reagan-era cuts we hear so much about, actually grew at a faster rate—21 percent between 1981-82 and 1986-87—than in the previous decade, when it increased by "only" 16 percent.

Naturally, the reform chorus tries to downplay the fact that spending is up, has always gone up, and given current trends, will continue to go up. Some of the more unscrupulous choristers use measures, such as year-to-year changes expressed as gross dollar amounts, to show that spending increases have been less than steady. That practice, of course, ignores the effect of the baby boom—there were significantly fewer students in the 1980s than there were in the 1960s. Adjusting for expenditure per pupil is the only way to relate spending to the number of students enrolled.

The National Education Association, however, is more careful about its statistics in this instance. Its most recent *Estimates of School Statistics* reports accurately that current expenditures per pupil (similar to the measure used above, but excluding such costs as school construction) have risen about 31 percent since 1978-79. That would seem to be a major increase, *after inflation*, but the NEA reports it as an increase of "only" 31 percent. The fact that American public schools have on average almost a third more resources to commit to teaching children today than they did only 10 years ago is treated as a failing of government. The NEA's perspective is, in a word, bizarre. In the text accompanying the data, the NEA remarks:

> The financing of public elementary and secondary schools presents several challenges to educators and policymakers in the current context of educational reform, state-local fiscal constraint, enrollment growth, teacher shortages, and the deficit-reduction policies pursued by the national government.

What's so challenging about learning to live with 31 percent *more* money per pupil?. . .

Spending and Learning Are Not Linked

Try as they may, researchers have not been able to prove the common assumption that the richer schools are, the better taught are their students. More precisely, while it is obvious that a school that spends $4 per pupil a year will probably do a poorer job than one that spends $4,000 per pupil, it's not so clear that a school that spends $2,500 per pupil is less capable of providing a good education than one that spends $4,000. That magnitude of difference does not appear to be a significant predictor of educational success.

Certainly the historical trends fly in the face of the spending-equals-learning thesis. As noted above, total real spending on education grew by 89 percent from 1965-66 to 1985-86. Yet during the same period, average Scholastic Achievement Test scores of college-bound high school seniors fell 16 points on the mathematics test and 30 points on the verbal test; the percentage of 17-year-olds who graduated from high school fell; and other measures of educational achievement also showed a downward trend.

The Washington, D.C., area is a perfect case in point. In 1987 D.C. public schools spent over $5,700 per pupil—compared with the national average of about $4,000. In the same year Maryland spent $4,400 per pupil and Virginia spent $3,800. But are D.C. students that much more educated than their peers in Maryland and Virginia? Quite the contrary: D.C.'s graduation rate was 55 percent, Maryland's was 75 percent, and Virginia's was 74 percent (the U.S. average was 71 percent). D.C. students had, on average, lower scores on the SAT and achievement tests as well. There is obviously a better prescription for educational success than government spending. . . .

Money-Based Reforms

Despite the stubborn refusal of the empirical data to support the spending-equals-learning thesis, the choral advocates of educational reform in the middle and late 1980s have maintained an inordinate focus on money. Let us briefly examine two of their proposals: teacher-related changes (pay hikes, workload, quality issues) and school district equity.

Polite Extortion

Opposition to education reform has surfaced as a voice advising that things might be fixed, they could be fixed, even they should be fixed, but they will require lots of money first. This is polite extortion. This most durable and persistent lament is nothing short of hijacking education reform and holding it for ransom. The American people have paid and paid dearly for education, but as yet they have not been given their money's worth. They have not been given the good results they and their children deserve.

William J. Bennett, *Our Children & Our Country*, 1988.

It is just plain common sense to examine the provider of a service—in education, the teacher—when the service is deteriorating. Thus, we have been bombarded with stories about teachers—stories that are cheered by teachers' unions and others that advocate "getting tough" with inferior teachers.

First, it is constantly asserted that teachers are "underpaid." Everyone has a teacher in the family who is only too happy to support that assertion with personal testimony; both my parents work in elementary education, so I've heard the complaints all my life. But the data show that teachers are reasonably well paid—they're not rich, but they are far from starving.

Most analyses of teachers' salaries leave out the fact that teacher pension plans are, on average, more generous than are those available to private-sector employees: 22 percent of salary compared with 19 percent for private workers. In some states, such as California and New York, teachers' pensions are 35 percent of salary. Keep in mind that those pension plans were established decades ago; the large increases in spending on education over the last few years may push pension figures even higher.

Teachers Work Less

One also has to take into account the fact that teachers are given summer and other vacations. They work about 180 days a year, and their regular workday, at least, averages less than the usual eight hours. It is true that night grading and other off-campus work should be factored into the equation, but one would be hard pressed to prove that teachers actually work more hours a week than many private-sector employees. (They do get up earlier than most, and working with kids all day long probably merits hazard pay, but the salary crisis is nevertheless overblown.). . .

In addition, the quality of teaching has become the subject of much discussion and experimentation. Merit pay, "master teacher" programs, and other reforms have been tried—despite the vehement objections of teachers' unions, it should be noted— but the results are mixed. Take merit pay, which sounds like a solid, market-based approach: pay the best teachers more and the inferior teachers less, and you'll have a better product.

In practice, there are a number of problems with implementing merit pay. Administrators don't want the extra responsibility of discriminating among teachers, which is understandable, but that creates real problems for merit programs in which outside evaluators judge teachers on the basis of one or two visits to the classroom. School districts are trying to superimpose a private-sector perspective on an enterprise that is still, in most areas, centrally controlled and financed. Unless principals can be allowed, and ordered, to reward their teachers on the basis of steady, day-to-day observation, merit pay will flop. Another approach, master teacher programs that increase the stipends of good, experienced teachers and give them some administrative duties, has also failed in real-world tests. Its chief failing is that taking the best teachers out of the classroom part of the time, even to give advice to struggling teachers, makes no sense at all.

Effects of Teacher-Based Reforms

Given the problems with teacher-based reforms, it should come as no surprise that studies have identified few benefits from them. Overall, according to Eric A. Hanushek's survey, 78 percent of studies on teachers' salaries found that they had no impact on students' performance.

The reform chorus has lately been singing the praises of equity reforms, which seek to equalize government spending on school districts throughout a given state. . . .
It's hard to believe the current focus on equity finance given the copious research on the weak link between expenditures and educational success. Equity reforms do everything that research says is wasteful and counterproductive: redistribute funds from rich to poor districts; increase centralized state control over curriculum and management; and focus public and governmental attention on teachers' salaries, class sizes, and per pupil spending. Unfortunately, more than a few proponents of equity reform see a parallel between equalizing spending across a state and equalizing spending nationwide. "Some students are more fortunate than others—simply by geographic accident," states Professor Allan Ornstein of Loyola University matter-of-factly. "State residence has a lot to do with the quality of education received.". . .

Increased Spending, Decreased Performance

For the last several decades, we've listened to claptrap by education experts and watched public schools deteriorate, while spending on education escalated. Just since 1982, per-pupil spending in public schools has risen 26 percent, and education bureaucracies have increased while student enrollment dropped. In Chicago, host to perhaps the nation's worst schools, between 1976 and 1986 enrollment declined almost 20 percent, but the number of public school administrators went up by almost 50 percent.

The education establishment and their political lap dogs say the solution lies in more tax dollars. But study after study shows little or no relationship between expenditure and pupil performance; nor between better school facilities, class size, and pupil performance.

Walter E. Williams, *Manchester Union Leader,* May 8, 1990.

Teaching reforms, equity financing, and other money-based detours have distracted American policymakers while more effective *structural* reforms have, with less publicity, proven their worth. Experiments in decentralization, local control of schools (in Chicago, by parent-teacher councils), and parental choice have been adequately reported elsewhere, but a few points about school finance and public opinion are in order.

Creating a Market for Education
First, the school districts that have had the most success with local control and choice, such as East Harlem, New York, started out at the bottom of the barrel in terms of per pupil ex-

penditure and student performance. Allowing choice to create a market for education, with the requisite gains in teaching effectiveness, management, and student achievement, is basically a revenue-neutral change. Since that flies in the face of all the assertions about underinvestment and spending causality, the NEA, the prestige press, and other members of the chorus must have either ignored or misunderstood the test cases. After all, the very foundations of their beliefs about education and government are called into question by choice reform successes. . . .

The American public, moreover, has not yet realized that the successful choice experiments (which they support) discredit the standard raise-taxes-to-invest-in-schools line (which they also support). According to the Gallup Organization's comprehensive 1987 poll on educational issues, 71 percent of respondents supported giving parents "the right to choose which local schools their children attend.". . .

At the same time, respondents wholeheartedly supported other reforms, such as national minimum standards, that would increase centralized control rather than weaken it. . . . In a 1988 Gallup poll, 64 percent of Americans said they were willing to pay higher taxes for better schools, a 6 percent increase since 1983.

Those results should not be interpreted as public endorsement of more spending for education. Americans are desperate; they know the public schools are failing to provide their children with crucial skills, particularly in math and science, that will determine their economic fate. In the absence of any alternatives, Americans will pay more taxes in hopes of improving schools.

Educational Marketplace Is Needed

Sadly, though, more money will not improve our schools. The history of funding for education over the last three decades, the overwhelming consensus of academic research, and the common sense principles of market efficiency establish that conclusion with undeniable finality. Only structural changes that give parents the power to demand quality in an educational marketplace will achieve real results. But this fact, supported by principle and experience, hasn't yet changed the reform chorus's tune. With knowing smiles, chorus members continue to call for more "investment," for "putting your money where your mouth is." They are smug—and they are wrong.

"I consider choice the cornerstone to restructuring elementary and secondary education in this country."

Allowing Parents to Choose Among Schools Would Help Children

Lauro F. Cavazos

Lauro F. Cavazos is the former secretary of education under the Bush administration. In the following viewpoint, Cavazos suggests that the best way to reform America's schools is to allow parents to choose which schools their children will attend. To keep their students and remain open, bad schools will have to improve, he believes, and schools will be forced to compete for students. Cavazos maintains that this competition is the key to improving all of America's schools.

As you read, consider the following questions:

1. Name the six examples of school restructuring Cavazos gives.
2. Why does Cavazos believe having a choice of schools will benefit disadvantaged children?
3. Why does the author believe parents will become more involved in their children's education if they are given a choice of schools?

Lauro F. Cavazos, "Restructuring American Education Through Choice," speech given to the Education Press Association, Washington, D.C., May 19, 1989.

This nation suffers from three deficits—a trade deficit, a budget deficit and an education deficit. All three of these deficits are linked and, I submit, that the trade and budget deficits will not be resolved until we overcome the education deficit.

One can quantitate the trade and budget deficits. It is done daily in Washington to the nearest million. I can quantitate the education deficit:

—27 million adults are illiterate

—28 percent of our students drop out of high school

—the national high school graduation rate is only 71.5 percent

—SAT and ACT scores have declined or remained static for the last three years

—U.S. students score low in math and science when compared to their peers in other industrialized nations.

By any measure one wishes to apply, we are failing or not making progress.

What is the solution? I believe that we must first have a national commitment to excellence in education and, second, we must restructure elementary and secondary education in this nation.

By restructuring, I mean developing and implementing strategies that will improve the educational process at the elementary and secondary school level. Some examples of restructuring include:

—curriculum reform that results in better education

—alternative certification of teachers and principals

—early childhood education to make every experience of young children a learning situation

—more educational decision authority for teachers and parents

—educational deregulation or cutting red tape

—choice.

Again, a total restructuring and we must start now. Time is against us and for too long decisions on what is taught by our schools have been the exclusive province of professional educators. We have paid a high price for that exclusivity in lowered parental interest and a boring sameness among our schools. Again and again, scholars studying American education have bemoaned a widespread lack of parental concern and involvement in the education of their children and noted a remarkable national uniformity in the methods and organization of our schools.

New Level of Diversity

But this is changing. Lately, we have begun to see glimmerings of a new level of diversity in American education, a diversity based on providing parents and students with an array of choices in both the form and substance of educational offerings. Whenever choice appears, commitment and involvement in education have been revitalized, and that revitalization sets the scene for a leap forward in achievement. It is that crucial next step, the provision of choice in education, that I would like to discuss with you today. I consider choice the cornerstone to restructuring elementary and secondary education in this country.

© 1985 John Trever/*The Albuquerque Journal.* Reprinted with permission.

Why do I believe so strongly in choice in education? Because I believe in young people like Andre Lawrence and Chris Schaefer.

Andre [attends] the Jose Feliciano School for the Performing Arts in East Harlem. This young man lives on the Lower East Side of Manhattan and must leave his home shortly after dawn each morning to catch the subway which takes him across the city to East Harlem. Andre could walk to a neighborhood school but it doesn't offer the curriculum that interests him and there are problems with drugs near the school. At the School for Performing Arts, he has grown academically and polished his considerable skills in music. And his musical talent would have gone untapped if he had not had a magnet school to attend. Thus, choice provided education and opportunity.

Chris Schaefer almost dropped out of school two years ago. To quote Chris, he was "sleepwalking through his classes" in his local high school, in a state of "educational depression." The choice reforms in Minnesota saved Chris as a student. With support from his mother, he enrolled at the Chisago-Pine Area Learning Center. In his new school, Chris developed his potential as a writer and his grades have improved.

Andre and Chris have had the advantage of choice in education. Working with their parents, they determined the school that would provide the best education for them.

Because of choice, we have seen remarkable changes in East Harlem. Test scores have risen and admission of students from East Harlem to the selective high schools in the city has climbed dramatically. It is axiomatic that good schools take care of and educate all students to their fullest potential. The blueprint is clear—all we need to do is to follow it to bring about positive change.

Success in Minnesota

Minnesota has been putting the nation's most ambitious statewide choice program into effect since 1985. This program offers open enrollment across district lines, post-secondary options, and area learning centers, like the one Chris attends. The successes here have inspired Iowa and Arkansas to enact open enrollment legislation, and it is reported that 21 states are considering choice programs.

All our young people should have the opportunities offered by choice that have benefited students like Andre and Chris. We must do away with ineffective conventional arrangements that only block reform.

It is expected that choice will promote school reform. Initially we tried to improve education by imposing regulations from the top down while leaving the basic structure of our schools untouched. Obviously, this has not worked.

In the current movement of reform, schools must be responsive to parents, students and teachers. To accomplish this, schools need the freedom to change and innovate.

Schools should remain accountable, of course, but accountable to parents, teachers and students as well as to central administrators.

In short, we must infuse our schools with the ingredients that are essential to any enterprise—entrepreneurship and accountability. Choice offers this opportunity.

The failings of our school system today affect all children, but none more severely than America's minority and disadvantaged young people. You are well aware of the tragic situation in some of our inner-city and rural schools where it is common for half or more of the minority students to drop out . . . and for those who do graduate to go out into the world unprepared for college and the workplace.

It's not enough to deplore the situation or to blame it on a supposed lack of money. We already spend more on our students than any major industrialized country in the world. No, as I emphasized earlier, I believe that we can no longer patch, adjust, tinker and complain. It is time to act. The solution is restructuring and the catalyst is choice.

Academic Needs

No child, no matter his or her circumstances, should be compelled to attend a failing school, or one that does not meet their academic needs. Choice offers parents, students and teachers the opportunity to select the better schools if the neighborhood school is faulty or if it cannot satisfy educational requirements. Through choice, we can exercise the same kind of judgment in selecting schools that we take for granted in making other decisions.

The Most Promising Reform

The most innovative and promising reforms to have gained momentum during the late eighties fall under the heading of "choice.". . .

This new movement puts choice to use as part of a larger set of strategies for reform *within* the public sector. It is not about privatizing the public schools, nor is it a surreptitious way of giving aid to religious schools. Choice is being embraced by liberals and conservatives alike as a powerful means of transforming the structure and performance of public education—while keeping the public schools public.

John E. Chubb and Terry M. Moe, *Politics, Markets, & America's Schools*, 1990.

Those who have benefited from choice are pleased with it. Yet, relatively few students have access to choice despite the benefits. This must be changed.

President Bush has called for "a second great wave of education reform" where choice is "perhaps the single most promising" idea. As David Kearns, the Chairman of Xerox, says, "To be successful, the new agenda for school reform must be driven by competition and market discipline . . . the objective should be clear from the outset: complete restructuring. . . . The public schools must change if we are to survive."

Where choice is used, it works. Charles Glenn, the civil rights director for the Massachusetts Department of Education, says choice can promote equity, ". . . by creating conditions which encourage schools to become more effective . . . by allowing schools to specialize and thus to meet the needs of some students very well rather than all students at a level of minimum adequacy, and . . . by increasing the influence of parents over the education of their children in a way which is largely conflict free. We have become excited about the potential of choice for public education."

Strength from Diversity

There are many reasons to be in concert with the innovations that choice can bring. This approach recognizes that there is no "one best way" for everyone. Children have different needs and learning modes. Teachers have different approaches. Parents have different philosophies. Choice allows schools to draw strength from diversity by developing different programs. It allows each school to excel. And, choice does something more: it empowers parents by bringing them into the decision-making process. It encourages teachers and principals to become entrepreneurs and structure their curriculum and standards; students are encouraged to become learners with options that direct and capture their potential.

A free and productive society thrives on empowerment of the people. The American economy and our democracy are products of empowerment, and this approach can revitalize schools around the country.

For an example of choice across a broad front, we only need to look at the system of postsecondary education in this country. At the postsecondary level, schools compete for students, offering a variety of programs to satisfy distinct needs. We have a fine system of universities and colleges . . . some say the best in the world. The rector of a university in Russia who was on a tour of our higher education system recently observed that "American universities are not good because the United States is rich. America is rich because it has good universities." That's quite an endorsement. And students from all over the globe come to this country to attend our universities and colleges.

My point is basic. . . . There are choices at the postsecondary level of education in this country and they have helped to produce the highest caliber educational system. I am convinced that the same approach can promote progress and success for our elementary and secondary schools.

Parent Involvement

The American public education system was once the envy of the world. Our past successes were built on a recognition that parents, teachers, students and local school administrators must work together to educate our nation's children. We strayed from this solid principle some time ago and placed our trust in processes and institutions that distanced parents and students from their educational systems. The concept of choice returns the crucial element of parent and student involvement. This involvement revives the relationship between parent and teacher, parent and principal, parent and student, and parent and parent, thereby rekindling community concern for education in this great country.

"He is free who lives as he chooses," a Greek philosopher wrote nearly 2000 years ago. Americans today still hold firmly to that ancient but timeless ideal. To be an American means to have choices. Yet, ironically, we are often powerless to make one decision with a profound and enduring effect . . . where to send our children to school.

"Choice. . .would appear to be a shaky fulcrum upon which to plan the turnaround of America's schools."

Allowing Parents to Choose Among Schools May Not Help Children

Paul Glastris and Thomas Toch

Allowing parents to choose their child's school is not necessarily the best solution to America's education problems, Paul Glastris and Thomas Toch maintain in the following viewpoint. While choice programs may work in theory, the authors argue, in practice such programs are flawed. The authors believe that few students take advantage of choice programs. In addition, they contend that some students choose schools that are less challenging academically, thereby harming superior schools. Paul Glastris is a domestic correspondent and Thomas Toch is an associate editor for the weekly newsmagazine *U.S. News & World Report*.

As you read, consider the following questions:

1. How can good schools be harmed by choice programs, according to the authors?
2. Why do the authors believe that voluntary choice programs lose their market incentives?
3. Why do Glastris and Toch argue that some bad schools continue to stay open even when choice programs are instituted?

Education Secretary Lauro Cavazos calls the concept of parental choice "the cornerstone to restructuring elementary and secondary education" in America. But if the nation's top education officer had done his homework before he traveled to Minnesota to promote that state's ambitious experiment allowing families to select among public schools, he might have muted his enthusiasm for the plan.

Under choice, not only are parents entitled to enroll their children in public schools outside their geographical district, but the state tax dollars go to the system that wins their enrollment. By creating market incentives, the thinking goes, academically superior schools should thrive while inferior schools would have to either improve their performance or face bankruptcy.

But so far, theory has not worked so well in practice in Minnesota, which is conducting the nation's largest, most sweeping experiment in "interdistrict choice." Under a law passed in 1987, Minnesota's school-district borders were opened up so that dissatisfied students could transfer to schools in other districts. . . . Iowa, Nebraska and Arkansas passed similar choice programs in 1989, while 11 other states have been considering the approach. "Choice has worked," President Bush proclaimed, "almost without exception, everywhere it has been tried."

Choosing Convenience

In fact, there is a conspicuous lack of evidence that statewide, interdistrict choice has worked as advertised. The reasons students opt out of one school for another are often unrelated to academics, and in some cases it is the academically rigorous schools, rather than failing schools, that suffer. Critic Dan Woll, a Wisconsin school-district administrator, went so far as to call Minnesota's choice program "the educational equivalent of cold fusion."

That may be too harsh, but the results of open enrollment have so far been less than impressive: Only 3,790 of Minnesota's 735,000 public-school students applied to transfer schools under open enrollment. Not surprising, the predicted marketplace effects are hard to find. Peggy Hunter, open-enrollment coordinator for the state education department, has received "more requests for technical and organizational assistance" from school administrators statewide, but she believes it is too early to know if the schools are really changing for the better.

One reason may be that plenty of parents choose schools for other than academic reasons. Mike Jacobson, who lives in suburban Eagan, says he drives his son Adam to an elementary school in South St. Paul "out of convenience"; the school is a block from the day-care center of his 2-year-old son, Kyle. Other parents pick schools near their work; still others because a neighboring district school is closer to home. In fact, Hunter's survey data indicate that 25 percent of parents using open-enrollment options do so for reasons of convenience rather than academic superiority.

Steve Artley. Reprinted with permission.

Convenience for families may not be a bad reason to choose a school, but it provides no incentive for schools losing students to make academic improvements. Under open enrollment, improving academics can even cost a district. After the Forest Lake district toughened graduation requirements, some students fled to other districts with lower standards, says Forest Lake Superintendent Gerald Brynildson.

Problems with Choice
Those parents who are eager to find better schools have a tough time in Minnesota, because no agency collects the basic data needed for informed decision making, such as the courses different schools provide. Most districts don't check student performance with standardized tests, and those that do often use different exams. "There's almost a conspiracy to keep that kind of information from being visible," complains legislative auditor James Nobles.

No schools have closed down because of the pressures of open enrollment, but one district that is teetering, Mountain Iron-Buhl in northern Minnesota, does not inspire confidence in choice. So far, 163 students have fled the district amid squabbling by parents over which town, Mountain Iron or Buhl—former athletic rivals forced to consolidate—would retain the high school. The exodus might have proved choice theory correct, were Mountain Iron-Buhl schools known for poor academic performance. But even Robert Krebsbach, a choice proponent and superintendent of the neighboring district that inherited most of the students, says that Mountain Iron-Buhl schools are academically sound, or at least were before the 1988 exodus.

John Gorsha, Jr., a 17-year-old at Mountain Iron-Buhl High, wants to leave but can't because of another problem with Minnesota's choice law: Lack of transportation. The state provides no bus service for those choosing to leave their districts. State funds can be used to transport students once they are within the receiving district, but that's often the shortest leg of the journey. Low-income students can get most of their car fare reimbursed, but that's not much help to people like Gorsha. He doesn't have a car. "What am I supposed to do," asks John Gorsha, Sr., a retired Marine living on a pension, "go into the hole to buy the kid a car for open enrollment?"

Choosing to Choose

The transportation dilemma is one reason why Minnesota's choice program is used least by those most in need of better schooling: Inner-city blacks. Whites in Minneapolis were twice as likely as blacks to apply for open enrollment in 1989. Critics argue that the state failed to spend enough to inform low-income minorities of their options. "Choice is great, but in Minnesota we didn't do our homework when it comes to equity issues," says Elaine Salinas of the Urban Coalition of Minneapolis.

State officials acknowledge that many of the disadvantaged students and parents open enrollment is intended to help have been receiving insufficient information about the program. To rectify the problem, the state sponsored the first of a series of workshops aimed at minority and disadvantaged students. The state is also publicizing the program through churches, welfare offices and even fastfood restaurants, since many of them employ minority students.

Minnesota's choice program has other conceptual flaws. Richard Elmore, a Michigan State University education professor who has studied the Minnesota effort, believes that the marketplace forces are weakened because the program is voluntary. "Students have to choose to choose," he points out, "and as a result a very small proportion of the system's students are involved." In contrast, Elmore points to "intradistrict" programs in

Cambridge, Mass., and East Harlem, where a student must pick a school within his or her community even if it means choosing not to transfer. "The stakes are much higher when all students are put in motion," he says. The relative strength of the marketplaces in these two cities suggests that, as a tool of school improvement, intradistrict choice may be more powerful than interdistrict choice. Desegregation orders, however, often limit the scope of choice in such programs. . . .

Expanding Choices

Practically speaking, in the lower grades where students' choices are often limited to schools that have vacancies, which many of the best schools do not have, choice's appeal may be largely rhetorical. Also, some parents are reluctant to send their kids to distant districts, no matter how bad their own district is or how good the transportation arrangements. That means bad schools are likely to limp along, rather than improve or close as choice theory predicts. That may explain why in recent decades few urban schools have improved, even under choicelike pressure from families fleeing to the suburbs.

Choice Is an Illusion

Choice is a political horse to ride. It gives the illusion of action but it is dangerous to hold it up as a panacea for the problems we have in schools today. There are families who are just scraping by. If they don't have a car to get to their child's school meeting across town, or need to hire a babysitter, how will they do it?

Gary Marx, *Fortune*, Spring 1990.

The answer to all these flaws, say choice advocates, is more choice. Students should be able to choose not only outside their districts but within their district. As a way of breaking down the geographic monopoly that school districts enjoy, some educators would even allow groups of teachers and parents to open independent schools anywhere they wish, using local taxes. In time, such a radical innovation might lead to a true marketplace for public education. But judging by the results of Minnesota's experiment, interdistrict choice, at least, would appear to be a shaky fulcrum upon which to plan the turnaround of America's schools.

"*Moral education is not only inevitable in schools; it is essential.*"

Moral Education Would Help Children

The Association for Supervision and Curriculum Development
Panel on Moral Education

The Association for Supervision and Curriculum Development
(ASCD) is an educational association that helps teachers and administrators select curricula. In the following viewpoint, written
by the ASCD Panel on Moral Education, the authors maintain
that because American society is becoming increasingly amoral
and materialistic, America's children need more moral guidance
in school. The authors believe it is possible to teach basic moral
values without offending the many different religious and cultural groups that make up the U.S. They suggest steps that society and schools can take to ensure that children receive this
moral direction.

As you read, consider the following questions:

1. Why do the authors believe that some teachers are wary
   of presenting even common moral values?
2. Explain what the panel means by the values clarification
   approach and the cognitive-developmental approach
   to moral education.
3. Why do the authors believe it is important for Americans to
   find common moral standards?

ASCD Panel on Moral Education, "Moral Education in the Life of the School," *Educational Leadership*, 45, 8: 4-8. Reprinted with permission of the Association for Supervision and Curriculum Development. Copyright © 1988 by ASCD. All rights reserved.

Moral education is whatever schools do to influence how students think, feel, and act regarding issues of right and wrong. American public schools have a long tradition of concern about moral education, and recently this concern has grown more intense.

Undoubtedly, alarm about the morality of young people is aggravated by a number of forces: fragmentation of the family, decline of trust in public institutions, increasing public concern about questionable ethical practices in business and industry, the impact of the mass media, and our gradually increasing affluence. All of these forces help foster a materialistic, "me first" attitude.

Finally, the increasing ethnic and social diversity of our population, while invigorating our nation, has brought with it an increasing variety of moral values that sometimes conflict. As a result, some educators, awash in a sea of pluralism, are wary of even trying to identify common moral values.

Yet there is increasing protest against the way values are addressed in schools. Public figures such as Secretary of Education William Bennett and New York Governor Mario Cuomo have stated that schools should pay more attention to students' moral development, and their comments have both reflected existing public opinion and triggered renewed interest.

Contemporary Issues

Issues that have confounded moral education over the past century are intensified today: How do we respond to disagreements about the proper methods of moral education? How does the school balance common values with pluralistic beliefs? What should be the relationship between religion and moral education in the public schools? What is the relationship between private and public morality? Should moral education emphasize indoctrination or reasoning?

How does moral education find a place in a curriculum already stretched to the limit? Should moral education be taught as a separate subject or infused throughout the curriculum? Should moral education take different forms for students of different ages? Who should teach about morality? How does one evaluate moral growth? And, how can schools build support in the community for moral education?

Historical Perspective

In earlier times, American schools did not find such questions troubling. The predecessors of today's public schools were founded under a Massachusetts law passed in 1647, 20 years after the first settlers landed. The law, which warned that "old deluder Satan" flourished on ignorance, was aimed at establishing schools that would deliberately foster morality. The academic learning transmitted in such schools was inextricably bound up with religious doctrine.

Feiffer

MY TEACHERS SAY I CAN'T TAKE CRITICISM. BUT ITS NOT TRUE!

I CAN TAKE CONSTRUCTIVE CRITICISM, - NOT HOSTILE CRITICISM.

I CAN TAKE CRITICISM THAT - APPRECIATES HOW HARD I'VE WORKED.

AND HOW MUCH IT MEANS TO MY PARENTS THAT I GET GOOD GRADES.

I CAN TAKE CRITICISM THAT ISN'T GOING TO MAKE ME FEEL LIKE - A CRIMINAL JUST BECAUSE I CAN'T FINISH THE THINGS THAT I START...

AND THAT I CAN'T BE EXPECTED TO DO HOMEWORK ALL DAY AND NIGHT. I'M YOUNG AND NEED MY FUN TOO!

I CAN TAKE CRITICISM THAT REALIZES I'M GOING TO BE RICH AND FAMOUS SO I'M NOT GOING TO NEED THAT MUCH MATH. I CAN HIRE PEOPLE FOR THAT.

YOU KNOW - THE KIND OF CRITICISM I CAN TAKE? I CAN TAKE CRITICISM THAT ADORES ME.

AND GETS ME MODELING JOBS.

Feiffer by Jules Feiffer. Copyright 1987 Jules Feiffer. Reprinted with permission of Universal Press Syndicate. All rights reserved.

Indeed, until the middle of the 19th century, public schools were typically pervaded with a strong, nonsectarian Protestant tone, which was reflected in Bible readings, prayers, ceremonial occasions, and the contents of reading materials. (In some communities where one sect was dominant, a more sectarian tone prevailed.) As Roman Catholic immigration proceeded, conflicts arose over moral and religious education. These disputes were circumvented by the creation of parochial schools.

By the end of the 19th century, public schools increasingly adopted a purely secular form of moral education, often called "character education". The character education movement identified a body of activities and principles by which moral education could be transmitted in a secular institution. The approach emphasized student teamwork, extracurricular activities, student councils, flag salutes and other ceremonies, and commonsense moral virtues like honesty, self-discipline, kindness, and tolerance. Some researchers concluded there was little connection between the character education approach and real-life behavior. Later researchers, however, have disputed this conclusion; furthermore, the research findings about how other forms of moral education affect conduct are equally inconclusive. In any case, schools still emphasize components of character education, and many of these activities are strongly supported by parents.

While character education was enjoying wide popularity during the first three decades of the century, John Dewey was articulating a theory of moral development that emphasized reflective thinking rather than moral lessons. According to Dewey, the proper way to resolve moral dilemmas in real life is to apply reason or intelligent thought. This theory of moral development would eventually become the main theme of the moral education efforts that emerged in the 1960s and thereafter.

Values Clarification

In the 1960s, Louis Raths and his colleagues, claiming to follow the work of Dewey, developed the values clarification approach. While this method was often viewed as a simple set of value-free activities, its original theory intended to help students make value decisions based on careful reasoning and democratic principles. In the 1970s, Lawrence Kohlberg proposed a cognitive-developmental approach to moral education based on the work of Dewey and Jean Piaget. Immensely popular in theory but difficult to apply in practice, this approach emphasized the application of thinking skills to the development of moral reasoning based on increasingly complex concepts of justice. In addition, it suggested that such thinking is influenced by the individual's stage of cognitive development and that such thinking fosters movement toward higher stages.

While these two approaches—values clarification and the cognitive-developmental approach—have received widespread attention, others have also been proposed and tried. Among these are the values analysis approach, the psychological education program and several more, including some of the current personal development and self-esteem programs that fall under the rubric of affective education.

It is crucial to understand that no single approach or program has gained complete ascendance in recent curriculum history. The values clarification and cognitive-developmental approaches have certainly enjoyed great popularity; however, character education has received renewed attention, and some public schools even persist in asserting a religious basis for moral education. Also, the revival of classical humanism has again brought forth the notion of moral education through literature and history.

Thus, we have a long legacy of theories, approaches, and programs, and the mixed results of research offer few definitive guidelines. Curricular decisions about moral education are currently based on a mix of moral philosophy and empirical evidence, impelled by public pressure for immediate action by the schools.

Morality and Religion

Religion is a major force in the lives of most Americans. Indeed, international studies continually report a comparatively high level of religious practice among Americans. Because religion is, above all, a meaning system, it naturally speaks to its adherents about right and wrong, good and bad. For many Americans, the first and foremost moral guide is their own religion.

While the theological doctrines of religions differ substantially, there is a great deal of overlap in moral theologies, particularly in their everyday application. Broad areas of consensus exist regarding concern for our fellow human beings, honesty in our dealings with one another, respect for property, and a host of other moral issues. These same issues are fundamental to the rules our nation has chosen to live by; in practice, the dictates of one's religious conscience and the precepts of democracy tend to reinforce each other.

Education Bankruptcy

An educational system that is amoral in the name of "scientific objectivity," thus devours its own young. They fall prey to a variety of predators that rob them of their confidence in the life of the mind, the significance of culture, the intrinsic worth of knowledge.

Moreover, permitting a generation of students to grow up as ethical illiterates and moral idiots, unprepared to cope with ordinary life experiences, is a declaration of education bankruptcy.

Norman Lamm, *The New York Times*, October 14, 1986.

There are many Americans, however, in whose lives religion does not play a significant role. There are others who, for a variety of reasons, are antagonistic to religion. For them, moral education based on religion and appeals to religious principles to solve moral issues are serious affronts. On the other hand, some religious people are equally affronted by public schools teaching students to look outside their religious tradition for moral guidance.

Need for Compromise

Public schools, committed as they are to serving all Americans, must approach this question with understanding, sensitivity, and willingness to compromise. Educators need to be sensitive to students' religious beliefs and respect their legitimacy, yet must not promote such beliefs in the classroom. Teachers should stress the democratic and intellectual bases for morality, but they should also encourage children to bring all their intellectual, cultural, and religious resources to bear on moral issues.

Appreciating the differences in our pluralistic society is fundamental to the success of our democracy. And tolerance must begin in the schools: If we are to survive as a nation, our schools must help us find our common moral ground and help us learn to live together on it.

Moral education is not only inevitable in schools; it is essential. Human beings vary tremendously and are enormously adaptable, and our broad potential requires that we teach the best of our inherited culture. That teaching begins, of course, in our families, but it must be supported by other agencies. A common morality should be developed while a society's future citizens are still children—before misdirected development leads them to harm themselves or others.

To accomplish this important task, all societies have public systems to help develop moral principles in children. In America, schools are a central part of that system. Our schools thus cannot ignore moral education; it is one of their most important responsibilities.

Recommendations

In recent years, the educational community has given substantial attention to excellence in our schools. An emphasis on moral education, we believe, is essential to that end. Moral education is not just another educational fad; it is an old and revered school mission. And with good reason.

At the heart of democracy is the morally mature citizen. A society whose citizens are not morally mature and cannot trust one another resorts to external force and can even evolve into a police state. Similarly, a school whose students are not morally mature is tempted to create an environment of repression. Schools must contribute to the development of morally mature individuals who, in turn, will help to ensure the existence of a just and caring society.

It is in this spirit that we make the following recommendations.

1. We urge all those involved in American education—from school board members to district and building administrators to individual teachers—to renew their commitment to promoting moral education in the schools. Indeed, we urge that moral education be made a powerful unifying and energizing force in the curriculum.

2. We recommend that educators form partnerships with parents, the mass media, the business community, the courts, and civic, racial, ethnic, and religious groups to create a social and cultural context that supports the school's efforts to develop morally mature citizens.

3. We recommend that schools define and teach a morality of justice, altruism, diligence, and respect for human dignity. These are universal moral values that coincide with traditional religious teachings but stand on their own as authentic secular

values. As part of a genuine respect for pluralism, schools should also teach students about the different ultimate sources for morality, including religion.

Bringing Values Back into the Classroom

Our public schools once placed the building of character and moral discernment on a par with developing the intellect. And they can once again. We *can* get the values Americans share back into our classrooms. And we will work to do this. Those who claim we are now too diverse a nation, that we consist of too many competing convictions and interests to instill common values, are wrong. Yes, we are a diverse people. We have always been a diverse people. And as Madison wrote in *The Federalist,* the competing, balancing interests of a diverse people can help ensure the survival of liberty. But there are values that all American citizens share and that we should want all American students to know and freely to make their own: honesty, fairness, self-discipline, fidelity, love of country, and belief in the principles of liberty, equality, and the freedom to practice one's faith. The explicit teaching of these values is the legacy of the common school, and it is a legacy to which we must return.

William J. Bennett, *Our Children & Our Country,* 1988.

---

4. We urge schools and school systems to make sure their moral education efforts extend beyond the cognitive domain to include the affective and the behavioral. Moral education must go beyond simply knowing what is good; it must also involve prizing what is good and doing what is good.

5. We recommend that moral education include, especially for younger children, socialization into appropriate patterns of conduct and, especially for older students, education for the critical thinking and decision making that are part of adult moral maturity. The latter may include examination of the complex issues that stir ethical debate in society at large.

6. We recommend that educators continually examine the institutional features of school life to ensure that climate and instructional practices contribute to the same moral growth.

7. We urge further research on what works in moral education, drawing on research findings from other fields and presenting those findings to the profession forcefully and clearly.

8. We recommend that educators regularly assess the moral climate of schools and the conduct of students and communicate the results of these assessments to their communities. Many schools take steps now, including notations about conduct on pupils' report cards, notes of praise or criticism to parents, and recognition for individuals or groups whose conduct is

praiseworthy. We acknowledge, however, that there is still much work to be done in the articulation of moral principles and the development of methods to assess their place in the school.

Moral Educators

9. We recommend that schools establish and convey clear expectations for teachers and administrators regarding their roles as moral educators. Furthermore, we recommend that their performance as moral educators be included as a regular and important part of their evaluation.

10. We recommend that teacher educators, both preservice and inservice, give major attention to moral education to ensure that teachers have the necessary knowledge, attitudes, and skills to fulfill their moral education responsibilities.

In these recommendations. . .we do not call for schools simply to return to the attitudes and traditions of the past; nor do we urge schools to attempt a new educational experiment. Rather, the moral education we call for is part of the living legacy of our nation. It is at the center of our evolving tradition as a national community. Our vision of the moral education children need is one that is basic to the survival of our culture, building on the past while preparing young people to deal with the moral challenges of the future.

6

"There's nothing neutral about the way values clarification is taught."

Moral Education Would Not Help Children

Phyllis Schlafly

In the following viewpoint, author Phyllis Schlafly argues that because common moral standards do not exist in America, schools should not attempt to teach morality to children. It is impossible for schools to teach neutral values, she contends, and therefore any moral instruction is an attack on the First Amendment rights of America's children. Schlafly is a well-known conservative writer who supports traditional family values.

As you read, consider the following questions:

1. What does the author state was the purpose of the Protection of Pupil Rights Amendment of 1978?
2. How does Schlafly define the word "family"?
3. How does the author believe many moral education courses attack religious beliefs?

Phyllis Schlafly, "The Teaching of Values in the Public Schools," *The Phyllis Schlafly Report*, October 1989. Reprinted with permission.

It's important to know what frame of reference I am coming from. I am not part of the religious right or a fundamentalist group trying to impose my religion on public school children. I come from a state where prayer was banned from the public schools at the time of World War I, and I am not seeking to put it back in. I am not an enemy of public schools. I had a very happy public school experience. I certainly believe in education. I come from a family where the women and men have been college graduates for more than a century. I wanted college so much that, having no money, I worked my own way through college without any aid of any type, in a grimy night job, 48 hours a week. My husband and I have financed six children through 38 years of university education at seven secular universities. So, indeed, I care about education. . . .

Two movements. . .are current in our society. On the one hand, we have those people who seem to believe that the public school child is a captive of the administrators of the public schools, and that the schools can do anything they want with the children, pretty much as though they were guinea pigs. Those people seem to think that, if parents presume to interfere with or criticize curriculum, they can be called troublemakers, mischief-makers, censors, bigots— the whole host of epithets spun out by the American Civil Liberties Union and People for the American Way.

On the other hand, there are those of us who believe that, since the children—and they are minor *children* in public schools—are a captive audience under compulsory school laws, the authority figure must be limited and restricted by two other factors.

Parents Are Primary Educators

First is the power and rights of the parents. It is good constitutional law in our nation that the parents are the primary educators of their children. They have the right to safeguard the religion, the morals, the attitudes, the values, and the family privacy of their children.

Secondly, the schools are subject to the taxpayers and the citizens of our nation. I come from the frame of reference that anybody who spends the taxpayers' money simply has to put up with citizen surveillance. The President has to put up with it. The Congressmen have to put up with it. The state legislators have to put up with it. And teachers, school administrators and librarians have to put up with it. This is one of the penalties of being able to spend the taxpayers' money. Those who don't like other citizens looking over their shoulders and second-guessing their judgment should really go into some other line of work where they're not spending the taxpayers' money. So we find it very distressing when schools resent parents and citizens looking over their shoulders.

Forty years ago it was not necessary to identify these different categories or types of rights because the public schools had a very high reputation in our land. I can remember that 40 years ago, when conservative speakers made some critical remarks about public schools, they were literally hooted down. Public schools then enjoyed a high reputation like the Post Office. They were sacred cows. Nobody could attack them and get by with it.

Children Are Not Taught to Read

That public confidence, frankly, is no longer there. Let me explain one reason why it's no longer there. Thirty-two years ago, I was ready to enter my first child in public school, thinking that the first task of the school was to teach the child to read. We now know that there are at least 23 million illiterates in this country, adults who have been through the public schools and didn't learn how to read.

Don Meredith. Reprinted with permission.

Well, 32 years ago when my first child was ready to start school, I discovered that the public schools didn't teach children to read. They only taught them to memorize a few words by guessing at them from the picture on the page. That is why I kept all my six children out of school until I taught them to read at home—so that they would be good readers, and so they would not be six of the 23 million functional illiterates in our country today. This is not a matter of Secular Humanism or morals, or affluence versus poverty, or anything else. No public school in my area taught children how to read. Schools only taught word guessing, which was a cheat on the taxpayers and on the children. We see the results today.

Thirty-two years ago I didn't know anybody else who taught her own child. Today there are about a million parents doing that because they feel cheated by the public schools.

Protection of Pupil Rights Amendment

In the mid-1970s something else came into the schools to use up the hours that could not be spent in reading the great books and the classics, which formerly children were able to do. This new element was best summarized and described by Senator Sam Hayakawa, who was a university president before he became a United States Senator. He called it a "heresy" in public school education. He said that, instead of teaching children knowledge and basic skills, the purpose of education has become group therapy. That's the best way to describe what has happened in the schools.

In public school classrooms, children are required to discuss feelings and emotions and attitudes. They are confronted with all sorts of moral dilemmas, instead of being given the facts and the knowledge they need. As a result, Hayakawa was a major promoter of a federal law passed in 1978 called the Protection of Pupil Rights Amendment, which said that schools should not give psychological testing or treatment to public school children on subjects that include family privacy, sexual and other personal matters, without the prior written consent of their parents. The purpose of this law was to prevent the schools from engaging in psychological probing, invasion of privacy, or manipulation of values.

The education establishment was so powerful that no regulations were issued on this law until 1984. But the parents were discovering what was happening to their children, and they didn't like it. They discovered that these psychological manipulations in the classroom constituted a continuing attack on their religion, on their morals, on their family, and even on parents. We believe that the continuing attack is so gross as to rise to the level of a violation of the First Amendment rights of parents and their children.

Values Clarification and Moral Dilemmas

What happened is best illustrated by the classic lifeboat game presented in Sidney Simon's book on Values Clarification, and probably used in every school in this country. I had a reporter tell me that she had some variation of it at every level of elementary and secondary education. This is the game where the child is taught that ten people are in a sinking lifeboat, and the child must throw five of them out to drown. Which five will you kill? Will it be the senior citizen, or the policeman, or the pregnant woman, or the college co-ed, or the black militant, or whoever? You pick *which* you will kill.

This "game" is played widely, in many variations—the fallout shelter, the kidney machine, starting a new race, and so forth. To explain what's wrong about this game, we have the example of the child who answered the lifeboat problem by saying, "Jesus brought another boat, and nobody had to drown." That child was creative but she got an "F" on her paper. That explains what values clarification does. It is not value neutral in any shape or form. It is a direct attack on the religion and the values of those of us who believe that God created us, and that it is not up to the child to play God and decide who lives and who dies.

Morals Should Be Taught by Parents

I do not want schoolteachers teaching my daughter values and morals. Their job is to educate my child to prepare her to locate, extricate and assimilate information to make up her own mind. And, it is hoped, they can teach her to communicate, so that she might share her mind with others. And I also expect them to have freedom to enforce the discipline necessary to maintain an atmosphere conducive to learning.

I feel that it is my duty and my privilege to teach my child values and morals at home. And I realize that the most effective, if not the only, method I have at my disposal is the example I set.

My advice to this "growing number of parents, worried that their children aren't building good character" is to take stock of their own lives. What kind of role models are they providing their children? Therein might very well lie the reason why their children appear to be lacking in "good character."

William B. Smith, *The Wall Street Journal*, May 17, 1990.

The curriculum is filled with these moral dilemmas. The reason we know about so many of them is that, in 1984, the Department of Education conducted hearings across the country, where parents could come and describe what had happened to their own children. Those hearings had no press, but you can read much of the testimony in my book called *Child Abuse in the Classroom*. They are the authentic testimonies of parents. They told how the children were given such moral dilemmas as: stand up in class and give a good example of when it's okay to lie; write a paper on when it's all right to steal; discuss which kind of drugs you will take, how much and how many.

These moral dilemmas never tell the child that anything is wrong. The child is taken through all the areas of sex, with obscene descriptions, discussions, role-playing, and other psychological manipulations in the classroom. You can call this secular humanism, you can call it situation ethics, you can call it group therapy, you can call it psychological manipulation, you can call it counseling. You can call it no-name. But whatever it is, it is pervasive in the public schools, and it is a direct attack on the First Amendment rights of those who believe that God created us and that He created a moral law that we should obey. There's nothing neutral about the way values clarification is taught. The option that we should abide by God's law is never offered.

The Alabama Textbook Case

The Alabama textbook case (*Smith v. Board of School Commissioners of Mobile County*) finally brought out of the closet a situation that has been going on for 15 to 20 years, without media coverage or public attention. A previous speaker said how surprised he was to discover that home economics is about sex. Well, if you've been reading the textbooks, you would have known that. And that is why parents are so upset.

The issue in the Alabama textbook case was, simply, does the child who believes in God have the same rights in the public school classroom as the atheist?

In the 1985 case of *Wallace v. Jaffree*, the Supreme Court held that little atheist Jaffree had the right to be in the public school classroom and not be embarrassed when his peers said a prayer or spoke about God. In the Alabama textbook case, the U.S. District Court decision simply gave the child who believes in God the same rights as the atheist (but that decision was overturned by the U.S. Court of Appeals). I believe that the child has a right to be in the public school classroom, and not have his religion, his morals or his family, belittled or harassed, or told that they are irrelevant, or be presented with moral dilemmas which tell him that he can personally decide what is moral or legal.

We hear about teaching the child to make decisions. Of course, the child, if accosted by the drug peddler, must make a choice whether to buy or not. But it is so wrong to tell the child in class that he is capable of making a choice on an issue which the law has already decided. The schools should teach that the law has already decided that illegal drugs are bad and that he must not take drugs.

Since the First Amendment seems to prohibit the public schools from teaching a belief in God and His moral commandments, the school must also not be permitted to teach that there *isn't* any God, that God did *not* create the world, or that God did *not* give us His moral commandments.

If you look at what was involved in the textbooks in the Alabama case, you'll find textbooks saying that "what is right or wrong depends more on your own judgment than on what someone tells you to do." That's a direct attack on religion. One book tells the teacher to design a bulletin board showing conflicting values held by young people and their parents. This is mischief-making between the child and his parents.

Indoctrination, Not Education

Moral education taught in the manner suggested in your article is nothing more than indoctrination. Indoctrination is not education. Furthermore, what makes us think that the moral and ethical decisions that our children will be making in the future will be at all similar to the decisions we are making today?

Ethical and moral decisions are becoming increasingly complex. Children need the tools and skills to make these choices, not indoctrination. They need to be taught the skills of ethical inquiry, skills that will improve their reasoning ability and help them make better ethical decisions not just today but tomorrow also.

Walter N. Plaut Jr., *The Wall Street Journal*, May 17, 1990.

Another textbook teaches that a family is a group of people who live together. That's not what a family is. A family starts with a marriage between a man and a woman. We find one textbook telling a child that, "in democratic families, every member has a voice in running the family, and parents and teenagers should decide together about curfews, study time, chores, allowances, and use of the car." Where does anybody get the idea that the school can tell the child that he's got a right to decide when he uses the car?

Here's another one. "Steps in decision-making can apply to something so simple as buying a new pair of shoes. They can also be applied to more complex decisions which involve religious preferences, use of alcohol, tobacco and drugs." Where did anyone get the idea that schools can teach children that the family should be democratic and that children should participate in making such decisions?

Here's a quotation from another Alabama textbook: "In the past, families were often like dictatorships. One person, or two, made all the decisions." Is that mischief-making? You bet it's mischief-making.

Here's a quotation from another textbook: "People who have strong prejudices are called bigots. Bigots are devoted to their own church, party or belief." That really puts your parents down, doesn't it!

Another textbook seems to say that it's okay if people want to experience parenthood without marrying. A long passage from another textbook says that divorce is an acceptable way of solving a problem. Then it calls on the class to role-play the circumstances that might lead the child to choose a divorce. The school has no right to attack the morals of children by telling them that divorce is acceptable.

Examples from Across America

Actually, the Alabama school textbooks are probably pretty mild compared to a lot of others we find around the rest of the country. In Seattle we found a textbook which said that promiscuity should not be labeled good or bad, that premarital sexual intercourse is acceptable for both men and women, that morality is individual—it's what you think it is, that homosexuality is okay, that prostitution should be legalized, that it is not deviant for teenagers to watch others performing sex acts through binoculars or windows, that alternatives to traditional marriage such as group sex and open marriage are okay, and then asks the child if he'd like to join such a group.

It took 18 months and finally some TV cameras, to get the curriculum committee to say the school would replace that textbook. It had been the textbook in a mandatory course in the Seattle public school system from 1978 to 1987.

Your New York City School Board video, "Sex, Drugs and AIDS," has been so controversial in New York that it is now being revised. But the original version has now gone all over the country. It blows my mind to think that anybody could believe it is constitutional to present a video in the public school classroom teaching children that fornication and sodomy are acceptable behavior so long as you use condoms, and telling them that homosexuality is all right, which is exactly what that video does. It is hard to believe that anybody could approve such an evil video for use in the public school classroom. The video is a direct attack on the First Amendment rights of those who believe that fornication and sodomy are wrong.

We want the same rights for people who believe in God and His commandments as the atheist has already established. Whatever you call it, this no-name ideology, it all boils down to an attack on religion, a war on parental rights, and a betrayal of trust.

7

"There would be less intolerance, violence, pranks, and disrespect if more students got whacked."

Corporal Punishment in Schools Would Help Children

Lawrence Wade

A lack of discipline in classrooms is one reason many of America's children fail in school, some experts suggest. The solution, Lawrence Wade contends in the following viewpoint, is to bring corporal punishment back into the classroom. Wade believes teachers should paddle disobedient students. This punishment, he argues, will instill respect and discipline in unruly students and bring order back into schools. Wade is a syndicated columnist whose articles have appeared in the *Richmond News Leader* and the *Baltimore Sun*.

As you read, consider the following questions:

1. What does Wade believe he learned from being paddled in school?
2. What is the worst kind of child abuse, in the author's opinion?
3. Why did America turn away from using corporal punishment in the 1960s and 1970s, according to Wade?

Lawrence Wade, "School Paddling Helps Young Learn Discipline," *The Richmond News Leader*, January 5, 1989. Reprinted with permission.

"Corporal punishment has no place in school," says Joan First, executive director of a Boston-based education rights group. Her group, the National Coalition of Advocates for Students, reports that blacks are paddled and suspended more often than whites simply because they're "different."

But there's no reason to end corporal punishment. Take this from a black who earned his share of paddlings.

If anything, there would be less intolerance, violence, pranks, and disrespect if more students got whacked.

Corporal punishment taught me to avoid anti-social behavior. And while a few students might be mistreated, I can't recall one paddling or suspension I didn't deserve.

What was "different" wasn't my color but my behavior.

The Author's Story

It all began one hot, spring afternoon at Alexander Hamilton Junior High in Cleveland. I believe that I was in the seventh grade.

Our school didn't have air conditioning. So, the big windows facing a busy urban street were wide-open. I heard a police siren as our young teacher scratched on the chalkboard.

I shouted, "They're coming to get you, Mr. Jones!"

His body shook. He dropped his chalk. The class roared. My timing was perfect.

For this harassment I got five swats *in front of everyone.* Do you know what hurt most? Seeing the blushing faces of two girls I adored.

But how much did such a harassment hurt our teacher's pride? Surely as much as it hurts authority figures whose effectiveness is diminished today by fools who can't resist a prank or joke.

I'm sure that it hurt as much as the pain felt by black students today who are called racist names on college campuses and Jewish female students who endure JAP (Jewish American Princess) jokes.

Mr. Jones' "swats" taught that you don't harass folks or disrespect authority. And no doubt there would be less of both if more students got their rear ends scorched.

Don't get me wrong.

I'm not for child abuse. Corporal punishment must be defined and within limits. But the worst abuse is to raise kids who don't know actions have consequences. Teaching this respect is love.

Disciplining Computer Hackers

Consider pranks, too. You've read the stories about computer whizzes who think it's fun to plant "viruses" in computer systems, break into hospital records or change bank files.

I wonder if these "hackers" would do this if, like me, they'd been caught and paddled for passing study-hall [notes] that read, "Stomp When the Next Dude Comes Through The Door!"

Dick Wright. Reprinted by permission of UFS, Inc.

How many students would start fights if, like me, they'd been paddled and suspended for it? Embarassment is a big guy—me —returning to classes with a huge bandage on his forehead caused by a little guy who got away.

These swats and suspensions taught that you don't use violence to settle disputes with friends and neighbors. But shortly after I graduated from high school, the "student rights" movement encouraged parents to tell teachers to lay off their kids.

The result: In New York City alone there were more than 500 attacks on teachers in the 1987-88 school year, *The New York Times* reports.

In Washington, there are so many "incidents" that the school board recently agreed to dramatically increase security forces and even considered metal detectors to stop guns and other weapons from entering school doors.

The Changing Attitudes of Educators

How did we get here?

Charles Payne, an Indianapolis eighth-grade teacher, writing in NEA Today, a publication of the National Education Association, says, "We turned away from corporal punishment in the

'60s and early '70s because society was so opposed to violence during the Vietnam era."

"Well, I've seen many educators' attitudes—including my own—change during my 20 years of teaching."

By the way, Payne is black.

As I said: It's not about color.

If more students were paddled, there would be more respect for the law.

8

"Corporal punishment is a failed practice—destructive to our youth and to our future."

Corporal Punishment in Schools Would Not Help Children

Bob Keeshan

For nearly thirty years Bob Keeshan has been well known as television's Captain Kangaroo. His program won six Emmy Awards and was honored for excellence in children's programming. In the following viewpoint, Keeshan demands that America end corporal punishment in its schools. Such punishment is child abuse, he maintains. Keeshan argues that children need love and support from their teachers, not physical punishment.

As you read, consider the following questions:

1. How did Keeshan's personal experience with corporal punishment affect him?
2. Why does the author believe some children are unruly in school?
3. Once corporal punishment is eliminated, what else must America do to improve its schools, according to Keeshan?

Bob Keeshan, "The Time Is Now." This article first appeared in *The Humanist* issue of November/December 1988 and is reprinted by permission.

An emergency room physician sees the welts and deep purple bruises on the thighs and buttocks of a twelve-year-old and does what he must do under the law: he reports a possible case of child abuse. The county social worker arrives and finds that the injuries did not occur at home but were the result of a spanking administered earlier in the day by a teacher who had used a wooden paddle. The boy had misbehaved in a gym class. The social worker told the boy's father that if *he* had beaten his son, he would probably be in jail. The teacher's abuse is protected by law. . . .

Corporal punishment of students is not an exclusive practice of the South or North or East or West. Corporal punishment is legal in most places in thirty-nine states. It is an outlawed practice in eleven states and in individual school districts in many others—St. Louis and Chicago, for instance. It is outlawed in New Haven, New Orleans, Phoenix, Portland, Little Rock, Dade County (Florida), and many other individual school districts within states where paddling teachers are otherwise protected by law. Despite these advances, over half of American school children sit in classrooms where the paddle is a threat and where their psychological well-being is in harm's way. According to federal estimates, corporal punishment is resorted to in this nation some three million times a year. . . .

Rationalizing Abuse

So often, defenders of corporal punishment in the schools will rationalize that they were beaten in the classrooms of their youth and ask others to just look at the good it did them. I understand what it is like to be slapped around in the classroom. I could live a life of five hundred years and never forget the sting of the heavy wooden ruler wielded by Sister Alonzo. She ruled over the eighth grade, but her terror was felt by first and second graders who knew well her cruel reputation. I can remember, in lower grades, averting my eyes lest in her capriciousness she would single me out for punishment for some unknown transgression. Did it do me some good, that stinging ruler laid upon my palm? If it did, I wish God, in his kindness, would make me aware of the benefits that did accrue. I remember the classroom of Sister Alonzo as being the most unruly, chaotic place I have ever been, despite the heavy wooden ruler and its frequent use. I can't remember what I learned there. I must have learned something other than the cruelty of violence. . . .

Corporal Punishment Does Not Work

The most astounding revelation for some of you may be that corporal punishment of students does not work, does not, in fact, achieve its stated goal of the establishment and preservation of discipline in the classroom to create an environment for learning. *It does not do what it is supposed to do.* Why, then, do teachers resort to corporal punishment? Do they enjoy beating children? Usually, no, but one of the great dangers of the practice is that some teachers and administrators do derive pleasure from beating children, and the most horrific results accrue from such aberrant behavior. Protected by law, such individuals can only be restrained by administrative procedure and, in extreme cases, by the courts.

Teaching by Fear

The essence of corporal punishment is the inflicting of pain and humiliation. It is teaching by fear. I cannot describe either pain or humiliation as being developmentally enhancing. The lessons learned by corporal punishment are short-term and will usually disappear when the threat of punishment disappears.

Frederick Green, *The Humanist,* November/December 1988.

Why, then, do otherwise enlightened and even kindly appearing teachers use corporal punishment to enforce discipline? The answer may be that it has always been available to them. It's a shortcut. It usually stops the unruly behavior at the moment, temporarily. It is a shortcut in the same way that corporal punishment by parents is a shortcut. It has no positive permanent effects that we know of. It has many negative effects. It teaches violence as an appropriate solution to problem-solving. It teaches this lesson to the child being beaten and to his or her peers even when the beating takes place outside their presence. They feel it in the next room or down the hall. Cruelty is not mitigated by distance; the psychological harm is done to all in the class and the lesson of violence is well learned. The most important point, perhaps, is that it does not achieve the stated purpose of maintaining discipline because it is treating the symptoms, not the underlying causes, of unruly behavior. . . .

A Cry for Help

The use of corporal punishment is a failed practice. The child displaying unruly behavior is a child crying out, "Help me! Help me!" He or she may be ill-fed, hungry, or physically or emotionally abused at home. The child may be abused by parents, siblings, foster parents, parental boy friends, girl friends, aunts, uncles, and every being in his or her life. The child comes to school and we ask him or her to be quiet, curious, and excited about learning, but such behaviors are foreign to the abused child's state. Unruly behavior is a cry for help, and we answer such pleas for compassion and understanding with the end of a paddle. Teacher or parent, you cannot whip the hurt out of this child. His or her behavior continues and worsens and leads to failure after failure. He or she grows to adulthood and becomes another of our modern and enlightened society's losers—miserable and a burden to all of us.

The Time Is Now

We must work toward our immediate goal: the elimination of the pernicious and failed practice of corporal punishment from every classroom in our land. Then, we can work to make our schools a vast family support system in which the emotional development of our children will be assured.

The time is now. The Netherlands, China, France, Spain, Austria, Denmark, Germany, the United Kingdom, Ireland, Switzerland, Sweden, and the Soviet Union have led the way. It is time for the United States to catch up with what the rest of the world knows. Corporal punishment is a failed practice—destructive to our youth and to our future. *The time is now.* Let us abandon for all time the corporal punishment of our children.

a critical thinking activity

Understanding Words in Context

Readers occasionally come across words they do not recognize. And frequently, because they do not know a word or words, they will not fully understand the passage being read. Obviously, the reader can look up an unfamiliar word in a dictionary. However, by carefully examining the word in the context in which it is used, the word's meaning can often be determined. A careful reader may find clues to the meaning of the word in surrounding words, ideas, and attitudes.

Below are excerpts from the viewpoints in this chapter. In each excerpt, one word is printed in italicized capital letters. Try to determine the meaning of each word by reading the excerpt. Under each excerpt you will find four definitions for the italicized word. Choose the one that is closest to your understanding of the word.

Finally, use a dictionary to see how well you have understood the words in context. It will be helpful to discuss with others the clues which helped you decide on each word's meaning.

1. When the *RECALCITRANT* administrators ignored the governor's order to improve the schools, he fired them.

    RECALCITRANT means:

    a) willing　　　　　　　c) helpful
    b) defiant　　　　　　　d) angry

2. New Mexico increased spending on schools. If the state is a *BELLWETHER*, other states will also increase spending.

    BELLWETHER means:

    a) leader　　　　　　　c) weather sign
    b) nation　　　　　　　d) follower

3. A *CACOPHONY* of angry voices filled the school's auditorium as parents and teachers argued about censoring textbooks.

    CACOPHONY means:

    a) pleasant sound　　　c) symphony
    b) harsh noise　　　　　d) harmony

4. Although many parents wanted to join the teacher's union, they were unable to because of the group's *EXCLUSIVITY.*

   EXCLUSIVITY means:

   a) messiness
   b) unimportance
   c) restrictiveness
   d) helpfulness

5. It is *AXIOMATIC* that schools should educate all students to their fullest potential.

   AXIOMATIC means:

   a) self-evident
   b) scientific
   c) obscure
   d) ignorant

6. Giving students a choice of schools cannot solve America's educational problems, and it is dangerous to view choice as a *PANACEA* for those problems.

   PANACEA means:

   a) poison
   b) cure-all
   c) genius
   d) obstacle

7. America's many religious, ethnic, and cultural groups make it a very *PLURALISTIC* nation.

   PLURALISTIC means:

   a) diverse
   b) angry
   c) boring
   d) common

8. Because early schools taught children to read by reading the Bible, education and religion were *INEXTRICABLY* bound together.

   INEXTRICABLY means:

   a) loosely
   b) temporarily
   c) pleasantly
   d) inseparably

9. Many atheists perceive moral education based on religion as a serious *AFFRONT* to their antireligious views.

   AFFRONT means:

   a) insult
   b) compliment
   c) answer
   d) belief

10. The *PERNICIOUS* practice of corporal punishment causes irreversible physical and emotional damage to children.

   PERNICIOUS means:

   a) unimportant
   b) necessary
   c) destructive
   d) uplifting

Periodical Bibliography

The following articles have been selected to supplement the diverse views presented in this chapter.

Clint Bolick	"A Primer on Choice in Education: Part I—How Choice Works," *The Heritage Foundation Backgrounder*, March 1990.
John G. Boswell	"Improving Our Schools: Parental Choice Is Not Enough," *The World & I*, February 1990.
Ezra Bowen	"Getting Tough," *Time*, February 1, 1988.
Ernest L. Boyer	"The Third Wave of School Reform," *Christianity Today*, September 22, 1989.
John E. Chubb and Terry M. Moe	"Choice *Is* a Panacea," *The Brookings Review*, Summer 1990. Available from The Brookings Institution, 1775 Massachusetts Ave. NW, Washington, DC 20036.
Fortune	"Saving Our Schools," special issue, Spring 1990.
Frederick C. Green	"Corporal Punishment and Child Abuse," *The Humanist*, November/December 1988. Available from the American Humanist Association, 7 Harwood Dr., Box 146, Amherst, NY 14226-0146.
Thomas Lickona	"How Parents and Schools Can Work Together to Raise Moral Children," *Educational Leadership*, May 1988. Available from the Association for Supervision and Curriculum Development, 125 N. West St., Alexandria, VA 22314-2798.
Sonia L. Nazario	"Schoolteachers Say It's Wrongheaded to Try to Teach Students What's Right," *The Wall Street Journal*, April 6, 1990.
New Perspectives Quarterly	"The Education We Deserve," entire issue on education, Fall 1990.
Newsweek	"How to Teach Our Kids," special issue, Fall/Winter 1990.
Samuel D. Proctor	"To the Rescue: A National Youth Academy," *The New York Times*, September 16, 1989.
Eleanor Smith	"The New Moral Classroom," *Psychology Today*, May 1989.
P.A. Zirkel	"You Bruise, You Lose," *Phi Delta Kappan*, January 1990.

How Can Children Be Protected from Abuse?

Chapter Preface

A father brings his sixteen-month-old daughter to the emergency room of a city hospital. The child has burns on her thighs, her legs, her hands, and her cheek. The doctor, suspecting abuse, notifies Child Protective Services. The father is outraged. Later, the doctor is told by CPS that there was no abuse—the child pulled her mother's hot curling iron off the vanity and burned herself.

On another day, the same doctor talks with the young parents of a thirteen-month-old boy. The child is perfectly healthy, but the parents have been arguing and seem upset. The doctor counsels them for several hours, and feels confident that they will be able to care for their son and make their marriage work. The next day the child is brought to the emergency room with a broken leg, the result of child abuse.

These true stories illustrate how difficult it is for those who work with children—health care professionals, teachers, social workers—to accurately and effectively respond to allegations and evidence of child abuse. One of every thirty American children are reported to CPS as suspected victims of abuse or neglect, but 60 percent of child abuse reports are determined to be unfounded. Another percentage of abuse cases are never discovered until the children are dead or permanently damaged. Richard Wexler, the author of *Wounded Innocents*, a book about child abuse, believes that the system created to protect children often accuses innocent parents of child abuse while overlooking children who are truly in danger. "Every year we let hundreds of children die, force thousands more to live with strangers, and throw a million innocent families into chaos. We call this 'child protection,'" Wexler writes.

Andrew Vachss, an attorney, novelist, and well-known advocate for abused children, believes that more resources need to be devoted to ending child abuse. Child Protection Services caseworkers "are underfunded, overburdened, undersupervised and disrespected," he writes. Many experts believe that America must increase the funding for programs that protect children and educate the public about child abuse.

Estimates of the extent of child abuse are conflicting. Some experts believe that about 200,000 children are sexually or physically abused each year, while others assert that the figure is closer to 2,000,000. But even the most conservative estimates—each year, 1,100 children die from abuse, 21,000 children are victims of serious physical abuse, and more than 100,000 are sexually abused—are cause for alarm. While experts may disagree about the extent of abuse and about how to combat it, most agree with Vachss' statement that "the reduction of child abuse is a moral imperative." The authors in the following chapter discuss how this goal can be achieved.

73

"The only pedophiles I have ever heard express remorse for their acts are those facing a sentencing court or a parole board."

Imprisoning Abusers Can Protect Children from Sexual Abuse

Andrew Vachss

Andrew Vachss is a New York City attorney, an author, and a well-known expert on child abuse. In the following viewpoint Vachss argues that the only way to protect children from child abuse is to imprison child abusers. He believes that longer sentences for offenders combined with increased penalties for child pornography can decrease the number of sexually abused children in America.

As you read, consider the following questions:

1. What does Vachss believe happens to many victims of pedophiles?
2. How does the author respond to the argument that pedophiles are addicted to their behavior?
3. Name three of the steps Vachss believes Americans should take to protect children from abuse.

Recently I had a conversation with a man I greatly respect, a man who once risked his life to protect this country and now devotes that life to improving it. We talked about child sexual abuse.

The conversation ended when he asked me a blunt question: What can be done about it?

A pedophile is an individual with intense, recurrent sexually arousing fantasies and urges involving prepubescent children. Such feelings are "sick." To act on such feelings, to make them reality, is evil. The predatory pedophile is as dangerous as cancer. He works as quietly, and his presence becomes known only by the horrendous damage he leaves. He (or she) may be a teacher, a doctor, a lawyer, a judge, a scout leader, a police officer, an athletic coach, a religious counselor. And he is protected not only by our ignorance of his presence, but also by our unwillingness to confront the truth.

Few Express Remorse

I have encountered many predatory pedophiles. Some boast of their crimes, claiming that only a rigid, puritanical society prevents children from "freedom of sexual expression." Some claim they are "addicts," unable to stop themselves from preying on children. But the only pedophiles I have ever heard express remorse for their acts are those facing a sentencing court or a parole board.

Predatory pedophiles are clever, calculating criminals. They stalk their victims with great care, working themselves into positions of trust. They study children as carefully as any psychologist, and their camouflage is our unwillingness to see the shark in our swimming pool.

The consequences of their depravity can be found in our psychiatric wards, our prisons and our graveyards. The runaway who turns to child prostitution, the violent juvenile criminal, the teenage suicide. . .all too many members of this army of victims can be traced to a predatory pedophile's original attack.

The ultimate protection of such criminals, the near-immunity they enjoy, is the perception that any individual who sexually molests a child must be "sick." That trump card is only played when they are caught and prosecuted. That rarely happens. And the "rehabilitation" of predatory pedophiles is fast becoming a growth industry.

Raise the Stakes

What can be done? The answer is simple: raise the stakes.

The essence of criminal rehabilitation is remorse. Even if it is true that predatory pedophiles are "sick," that does not mean they can be treated. But, sick or not, they are certainly contagious.

Sexual molestation of children is a volitional act. It is a matter of choice.

Kiddie pornography is not a "first amendment" issue. It is a picture of a crime.

Fear of her abuser is shown in this self-portrait by a 7-year-old.

Reprinted with permission of *Parade* magazine.

Incest is not "family dysfunction." It is rape-by-extortion.

Most child molesters are not strangers to their victims. We are far more endangered by those who have our trust than by the relatively rare kidnapper.

Pedophiles do not regret their actions, they glory in them. They regret only the possibility of consequences to themselves, not the certainty of damage to their victims.

Pedophiles are not "homosexuals." We would not call a man who molested a five-year-old girl a "heterosexual." Whatever the sex of the adult and the child, the proper description is simple: the adult is the perpetrator, the child is the victim.

The "Addiction" Defense

The new pedophile defense is "addiction." They cannot help themselves. If true, such individuals will remain dangerous, and must be treated accordingly.

If we had an amnesty, allowed predatory pedophiles to turn themselves in, promised immunity from prosecution upon an agreement that they volunteer for treatment, I believe we would have no candidates.

We debate "solutions" to the narcotics problem. The solutions come down to two: interdict or legalize. Neither is possible with predatory pedophiles. Therefore, if we cannot eliminate the evil, we must increase its consequences to the perpetrators.

This is how we raise the stakes:

• Significant incarceration for offenders. Child molesters are among the least likely criminals to be prosecuted and, when prosecuted, are first in line to receive "alternative" sentencing options such as probation with psychiatric treatment. We have no problem with treatment programs for addicts. But we also have no problem with criminal sentences for those addicts who commit crimes to "support" their addiction. Nor do we have a problem with life sentences for those who traffic in narcotics. Is child sexual abuse a lesser threat to the youth of this country?

• The crime of "incest" should be eliminated, and replaced with a flat law against sexual intercourse with minors, regardless of the biological relationship between perpetrator and victim. An offender should not enjoy a lesser exposure to prison simply because he grew his own victim.

• Enhanced penalties for child sexual offenses involving more than one victim, and for more than one offense against any victim. Second offenses must result in mandatory incarceration.

Penalties for "Networking"

• Increased penalties for "networking" of any kind, including: child sex rings, trafficking in children, distribution of kiddie pornography (and the use of telephone and computer lines to promote or distribute the same).

• National registration of convicted child molesters, with agencies and institutions that work with children required to check each potential employee.

• Intensive probation supervision for released child molesters, with specialists assigned to each.

• Increased use of federal resources for interstate crimes involving child sex abuse, including use of the RICO [Racketeering Influence and Corrupt Organizations] racketeering statutes for prosecution of child sex abuse rings.

• Training of specialized law enforcement units, both investigative and prosecutorial. Increased support for those already in existence.

• Development of new weapons and adaptation of existing ones to this vital task. For example, a regulation bringing child prostitution and pornography within the scope of the child labor laws. This would require only the passage of a regulation, not legislation, and would give federal authorities immediate access to the child exploitation industry. If child prostitution and pornography are not hazardous occupations, what is?

• Let all "rehabilitative" experiments with predatory pedophiles continue. But let them continue behind bars.

Trend Toward Accountability

Some predatory pedophiles will be deterred, and children will be spared. Some will not, and the enhanced penalties will keep them away from their new victims for much longer periods of time. Either way, we benefit.

The trend today is toward accountability. It seems the ultimate irony that while some are demanding children be tried as adults on ground of "accountability," there is still no groundswell of support for the proposition that predatory pedophiles are responsible for their crimes. If we are truly concerned about crime in America, if we truly understand that today's victim is tomorrow's criminal, we must act.

We must raise the stakes in this most evil of games. The predatory pedophile has upped the ante to include not only our country's children, but its future as well. It's time to call, or fold.

"The child may suffer deep distress when the outcome of the prosecution is that the abuser goes to prison. "

Imprisoning Abusers Cannot Protect Children from Sexual Abuse

Danya Glaser and J.R. Spencer

Imprisoning child abusers cannot protect children from abuse and will most likely result in increased child abuse, the authors of the following viewpoint believe. Danya Glaser is a child psychiatrist at Guy's Hospital in London, England, and J.R. Spencer is a law lecturer at Selwyn College in Cambridge, England. They contend that the threat of imprisonment prevents abusers from confessing their crimes and seeking rehabilitation. In addition, Glaser and Spencer assert that abused children do not benefit from the guilt and loss they feel when an abusive parent is imprisoned.

As you read, consider the following questions:

1. How do the authors say other inmates treat imprisoned child abusers?
2. How do Glaser and Spencer support their belief that imprisoning the abuser only harms the abused child and his or her family?
3. What do the authors view as the aim of the rehabilitation of child abusers?

Danya Glaser and J.R. Spencer, "Sentencing, Children's Evidence, and Children's Trauma," *The Criminal Law Review*, June 1990. Reprinted with permission of Sweet & Maxwell Ltd.

It is first necessary to consider some background information relating to child sexual abuse. . . .

(a) The abusers of most (over 80 per cent. of) children whose abuse is declared, are either family members or acquaintances of the abused children. That they often have a caring role in relation to the abused child is in contrast to many offenders abusing and raping adults. Child sexual abusers therefore form a group distinct from these.

(b) The average age of abused children is 10 years, with significant numbers coming to light before the age of seven.

(c) When child sexual abuse comes to light, the majority of alleged abusers deny the abuse. Many criminal lawyers may be surprised at this, because the overwhelming majority of those who come before the criminal courts for sexual offences against children are convicted on a plea of guilty.

(d) . . . By and large, only those who admit the offence are prosecuted. In the face of denial the probability of a completed prosecution diminishes significantly. At present, therefore, only a small proportion of declared cases of child sexual abuse result in a prosecution.

(e) One reason for this low rate of prosecution is that the police sometimes decide that a prosecution, although feasible, would do more harm than good. However, the main reason is that in many cases prosecution is thought desirable, but not enough of the evidence is legally admissible to give the faintest chance of securing a conviction, let alone the "realistic prospect of conviction" which must exist before it is considered proper to institute criminal proceedings.

Little Evidence of Abuse

The difficulty is that in most cases of child sexual abuse there is little evidence of what happened apart from the word of the child or of a number of other children. Less than 50 per cent. of sexually abused children show any positive physical signs of abuse at the time of examination and even when these are present, usually they are only compatible with abuse, rather than positive proof of it. . . .

(f) If anyone does get convicted of a sexual offence against a child, he runs a high risk of being sent to prison, and one that has steadily risen as the courts have become more and more severe in their sentencing. . . .

Imprisonment for someone convicted of sexual offences against children is likely to be a particularly unpleasant experience, because the thieves, burglars and unlawful wounders who make up the bulk of the prison population share the general public's disgust and horror at child sexual abuse, and often show it by acts of violence. Thus there can be little doubt that the potentiality of imprisonment if convicted is another very powerful encouragement for perpetrators to deny the offence.

(g) The majority of sexually abused children feel guilty for the abuse, as well as not infrequently being blamed for the disclosure and its consequences. Some children are not believed by their non-abusing caregivers (e.g. mothers). . . .

(h) Where the child sexual abuse is followed by criminal proceedings these often inflict further emotional damage on the child, particularly where the person prosecuted is a close member of the family. . . .

Prison Perpetuates Violence

Sexual abuse scandals have been convenient launching pads for . . .promotion of cops and courts and prisons as a solution; predictably, the Right doesn't. . .care to mention that abuse perpetrators can't be isolated as "criminal types," that the criminal "justice" system weighs most heavily on poor people and communities of color while letting perpetrators who are affluent and/or white go unnoticed, or that the prison system only serves to perpetrate institutionalized sexual violence.

Pam Mitchell, *Resist,* January 1989.

The child may suffer deep distress when the outcome of the prosecution is that the abuser goes to prison. Although some children who have been sexually abused within the family hate their abuser, many hold ambivalent feelings towards him and others still love him and feel concern for him. These children usually wish the abuser to take responsibility for the abuse, but do not wish for him to go to prison. Finding themselves instrumental in the defendant's incarceration then further increases the child's sense of guilt, rather than affording relief in the safety the child has gained. Adding insult to injury, some children also find themselves facing the displeasure of the other members of their family for the disaster they are felt to have brought about. A prominent feature of criminal justice is that the victim of the offence is officially a nobody: he cannot directly make his own views on sentence known to the court, and the courts currently appear uninterested in them, even when offered by witnesses. . . . Children (and often their relatives who are expected to support them through the ordeal that follows disclosure of the offence) often find this failure to pay any attention to their declared wishes in relation to the abuser quite incomprehensible. Indeed, when it issues a custodial sentence, the court's apparent lack of response to the child's wishes is often perceived by the child as an extension of his or her powerlessness, of which the abuse had been a previous expression. . . .

A prison sentence is presumably intended to serve several functions.

It is meant to express society's and the victim's assumed wish for retribution. The problem here, as we have seen, is that society's real or assumed needs in the matter are usually given precedence over the wishes of the victim, sometimes to the victim's considerable distress.

Imprisonment Offers Protection

Imprisonment is also designed to offer protection, both to the victim and to society in general. A prison sentence is undoubtedly effective in this respect for as long as the defendant stays inside, but unfortunately it does nothing to protect anybody from him after his release. Recidivism rates for this addictive problem are thought to be high without effective treatment, which is not included in imprisonment practice. If full protection from further abuse was seriously contemplated as forming the paramount consideration in the determination of the sentence, then the only way to achieve this with certainty would be by the imposition of very long or even indeterminate sentences on abusers, a suggestion which lacks regard for the human rights of the abusers, and which would create a public outcry for that reason. There are, however, exceptional cases where harsh as this would be, it would be more sensible than the approach, in which the duration of the required protection from the abuser is usually set quite arbitrarily, and with no regard for ensuring the safety of his previous and future victims. In the absence of any meaningful plans for developing and offering treatment for abusers as part of their imprisonment, there can be little reason to assume that the abuser will undergo any positive changes while in prison. Indeed, there is increasing evidence to suggest that the necessary herding of sexual abusers together offers reinforcement in the form of opportunities for further sexual excitement and sharing of their sexual experiences.

Imprisonment is also designed to act as a deterrent to potential abusers. To some extent it may do this, but the experience of many sexually abused children is that the intended deterrent of a prison sentence seriously misfires, because abusers often successfully use the threat of their own imprisonment if they are found out, as a way of persuading the child not to tell anyone about the abuse. Indeed, rather than deterring abuse, imprisonment seems far more likely to deter reporting of the abuse.

Lastly, there is the potential for rehabilitation. The aim here is to lead to the cessation of sexually abusive activity and the assumption of true responsibility for all aspects of the abuse. In the absence of treatment, and in view of the considerable propen-

82

sity for denial of responsibility by abusers, imprisonment actually serves to increase the sense of victimisation and powerlessness of the abuser.

If a judge is reading this paper he will probably be thinking thus:

> It is easy enough to say that we should not send intrafamilial child abusers to prison, but what else can we do with them? These cases are usually far too serious for a fine. We cannot simply let the matter pass. What alternative is there?

In a number of the most serious cases, sadly, the answer must be that there is no alternative to prison. But in others there does exist a possibility of ordering treatment under a named psychiatrist by means of a carefully constructed Psychiatric or other Probation Order, with a condition of residence away from home. . . .

A Stick and a Carrot

If the criminal law is to deal effectively with the problem of child sexual abuse, it needs both a stick and a carrot to persuade the guilty to admit what they have done. The stick should not take the form of increased prison sentences, but rational changes in the law of criminal evidence to increase the chances of convicting the guilty. We need to alter the present state of affairs so that there is a realistic likelihood of convicting a guilty person even where he does not confess, so that there is less point in denying his offence. The carrot should be less reliance on imprisonment, and greater use of treatment, for those who are prepared to admit their guilt and accept responsibility for their behaviour. If a coordinated approach meant more admissions, it might mean less need for criminal proceedings in a number of cases where they would otherwise be necessary (e.g. through the use of police cautions where the abuser agrees to undergo treatment). It should also mean that insofar as more child abuse cases do result in criminal proceedings there is not an enhanced proportion of "not guilty" pleas among them. . . .

A probation order with conditions attached may be the right method of dealing with a father who has pleaded guilty to incest, bearing in mind his good character, his immediate admission of guilt, and the fact that sending him to prison would have serious ill-effects for the victim and the rest of her family. So there is room for hope.

"Research findings offer compelling evidence for continuing our efforts to educate all children, even preschoolers, about [child abuse]."

School Prevention Programs Can Protect Children from Sexual Abuse

Deborah Daro

School programs that teach children about abuse can help them identify and prevent such abuse, Deborah Daro contends in the following viewpoint. Daro maintains that child abusers are deterred by children who have been taught in school to resist abuse. In addition, some abused children will be more willing to reveal their abuse if the subject is discussed in school. Daro is the director of the Center on Child Abuse Prevention Research for the National Committee for Prevention of Child Abuse in Chicago, Illinois.

As you read, consider the following questions:

1. Why does the author think that school prevention programs are controversial?
2. What factors does Daro believe determine why some children learn more from prevention programs than others?
3. How does Daro think prevention programs can help educators, parents, and children?

Deborah Daro, "Child Sexual Abuse Prevention: Separating Fact from Fiction," a position paper from the National Committee for Prevention of Child Abuse, published December 1989. Reprinted with the author's permission.

The prevention of child sexual abuse presents a major challenge to our society. One of the most common strategies to combat this particular variant of the child abuse problem has been the provision of classroom-based instructions for children of all ages on how to protect themselves from sexual assault and what to do if they experience actual or potential abuse. In addition, these programs provide educational opportunities for teachers and parents to review curriculum content, child abuse reporting procedures, and local service resources.

Sharp disagreement has emerged among professionals as well as parents regarding the overall merits of these efforts. Of particular concern has been the worry that the programs raise unnecessary anxiety among children, particularly young children, regarding the safety of their own homes. Further, critics argue that these programs raise unrealistic expectations that children, once educated on the topic, can fend off abuse.

Gains Undermined by Debate

Both proponents and critics of these programs have cast a scientific aura over the debate, drawing on a variety of research efforts and theories of child development to support their particular conclusions. This strategy, while appearing rational, has polarized even thoughtful observers into extreme positions. Rather than moving the field toward a deeper understanding of the issue, the present debate has confounded the public's understanding of child assault prevention programs and has undermined the gains that have been made in the public's recognition of sexual abuse.

The simple fact is that limited research findings exist on both the positive and potential negative effects of child assault prevention education. Relatively few evaluations have employed experimental designs, compared the relative merits of different intervention strategies and utilized sample sizes greater than 100 children. The vast majority of these efforts have samples of less than 50 children and draw their conclusions from the differences noted on knowledge and behavioral tests given prior to and shortly after the intervention. Progress is measured in terms of average group performance between these two testing periods. While such comparisons are useful in determining if a specific curriculum has any notable impact on a child's attitudes, knowledge or behavior, this type of research cannot inform policy makers about what types of children may have difficulty learning or what presentation methods are most effective.

However, those few evaluations which have compared the performance of different groups of children to various types of programs offer useful insights. Such studies have repeatedly found that children do learn the concepts presented in these courses, even those presented over a very limited period of time. As with all interventions, this learning is uneven. Factors which have been associated with some children learning more than others include the child's level of self-esteem, prior exposure to the concepts, and age, with older children (i.e. fourth to sixth graders) learning more complex concepts than younger children (i.e. kindergarten through third grade). The one exception to this pattern was an evaluation of a behavioral-based curriculum with 670 children ages three through 10 which found that preschoolers demonstrated learning equal or superior to first, second or third graders.

Fear and Anxiety

A small group of studies have found some children more leery of strangers, more uncertain about types of touches one might view as benign (e.g. bathing and tickling) and occasionally anxious about the realization that they might be abused by someone they know and trust. Three studies found that a small percentage (5%) of participants experience more notable degrees of fear and anxiety as evidenced by increased reports of nightmares, bed wetting and changed reactions to physical affection. However, no study has documented that such effects last beyond the period immediately following the program.

Helping Children to Say "No"

Child sexual abuse prevention programs aimed at school-aged children appear to be useful in helping children avoid sexually abusive situations and say no to inappropriate touch by adults.

U.S. Department of Health and Human Services, *Child Abuse and Neglect: A Shared Community Concern*, March 1989.

Just as all children do not have the same reaction to these programs, the wide range child assault prevention programs available throughout the country are not interchangeable. Programs which generate the greatest controversy and, in some instances, the fewest gains are those which present concepts too abstract for the target audience, encourage children to utilize self-defence techniques to fend off abusers, and are imposed upon communities rather than selected by them. In contrast, program features found most useful in conveying knowledge and in building skills include tailoring material to a child's cognitive characteristics and learning abilities, presenting material in a stimulating and varied manner, and providing children opportunities to rehearse prevention strategies through staged interactions. More recently, the most effective of these programs have shifted away from stressing abstract concepts such as "good touch" versus "bad touch" and now emphasize building specific skills in such areas as assertive behavior, decision-making and communication.

Compelling Evidence for Education

While we lack solid empirical evidence on the merits and drawbacks of these programs, other research findings offer compelling evidence for continuing our efforts to educate all children, even preschoolers, about this topic. First, we know that child sexual abuse has devastating consequences for children, many of whom carry enormous feelings of guilt and responsibility for their victimization throughout their childhood and adult lives. Low self-esteem, clinical depression and an inability to have positive and satisfying personal and sexual relationships are characteristic of many victims. While it is difficult to document the degree to which child assault prevention instructions prevent initial victimization, the programs do provide children an opportunity to disclose prior or ongoing abuse thereby reducing the possibility for revictimization and minimizing the emotional trauma associated with being unable to discuss the abuse.

Second, the behavior and comments of perpetrators suggest the programs are indeed having a positive impact. Sexual abuse offenders interviewed by various researchers report that they are deterred by a child who indicates that he or she would tell a specific adult about the assault. Perpetrators seek out passive, troubled or lonely children and increasingly younger children, who can be counted on to maintain the secret of an abusive relationship. Regardless of the ability of child assault prevention programs to successfully convey all of the concepts they cover, teaching young children the simple task of telling an adult when a situation confuses them may justify retaining these programs.

In the absence of clear scientific proof regarding the efficacy of these programs, opponents and advocates have attacked each other with dramatic stories, misused statistics and gross generalizations. Some opponents have sought to dismantle all classroom-based instruction on the grounds that such efforts are both ineffective and dangerous. Many advocates have argued for the retention of all programs as if all existing curricula were equally effective. Neither of these two positions are empirically defensible nor are they solid public policy. Not all programs are good. Not all are bad. Some preschoolers learn. Some do not. These programs do tell children that their own parents might abuse them. For some children, this message unfortunately is true. It is not fair to say that these programs unnecessarily scare children. Sexual abuse is a reality and it is a reality for very young children.

No one has ever claimed that child assault prevention instructions should be the sole emphasis in preventing child sexual abuse with children of any age. Prevention efforts need to target simultaneously the potential victim, potential perpetrator, and those aspects of the social fabric that nurture abusive behaviors. Child assault prevention education should do more than instruct children in safety skills. The intervention can offer an opportunity for educators and parents to work together in creating safer environments for children. Training parents as well as teachers on the topic of sexual abuse has resulted in more open discussions regarding this topic between parents and children and teachers feeling more confident in discussing the concepts with their students and their colleagues.

"The only reasonable step that school systems can undertake. . .is to place an immediate moratorium on all [child abuse prevention] programs. "

School Prevention Programs Cannot Protect Children from Sexual Abuse

W. Allan Garneau

W. Allan Garneau has been an elementary school principal for twelve years and an educator for twenty-five. In the following viewpoint, Garneau argues that school abuse prevention programs frighten children unnecessarily and do nothing to prevent child abuse from occurring. Children are often confused by the information presented in such programs, he maintains, and this confusion can harm many children. Garneau believes that the risks presented by prevention programs far outweigh any benefits to children.

As you read, consider the following questions:

1. Why does Garneau believe abuse prevention programs were first developed?
2. What effect does the author think abuse prevention programs have on families?
3. What does Garneau say schools should do if some parents insist on continuing abuse prevention programs?

W. Allan Garneau, "Focus: Child Sexual Abuse Awareness Programs," *Education Reporter*, February 1989. Reprinted with permission.

Programs to deal with the prevention of child sexual abuse, generally accepted by parents and educators 'til now, are beginning to experience a backlash. Increasing numbers of parents are pulling their children out of programs at school, and along with others whose children have participated with negative results, they are calling for an end to the programs. Objective consideration of the programs is essential by everyone in a position of responsibility in our school system.

Why were the programs developed in the first place? First of all, our attention was drawn to the problem of child sexual abuse by what seemed to be a proliferation of cases, many of them quite repugnant to our sensitivities. Reaction quite naturally included an interest in seeking some means to avoid such events from reoccurring. Since the actual rate of incidence was somewhat obscure, "experts" began to guess, projecting figures from the known to the unknown. Once some of these guesses were revealed, they took on a legitimacy that was probably quite unwarranted.

Well-meaning people, motivated by fright and having their fears reenforced by the overwhelming media coverage of a few cases, continued to encourage development of programs they hoped would rid us of this horrible situation for our children. It seemed natural to want the school, with its captive audience, to take on the task. Not surprisingly, every child was seen as a potential victim, overlooking the fact that using the broadest definition of abuse, about three-quarters of our children would never be sexually abused. With the victim in mind, no thought seemed to have been devoted to how the innocent, non-victim might react to the program.

Good and Bad Touching

The initial thrust was based on the touch continuum, that is a range of 'touching' from good to bad, along with another unwarranted assumption that children would automatically sense that abusive touching would feel bad, and that appropriate touching would feel good. Did no one realize that the young, rejected 14-year-old might actually accept the attention from an exploiter as a "good" touch, since it could be perceived as affection? Or that the mushy kiss from a dear aunt at the airport would be warded off by the ten-year-old boy armed with the knowledge that if you don't like it, it must be abusive? A pioneer in the field who developed this concept has changed her mind about the value of programs based on her good-bad touch ideas. Cordelia Anderson (Kent), from Minnesota, now wishes she hadn't thought of it, since it oversimplifies the concept and makes it an easy answer to give kids; the majority of touch is, she now accepts, confusing.

There is no indication that anyone did any prior research into outcomes that might be experienced by the child who cannot relate to program information because he/she is not, nor would likely ever be, in a sexually exploitive situation. Young children have difficulty dealing with abstract thought, and consequently, their imaginations can be quite unpredictable. One immediate reaction among children is the surprising number who engage in play-acting and demonstrating situations with each other.

Courses Confuse Children

Parents claim that the [child sexual abuse prevention] course confuses children as to whom they can trust, arouses a curiosity about their bodies that is unnatural at their ages, and above all is not suitable for such young children. They also fear that [it] may have long-term negative effects that later would prevent the children from having a normal sexual life because it presents sex as dangerous and frightening.

Phyllis Schlafly, *The Washington Times*, February 28, 1989.

The most serious reaction to the programs, though, is the confusion created over what constitutes normal family affection and interaction. The emphasis placed by most programs on the lack of trust that can be placed on family members has caused an untold number of children to shun their parents', particularly father's, normal affection. Several quite tragic occurrences have become known to the writer; the worst feature of these events is that the normal family relationship that pre-existed has been unalterably destroyed.

Parents Become Suspects

Parents concerned about these and other reactions have withdrawn their children from the school program (or the school). Yet, even though some of them are told that this is a legitimate option, an immediate suspicion is cast upon any parents who do so. After all, there must be something to hide. In literature which accompanies some of the programs, teachers are told of this possibility, so that parents who decline participation are suspected or even being reported and investigated for child abuse on the sole evidence of their refusal!

Even a child who has been abused can be a victim of the programs. The programs anticipate that a sexually abused child will acquire the skills to blow the whistle on the situation. What is the probable effect on a girl who has been through an abusive situation, and is now well into the healing process? What is she to think when a teacher tells the class that one can just say NO, when that was not likely the case involving her?

Another unwarranted assumption is the idea that a child can deter sexual abuse by becoming assertive and just saying NO. Who would even suggest that tactic for the child who is regularly physically or verbally abused? Why would we think that sexual abuse is any different? Not only does it likely create a false sense of security, but is it really a practical alternative for the young girl to deal with an older, physically superior male?

Returning to families, one must question the emphasis on incest found in most programs. The way in which statistics about the incidence of sexual abuse are thrown around would lead one to think that incest is quite a common form of abuse. In fact, the teachers' guide to the C.A.R.E. [Child Abuse Resource and Education] program makes that very statement. If sexual abuse is experienced by one in four, what portion of those are incest? The field at the moment is somewhat vague on this, but the general rate agreed to by researchers is about one per *thousand*. That seems hard to believe, given the attention paid to abuse by family members in programs. Further information suggests that two-thirds of the cases involving "father" mean someone other than the biological father—mother's boyfriend, stepfather, etc.

One other interesting statistic given by researchers in this field is that any intervention program puts participants at some risk of unintended, damaging reaction. The acknowledged rate of such damage is said to occur to about 3 percent of the participants. It might be concluded from this that programs which focus on incest risk damaging 30 children per thousand, in an effort to reach a target of one.

While many outcomes are possible, the most serious damage that can occur is that of the destruction of the family through the mere suspicion of abuse. Normal relationships are at risk, putting fathers, grandfathers, uncles, cousins and brothers in a suspect position.

Where is the child encouraged to seek help? In other words, who can the child trust? Well naturally, programs emphasize teachers, police, and social workers, and so on. Parents are rarely seen as useful allies in these programs, implying that parents are the majority abusers. The number of cases that end up in court, however, seem to involve the trusty caretakers as much as, if not more than, the untrustworthy parents.

Harm to the Family

The effect these programs have on family integrity is something that will only show over time, but my guess now is that it will be quite significant. Do schools have the right to put children through a program that causes them to question their family's beliefs or traditions? Dr. James Krivacska puts it this way: "The imposition of a value system that changes a child's interpersonal interactions with family members is an infringement on family privacy, the right of a parent to inculcate their child with their family's value system."

Children Avoid Normal Affection

Child abuse prevention programs are ineffective and should be eliminated and efforts to teach very young children the difference between "good" and "bad" touches confuse children and may frighten them away from normal affection.

Education Reporter, February 1989.

Aside from this, one must not overlook the effect on any typical child. At the outset, I suggested that we often treat children as more sophisticated than they really are, and in the process, deny them a real childhood. The loss of innocence is something all of us should be examining in the light of recent evidence. Most young children are not capable of the abstract thought and ability to use adult virtues in their reactions to the training in the programs. We might then expect the results to be not just different from what is intended, but harmful as well. Research has shown that scare tactics, or instruction in preventative techniques beyond the child's level of understanding or ability to implement, actually increase the child's vulnerability. Children have a basic right to grow up believing that their world is fundamentally a nurturing place, to be free from undue worry or anxiety. Young children need security above all; most teachers know this. So why do they engage in a program designed to supplant this necessity?

Body Ownership

Children need to be given sound and reliable information. One of the concepts of abuse prevention is to convince the child of body ownership. However, the concept of body ownership belies the reality that we do not allow children the right to control access to their bodies on many occasions. They must go to the dentist, wash behind their ears, which, by the way, they cannot poke full of holes at will. We understand the difference; do they?

In the long range, can we be certain that the introduction to ideas now will not have long-lasting negative effects on them as adults? Several researchers are concerned that the young child's first exposure to any discussion of sex being solely within the extremely negative context of abuse will lead to warped sexual relationships as adults.

One other question that occurs to me, and I am surprised that not many have brought it up, is the amount of time devoted to the topic in school. With the demands on the school day increasing, and time for the basic curriculum at a premium, why have teachers not been more verbal in their objection to this? Just how much time is needed for anyone to get the message across to children about their right to protect their "private parts"? It sure doesn't take ten formal sessions at home to accomplish the task.

One unintended outcome of the programs is to give children a vocabulary with which to fabricate stories about abuse. Once it was said, and probably with some truth, that children do not lie about these things. That, as several visible, and not-so-visible court cases (over child custody) have shown, is no longer the situation.

As a school principal who takes seriously the responsibility we have for the well-being of our young children, and as a parent who has high regard for the integrity of the family, I cannot justify the undertaking of an activity which threatens both. The victims are children, but the responsibility is ours. Children send a variety of signals that something is going on, even if the message is obscure. Why cannot we spend what resources we have to better equip parents, teachers and other adults how to read the signals?

Immeasurable Damage

In the meantime, who can really measure just what damage is caused to any child who suffers some form of sexual abuse? For some, it is tragic and long-lasting; for others, the healing is quick. But how do we compare that to the damage possible among normal children because of a well-meaning attempt to protect them? To continue the proliferation of some of the programs we subject our children to is a betrayal. The loss of trust and closeness among a happy family cannot be justified on the basis that someone had good intentions. As G. K. Chesterton has observed, "we have this modern and morbid habit of sacrificing the normal to the abnormal."

The onus is on those who feel that these programs are safe and effective to produce sufficient evidence. Any research that purports to demonstrate the positive effect of the programs seems limited to measuring gains in knowledge, but the researchers fail to demonstrate how that knowledge is of any benefit.

In the meantime, the only reasonable step that school systems can undertake in the wake of the rapidly building file of negative reaction is to place an immediate moratorium on all such programs (even though I believe enough evidence exists to cancel them altogether). It is my opinion that, not only will evidence justifying the programs not materialize, but that any attempt to "fix" them will not succeed. When something is fundamentally wrong because the inherent philosophy is faulty, then tinkering with the parts will get nowhere.

Optional Programs

In spite of the indicators which merit some attention, many teachers and parents will still believe that the way to deal with the serious problem of sexual abuse of children is to continue and expand the "prevention" programs. If, with the evidence accumulating, some are not compelled to change the approach, then the information available must be made known to parents and teachers before any program begins (the concept of informed consent). Then, those who still wish their children to participate should be given the option of doing so, but only on an "opt-in" arrangement.

David Finkelhor, one of the proponents of such programs for children, acknowledges that reasonable questions have been raised about the effectiveness of these programs and possible negative side effects. He admits that the present positive effects are measured merely by "enthusiastic response," and makes this incredible statement: "sexual abuse prevention promises to be one of the great social experiments of the decade." How can we continue to make guinea pigs out of our young children?

The resources spent on the programs for children must be turned toward programs which increase the awareness of adults, to better interpret the messages children send, and to bring about effective prevention. With what is at stake for our children and their families, it is vital that we change our focus soon.

"There is still a great demand for foster care."

Foster Care Can Protect Children from Physical Abuse

Barbara Kantrowitz with Patricia King

Barbara Kantrowitz is a senior writer and Patricia King is a news editor for *Newsweek,* a weekly newsmagazine. In the following viewpoint, Kantrowitz and King maintain that foster homes can nurture abused children and protect them from further abuse. The authors contend that abused children need to feel the security and comfort of being part of a stable family, and foster homes meet this need.

As you read, consider the following questions:

1. Why do the authors believe the foster parent's job is becoming more difficult?
2. What do Kantrowitz and King think motivates people to become foster parents?
3. Why do the authors believe more specialized care could improve the foster care system?

The nearly 50 foster children who have passed through JoAnn and Jim Miller's home were the walking wounded, victims of neglect or abuse by their families and sometimes also of a child-welfare system that can seem worse than the ills it tries to cure. Eight-year-old Elizabeth's previous foster family had given up on her after she killed a kitten. A victim of sexual abuse by her father, she refused to wear underwear and exposed herself on the school bus. Chris was a precociously independent six-year-old, used to looking after himself and his brother when his mother left the house for days at a time; he had a hard time being part of a family. An inexperienced caseworker insisted that 13-year-old Tammy be taken away from the Millers and returned to her step-father, who then sexually abused her.

Doors Remain Open

The Millers have seen shocking things in the 15 years that they have been foster parents but the doors of their Elkhart, Ind., home have remained open to youngsters who need help. "I want the children to feel they are loved, no matter what," says JoAnn, 35. She and her husband, a 37-year-old aircraft mechanic, are among the approximately 200,000 foster families in this country. They form a vital link in the foster-care system. Children end up in foster care for a variety of reasons; the most common is abuse or neglect. Social-service agencies place them with the foster families or in institutions and group homes. While the larger facilities may be appropriate for children with particular problems, most kids want to feel they are still part of a family even if it isn't their own. "You want to be able to call someone 'Mom' and 'Dad'," says Eric Brettschneider, a consultant and former New York City deputy commissioner for human resources. "You don't want to feel like you're Little Orphan Annie."

In the last few years, the job of the foster parent has become increasingly difficult. Spurred by changes in federal law and a widespread movement for reform of the foster-care system, child-welfare agencies in many parts of the country have made a greater effort to help natural families stay together. The theory is that children should be separated from their parents only in severe cases of neglect or abuse. As a result, children who do end up in foster care often come from the very worst home situations. In some cities, there has been an increase in the number of children who are separated from their families because the parents abuse drugs or alcohol. These children can have serious emotional and physical problems. A shortage of foster families has meant that many foster parents are overburdened. . . .

Even under the best of circumstances, foster parents must maintain a precarious balance between providing love and yet not becoming so deeply attached that letting go becomes unbearable. Foster care is supposed to be a temporary solution. In recent years, according to Toshio Tatara of the American Public Welfare Association, over half of the more than 250,000 children annually in foster care have been eventually reunited with their natural families; an additional 10 percent were adopted. In general, a child's chances of being returned to his parents diminish with each year that he is in foster care, says Marcia Robinson Lowry, director of the American Civil Liberties Union's Children's Rights Projects.

Holding On

In many cases, the natural parents still maintain some contact and good foster parents are sensitive to the children's need to feel connected to their families during the separation. JoAnn Miller remembers one pitifully abused 18-month-old baby who weighed only 14 pounds and had a broken arm and a bruised body. Yet the baby reached out to her mother when she came to visit although she held on to JoAnn tightly as well. JoAnn tries to work with the natural parents although she often feels angry about the way they treat the children. One four-year-old boy refused to turn five because his mother hadn't given him a party. JoAnn finally gave his mother a cake mix so his life could go on. Another child fell asleep with his chin on the windowsill waiting for his father—who showed up three days later. The success stories make it worthwhile. One drug-addicted couple spent four years kicking their habit before they got their children back. Says JoAnn: "Four years is nothing if it works."

A Different Kind of Home

After spending time [in a foster home], children learn for the first time that they're hit and abused not because they're horrible and worthless children, but because of a madness in their home. They'll learn that a house can be different—that there are adults to trust and rely on who will never beat you or blame you, but comfort you instead.

National Foster Parent Association, "A Foster Mother's Story," 1988.

Foster parents have recently suffered from a generally negative public perception that many of them are in it only for the money. But social workers say that although there are some people who take in kids just to get the stipends (which generally run from about $5 to $12 a day for children without special needs), the money is usually barely enough to cover the cost of feeding and clothing a child. More often, people become foster parents out of altruism. "The vast majority of foster parents see this as part of their life's work," says Jim Lardie, president of the Association of Child Advocates. "They say that this is what they were put on earth to do."

The Millers became foster parents when they thought they wouldn't be able to have children. Although they now have five children of their own and have adopted two former foster children, they have never stopped taking in foster children and the household now includes three. Jim says that the guiding principle of the disparate clan is: "Treat the foster children like your own." The rules are the same for everybody, and all the children have regular chores and responsibilities. Larry Mandt, a psychologist who has worked with two of the Millers' foster children, says living in a solid family setting was more therapeutic than weekly counseling sessions. After three years with the Millers, Elizabeth, the little girl who had been so unmanageable when she first arrived, had become an integral part of the Millers' extended family. It wasn't easy; there were many angry confrontations and tears and hugs afterward. But the combination of love and structure worked. There were tears in everyone's eyes when she left for an adoptive home where she could be with her older brothers.

For many foster parents, getting through the complex child-welfare system can be as daunting as handling troubled children. Understaffed agencies often don't have the resources to provide the support services and training programs that parents need. Some experts think that more specialized foster care would help; parents could be trained to handle children with specific emotional or physical problems. A multilayered system is another approach, says Theodore Stein, a professor of social policy at the State University of New York. Certain foster parents could be targeted to receive children for short-term stays; other parents would receive only youngsters who were likely candidates for eventual adoption.

Staying Together

Keeping children out of foster care in the first place is the long-term goal of many children's advocates. A number of innovative programs aimed at family preservation have been started in the last few years. At Kingsley House in New Orleans, for example, families receive intensive counseling for six to eight weeks in an effort to get them through an immediate crisis—such as loss of housing—that might have split up the family. Maudelle Davis, the assistant executive director, says that of the 90 families served by the program since late 1985, 94 percent are still together.

"Foster care is not safe."

Foster Care Cannot Protect Children from Physical Abuse

Michael B. Mushlin

Abused children are more likely to be harmed than helped by foster care, Michael B. Mushlin argues in the following viewpoint. Mushlin believes that many foster parents are child abusers. A better system of care must be created to treat abused children and to protect them from further abuse, he contends. Mushlin is a law professor at Pace University in New York City.

As you read, consider the following questions:

1. What does the author believe is the reason for the increased rates of foster-care abuse and neglect of children?
2. What evidence does Mushlin give showing that foster care does not protect abused children from further abuse?
3. How does physical abuse affect a child's development, according to the author?

In a midwestern community not long ago, a one-year-old girl who required constant medical attention for epileptic seizures was sent by a state child welfare department to a foster home known by the state to be inadequate. In fact, the caseworker assigned by the state to supervise the home had recommended that the department not use this "marginal" setting except on a temporary, short-term basis. Children sent to this home in the past had been "ill clothed" and had not received attention for medical problems. The warning was ignored. When the child's caseworker reported that the foster parents were not bringing the child to her scheduled medical appointments, again the child welfare department did not respond. Finally, after two and one-half years and pressure from the child's physician, the child was removed from the foster home. By this time, the child, now three and one-half, had not received treatment for her epilepsy and was also experiencing other medical problems. Even after an official finding of abuse by the state was registered against the home for its failure to care for this child, the state continued to use the foster home without interruption as a placement for abused and neglected children.

Other Incidents of Abuse

In the same state, another foster child was assaulted while in foster care. The state knew of the attack, but did nothing. Within four months, the child was sexually abused by the foster father in the same home. In a third foster home, a four-year-old girl was whipped by her foster mother and made to stand with her hands extended over her head for thirty minutes. The child was being punished for being dirty. Although the caseworker determined that the child had been beaten, and reported this to her superiors, no action was taken and the child was returned to the home.

In another part of the country, a troubled young boy who wet his bed was placed in a foster home. The foster mother, frustrated at her inability to control his behavior, sought help from the state's child welfare agency. Her pleas were ignored. The situation deteriorated until one night the foster mother forced the child to "drink his urine."

None of these cases received public attention, nor were any of them the subject of reported court decisions or large damage awards. Each, however, is an example of the stark reality of life in foster homes for too many of the nation's half-million foster children. . . . In the last twenty-five years, the number of children in foster care has increased fivefold. The foster care program now ranks with prisons, mental institutions and juvenile detention and treatment centers as a major state-operated custodial program. . . .

Foster care is intended to provide a temporary, safe haven for children whose parents are unable to care for them. Too often, however, this purpose is not realized. Frequently, foster children are exposed to abuse and neglect by foster parents, and to serious injury due to the failure of the system itself to provide for stable care, or to attend to the children's medical problems. The failure of foster care programs to follow appropriate minimum standards that would ensure the care and protection of children has led to increased rates of foster care abuse and neglect. Despite the considerable costs, to both the children affected and to society generally, the political process has been unresponsive to calls for reform of foster care systems.

© Graston/Rothco. Reprinted with permission.

Whatever the reason for placement, foster children have not had a normal upbringing. By definition, the bonds to a foster child's permanent family have been disrupted. Foster children suffer disproportionately from serious emotional, medical and psychological disabilities. To compound matters, it is well-established that they are at high risk of further maltreatment while in foster care. Foster children, therefore, are especially vulnerable individuals, prone to become victims unless special care is taken to protect them. . . .

No one knows how many children are abused or neglected while in foster care, but the problem is more widespread than is currently acknowledged. Children in foster family care have been reported severely beaten and killed. In addition, cases in which children have been subjected to bizarre punishments or parental neglect are common.

Foster children seem peculiarly vulnerable to sexual abuse. This is a special problem because, by definition, there is no permanent kinship bond in foster care. As a result, the traditional incest taboo does not operate. The lack of permanent ties combined with the cultural and class gaps that often exist between foster families and foster children also can create an explosive environment in which expressions of verbal hostility often erupt.

High Rates of Abuse

While foster care has been frequently criticized for other reasons, some observers claim that, at the very least, children in foster care are protected from a high risk of abuse and neglect of the type just described. The evidence, however, does not bear out these hopes. One study reported that the rate of substantiated abuse and neglect in New York City foster family care was more than one and one-half times that of children in the general population. A national survey of foster family abuse and neglect, completed in 1986 by the National Foster Care Education Project, revealed rates of abuse that, at their highest, were over ten times greater for foster children than for children in the general population. . . .

The actual amount of abuse and neglect may be much greater than anyone imagines. One study attempted to account for unreported or uninvestigated abuse and neglect in assessing the risk of abuse and neglect in foster boarding home care. The study concluded that forty-three percent of the children studied had been placed in an unsuitable foster home, and that fifty-seven percent of the children in the foster care system who were examined were at serious risk of harm while in foster care. . . .

A Right to Safety

The time has come to recognize that foster children have a right to safety while in foster care. Foster care is intended to be a temporary refuge for children whose parents cannot care for them. But in practice, more often than has been acknowledged by many observers, foster care is not safe. Abuse and neglect of foster children occur at levels that far exceed in quantity and magnitude what a reasonably run system of care should produce. State-countenanced mistreatment of innocent children has serious ramifications for society. The infliction of harm on children who have suffered the trauma of parental default retards or even eliminates their potential for normal development. However, the political process has proven to be ineffective in alleviating this problem. Foster children, drawn largely from the disadvantaged and from minority groups, simply do not have access or influence to move the executive or legislative branches of government to increase the funding needed to bring about change. As a practical matter, the courts must become involved if foster care is to function as it is intended.

"Acting on behalf of a child may well save her from future abuse or even save her life."

Intervention by Strangers Can Protect Children from Physical Abuse

Joanna Simms

Many Americans are reluctant to act when they see a parent abusing a child in public. In the following viewpoint, Joanna Simms argues that this reluctance to become involved in another family's problems must be overcome to protect children from abuse. She believes that confronting the parent or calling the police may save a child from a life of abuse. Simms is a freelance writer and contributor to *Parents* magazine.

As you read, consider the following questions:

1. What five reasons does Simms give to explain why people are unwilling to become involved when they see a child abused in public?
2. How might an abuser react when confronted by a stranger, according to the author?
3. What does the author think about false accusations of child abuse?

Joanna Simms, "Witness to Child Abuse," *Parents*, May 1989. Reprinted with permission of the author.

As much as child abuse has always saddened me, I had never really considered it my problem; after all, I didn't abuse my children, nor did I know anyone who did.

That was before my thirteen-year-old daughter, Katy, and I became unwilling spectators of a vicious case of child abuse not long ago. She and I *did* act, and according to the police department, what we did was proper and sufficient. Yet we have been haunted by the feeling that we did not do enough.

We had made a late-afternoon stop at a supermarket in our Denver suburb, and as we approached the store we heard piercing screams coming from a dilapidated old-model car. A child's voice was pleading, "No! No! Please . . . don't. Don't, please!" The cries were punctuated by the sound of sickening thuds, and we saw a large, bearded man in the front seat of the parked car punching the child with terrific force with his clenched fist. Although we could not see enough of the child to determine his age or even his sex (he was lying on the front seat), our guess was that he was a five- or six-year-old boy.

After several punches the child was silent, but his attacker continued to beat him. Then he turned to the backseat and proceeded to hit something there. Was it possible, we wondered, that there was another prostrate child in the back?

Call to Police

In a state of shocked disbelief, we considered what to do. Almost automatically my daughter walked toward the car, intending to open the door on the passenger's side to rescue the victim. I cried out, "Katy, get back!" She did, but reluctantly. With the fearlessness common to youth, she was certain that she could save the helpless youngster. I, on the other hand, was afraid of Katy's being attacked.

We wrote down the license-plate number and a description of the car and then hurried to call the police. Before the officer arrived, however, the abuser and his victim were gone.

On the way home Katy cried. She blamed me for not allowing her to open the car door in an attempt to get the child. "I just know I could have saved that little boy, Mom," she said. "I hate it that he thought no one cared!" I felt like crying, too, for it seemed we had actually witnessed a crime and had done little to stop it.

The officer had assured us and the two other witnesses who had come forward that we had acted correctly in promptly notifying the police department. He had said there could have been legal problems if we had snatched someone else's child. Still, Katy and I felt we could have done more, and I told myself I would never again witness child abuse without trying to stop it.

Since then I have observed two other incidents of abusive behavior toward children. Both times I confronted the abusers, in one case provoking a physical attack upon myself.

The first incident occurred after an event at the Denver Coliseum. As the crowd quietly filed out of the building I heard shouting on the sidewalk out front. Expecting to see a fight developing, I was astonished to find a huge fellow yelling at a baby who couldn't have been more than eighteen months old. He was shaking her stroller roughly and ordering her to stop crying. Several people in the exiting crowd stopped to stare. No one, however, did anything. When I could stand it no longer, I walked over to speak to him.

"Please don't treat your little girl like that," I pleaded, almost in tears. "She's only tired, you know."

Signs of Possible Child Abuse

	Physical Abuse	Physical Neglect
Physical Indicators	• unexplained bruises (in various stages of healing), welts, human bite marks, bald spots • unexplained burns, especially cigarette burns or immersion burns (glove like) • unexplained fractures, lacerations or abrasions	• abandonment • unattended medical needs • consistent lack of supervision • consistent hunger, inappropriate dress, poor hygiene • lice, distended stomach, emaciated
Behavioral Indicators	• self-destructive • withdrawn and aggressive—behavioral extremes • uncomfortable with physical contact • chronic runaway (adolescents) • complains of soreness or moves uncomfortably • wears clothing inappropriate to weather, to cover body	• regularly displays fatigue or listlessness • steals food, begs • reports that no caretaker is at home • self destructive • school dropout (adolescents)

U.S. Department of Health, Education, and Welfare, 1979.

He looked at me in silence, lips pressed tightly together in that telltale line of rage. Slowly he got up from his crouched position and drew himself up to his full height directly in front of me. For a few seconds he just stared, and I thought he might hit me. Then suddenly his posture changed, and he backed away. Taking the handle of the stroller, he walked off as if nothing had happened, chatting pleasantly with the woman and another couple who were with him. Unbelievably, not one of the three people with him had intervened to stop him from hurting the baby.

The other incident happened at another supermarket. As I was leaving I noticed a young woman with a boy, who was perhaps seven years old, in tow. She jerked his arm and dragged him along, screaming that he was worthless and the cause of all her problems. She seemed out of control as she lashed out in frenzied verbal abuse. The youngster just stared at her, eyes wide with fear. "I love you, Mommy," he said, hoping, I suppose, to placate her somehow.

Once again a few people stopped and muttered among themselves about the woman's behavior, yet no one moved to stop her. As her tirade continued I approached her and asked her to stop mistreating her son. Turning toward me, she shouted an obscenity and slapped me hard across the face. Then she quietly hustled her child away. It was as if the slap had dissipated her anger.

What most astonished me about these incidents was that although they all occurred in well-traveled areas, few passers by showed any concern. Why, I wondered, would normally caring individuals show such a disinclination to get involved in something so serious?

Reasons for Uninvolvement

According to Donald W. Bechtold, M.D., director of the child psychiatry clinic at the University of Colorado's Health Sciences Center, there are a number of reasons:

Lack of consensus. People do not always agree on what constitutes child abuse. Spanking, for instance, is considered acceptable by some, while others think it is abusive. Nelson L. Nadeau, director of the Jefferson County, Colorado, Department of Social Services, tells of one case in which a twelve-year-old girl had 109 welts on her body from a strap, and yet at her father's trial the courtroom was overflowing with his supporters (perhaps not realizing, prior to the trial, the extent of his abuse) defending his right to "discipline" his child.

Although physical abuse is sometimes considered to be anything that leaves a mark, clearly that definition is not all-encompassing, nor does it address psychological abuse, which is much harder to prove yet just as serious. As Nadeau explains, "Children often recover well from physical abuse, but emotional abuse lasts and lasts."

Ignorance. Sometimes people are not aware of child-protection statutes, or they might not know where to report abuse. In metropolitan areas, where there are often several child-protection agencies, a witness might be confused about whom to contact. Generally either a law-enforcement department or a social-services agency can be notified.

Frustration with the system. Some witnesses may hesitate to report abuse because they feel that justice will not be done and that nothing will happen to the offender, anyway. Furthermore, they may be hesitant to become entangled in the legal system. Dr. Bechtold says, "It is a bit analogous to certain cases of rape in which some women may be concerned about what may happen to them if they actually press charges."

Fear. This often plays a part in nonreporting of abuse, especially if the witness knows the abuser. Some witnesses are afraid the abuser will seek revenge. If this is a worry, the report of abuse can be made anonymously. Others fear the possibility of having to testify in court. Another concern, though unfounded, is that if the allegation turns out to be untrue, the witness himself might be prosecuted. Dr. Bechtold emphasizes that a witness is immune from legal prosecution even if the allegation, made in good faith, is found to be without basis. Also, the police must follow up even if the report is anonymous.

Apathy. Witnesses of child abuse sometimes just don't care to get involved. They may not want to take the time, or they may feel that they have no right to interfere in someone else's private life.

Witnesses Should Act

Detective Cleo Wilson of the Denver Police Department's Crimes Against Persons Bureau has investigated hundreds of incidents of child abuse since 1981. She notes that average citizens, unlike medical personnel, are not required by law to report child abuse. But her department requests that witnesses act if they observe abuse.

"I tell them," Wilson says with intensity, "it's your home, it's your city, it's your environment. It's going to be what you make it. I feel there is a moral obligation to intervene. I could not deal with my own conscience if I were to observe something like that and not intervene in some way." She suggests several courses of action for witnesses of abuse.

If the abuse does not appear to be severe enough to warrant a report, a witness can merely speak to the offender. Often a word from a stranger or a friend will bring an abuser to his senses and give him an opportunity to alter his behavior. Dr. Bechtold points out that while an abuser may not appreciate the interference at first, later he may realize, I really needed that! He explains that public abuse may be a veiled plea for help.

"With many of these parents," he says, "there is a side to them that recognizes that this is not right. I think that's one reason we see a wide range of pathological things people do in public places. Part of the message may be that they're asking for help."

Nelson Nadeau indicates that seemingly moderate emotional and physical abuse in public is often indicative of worse abuse in private. Also, an abuser may feel that his behavior is normal, perhaps having been abused himself, and it is helpful if he sees that society disagrees.

If the abuse is more serious, possibly endangering the health of a child, a witness can try to detain the abuser, perhaps enlisting the aid, for example, of store security personnel or someone else in authority, until the police can respond. As Detective Wilson notes, "If one person cares enough to act, often it will have a kind of snowball effect. If someone will just make the first move, a lot of others will often follow."

Notify Authorities

A witness can also get a license-plate number, a description of the abuser, an address, or any other pertinent information and then call a law-enforcement agency. Even if a witness reports abuse anonymously, which makes prosecution much more difficult, the report will still be investigated, and at least a message will be sent to the offender that someone has noticed his behavior. Also, the abuser can then be advised by the agency on where to get help.

Whether we witness abuse by a stranger or observe abusive behavior by a family member or acquaintance over a period of time, we should recognize that acting on behalf of a child may well save her from future abuse or even save her life. Detective Wilson observes ironically, "I have seen more people intervene on behalf of animals than on behalf of helpless children."

Several years ago a friend related a humiliating experience. She said her husband had disciplined their four-year-old son for misbehaving, and the angry child had loudly wailed his displeasure. A short time later there was a knock at the door. It was a police officer, informing them that someone had reported them for child abuse. Even though the officer found no basis for the complaint, my friend was mortified.

A Small Price to Pay

At the time I was outraged that she had had to endure that ordeal without justification, merely because a neighbor had misconstrued the child's crying. Now, however, my perspective has changed. Although I do sympathize with the person who has been wrongly accused, I believe that occasional overreporting is a small price to pay if children's lives can be improved, or even saved, by a concerned public.

"We must ask for a higher standard from our leadership, demand that they express an ethic of nonviolence."

Creating a Less Violent Society Can Protect Children from Physical Abuse

James Garbarino

James Garbarino, an author and editor, is president of the Erikson Institute for Advanced Study in Child Development in Chicago, Illinois, a private graduate school and research center specializing in issues of child development. In the following viewpoint, Garbarino maintains that the U.S. is a violent society and that child abuse is one result of that violence. To end child abuse, he believes that Americans must become less violent and that all physical discipline of children, including spanking, must end.

As you read, consider the following questions:

1. The author's daughter was surprised when she learned that some children are abused. What two meanings does the author give to her surprise?
2. What does Garbarino see as the difference in the way Americans perceive physical abuse and sexual abuse?
3. Why does the author believe it is unnatural to ask people to parent on their own?

James Garbarino, "Child Abuse: Why?" This article appeared in the June 1990 issue and is reprinted with permission from *The World & I,* a publication of The Washington Times Corporation, copyright © 1990.

It is easy to be against child abuse. What is difficult is to see the connection between "normal" punishment and the problem of child abuse. I believe physical punishment in the home is a bad policy because even nonabusive "corporal punishment" and verbal assault set a bad example, are unnecessary, and contribute to greater violence in our society. Once people imagine a different way to live with children—or see it manifest in another society—they can set about making that alternative vision a reality. Imagine what it would be like to live in a society where it was not routine and normal to physically and verbally attack children. Difficult to imagine? This is the difficulty we face, not only as individuals and professionals but also collectively, as a society.

However, we need not be totally discouraged about this, even in a violent society such as our own. When I first began flying, I was greatly bothered by people smoking cigarettes right next to me. At the time it seemed almost inconceivable that within two decades we would be within sight of a law prohibiting smoking on airplanes entirely. How did this happen? Certainly it required a systematic, coordinated assault on a set of values, a set of assumptions about what people's rights were. The right to smoke—which seemed fundamental twenty years ago—has been abridged, and we can hope that before too long smoking will be considered a deviant behavior that we suppress because it is a health hazard. Achieving such a consensus is the goal in our efforts to stop assault against children.

Glimmers of Hope

In some of our families and communities, we have begun to see glimmers of hope. In 1988, the *Chicago Tribune* ran a story called, "To Spare the Rod: The Case Against Corporal Punishment." One evening, as I was reading some of this article aloud, my six-year-old daughter asked, "You mean people hit children? Teachers hit children? That's terrible," she said. "Don't they realize they'll learn to hit other kids and they'll grow up to hit their own kids?"

Her response has two meanings. First, as a child, she is struggling with the issue of how to deal with aggression, in her own behavior and in the behavior of others. She needs all the help she can get in responding to her own aggressive impulses. She needs role models and cultural support for learning nonviolent ways to respond when she is frustrated, angry, or simply wants to exert her will. If the adults in her life use assault as a tactic under those conditions, how is she, a young child, supposed to "know better"—and do better? The prospect of adults hitting children is frightening to her as one trying to learn how to manage her life.

But there is also a second meaning to her response. The fact that physical abuse is inconceivable to her, that people can get along *without* verbally and physically assaulting kids, is evidence that we *have* made some progress on this issue. Many of us have in our personal lives. We have institutionally, when we note that a majority of American schools prohibit "corporal punishment." And a national survey found that 74 percent of American adults said they thought "repeated yelling and swearing" would lead to "long-term emotional problems" for the child. I think we must acknowledge and promote public consciousness of that progress.

© Canton/Rothco. Reprinted with permission.

The question is not simply whether we can eradicate physical and verbal assault against children in one fell swoop but whether we can tip the balance in the American value system in the coming years so that we will be where we are with smoking now; maybe it will be ten years, maybe twenty years. By marshalling scientific evidence, by personal testimony, and by group demonstration of "a better way" we can build a credible cultural foundation upon which to proceed with policies to regulate, confine, and gradually eradicate assault against children.

The tactical and the strategic issues we face can be broken

down into several areas. One is the issue of language, the power of language to push people's consciousness in the direction we want. Redefining the vocabulary of violence means speaking of "assault against children as punishment," instead of "discipline" or "corporal punishment," or even "physical punishment," because lots of physical punishments do not involve assault. Picking up a squalling two year old in the midst of a temper tantrum, sitting him down, and saying, "You will stay here because this is no way to be" is certainly physical control. Restraining a child who's fooling around is a kind of physical punishment, but it is not assault. Focusing on "assault" as "discipline" clearly disorients many people; but that, of course, is what we have to do—disorient people, remove the comfort of familiar terms like "a good licking."

Again we might look to other campaigns for social change, like the antismoking movement. We know we must challenge the advertisements that portray smoking as glamorous and instead show what smoking really does—to the lungs, for example.

Discipline or Abuse?

A second issue we must address is the view that physical child abuse is simply too much of a good thing. Is physical child abuse something qualitatively different from normal "physical discipline" that most American parents use as part of their child rearing? Do we have a continuum on which, when the behavior reaches eighty-five on a scale of one hundred, it is then considered child abuse? Or are "physical punishment" and child abuse fundamentally different phenomena?

One way to look at this question is to contrast the way we look at sexual abuse with the way we think about physical abuse. In the case of sexual abuse we base our definition on two clear statements: First, children are off limits to adults. Second, normal affection is different from sex (and indeed, the more normal the affection, the less likely that sexual abuse will occur). We don't have the sense that sexual abuse is too much of a good thing—simply crossing a line. We don't say that it's good to have sexual contact with children but stop at intercourse. But our approach to physical child abuse is very different. The evidence tells us that the more "normal" assault is present in a parent-child relationship, the more likely it is that there will eventually be abuse.

Stopping child abuse is about setting minimal standards of care for children. Underlying the process of setting minimal standards of care is the question: Does all violence lead to more violence? Based upon his review of the evidence, psychologist Jeffrey Goldstein adopts the following position: "Aggressive behavior used to achieve a personal goal, such as wealth or power, and that may be perceived by the actor as justified, or even as

114

nonaggressive, is a primary cause of aggressive and criminal behavior of others." His model leaves a kind of loophole—"to
achieve a personal goal." It is not a simple model that *all* violence leads to violence. It leaves open socially defined violence
as possibly noncontagious.

Violence Produces Violence

Another view, commonly associated with Murray Straus of
the University of New Hampshire, offers a more straightfor-
ward one-to-one correspondence model: All violence produces
violence somewhere down the line. Goldstein has pulled back
from this "radical" view to allow the possibility that violence
can be confined to social purposes without spilling over into
other contexts. But from a child's point of view, the whole
world is "personal." Certainly a child's relationship with his or
her parents is profoundly personal. In their future behavior and
their worldview, children tell us that hitting them increases the
likelihood that they will hit others. Nonetheless, there's certainly a lively debate on this topic.

A Common Voice

When we view the current status of children and families in our
nation as not only economically costly but morally unacceptable,
when we perceive our treatment of children and families not only
as a national problem but a national tragedy, then we will find a
common voice to speak and a common body to embolden our
steps toward a path of social change.

Nancy McDaniel, American Association for Protecting Children, 1990.

It's obviously an important question, because if it is possible to
confine violence to socially approved settings eliminating assault
against children by parents may be less strongly tied to general
efforts to reduce violence in American life than some of us hope.

If social injustice is an engine that drives the level of violence,
and if violence is contagious across all systems in the society,
then our efforts to reduce or prevent it between parents and
children may be fundamentally different from those to eliminate smoking. Smoking may well be something that can be confined, that has what psychologists would call "functional autonomy" (i.e., it can be separated from all the other contingencies
of one's life). Violence may not be functionally autonomous; it
may be so rooted in all the other features of life that it cannot
be plucked out without major social changes. One such change
is the overturning of the popular contention that child rearing is
a private matter.

An article published twenty years ago, "A Bio-social Perspective on Parenting" by sociologist Alice Rossi, argues persuasively that parenting evolved in our species in a situation of stable, close, intimate relationships with monitoring by others, shared responsibility for child care, and supportive feedback about child rearing. Her point is that as a species we developed the capacity to parent in that kind of environment, which makes it "unnatural" to ask people to parent on their own—perhaps as single parents living in single houses or as nuclear families living without community interconnections.

We've erected a cultural superstructure around privacy and autonomy that is fundamentally not in the best human interest because it asks people to do something unnatural. If that's true, then we do indeed have a big agenda in changing this orientation, an orientation that says that children are the private matter of their parents. We have to see that child rearing is a social matter and that being a parent is a social act.

Taming the Monster

We do have some evidence that intervention programs that take this kind of social connection, social support, and social control function can have an effect on family violence. I am thinking particularly of the Home Health Visitor Study of David Olds, a psychologist at the University of Rochester School of Medicine, in which one of the findings was that a nurse, working with high-risk mothers from the time they were pregnant, was able to virtually eliminate spanking at six months of age in a population that, without that intervention, was spanking once a week at six months of age. That's an encouraging note from a programmatic perspective. Support programs can change attitudes and behavior. Finally, we have to look to national and local professional, political, and spiritual leadership for an ethic of nonviolence. We must ask for a higher standard from our leadership, demand that they express an ethic of nonviolence. Like my young daughter, we are all struggling to find a way to deal with aggression in our lives and in ourselves. Every little bit matters. I believe making a commitment to end assault in the home—under any name, under any circumstance—is something we all can do to tame the monster of human violence.

Recognizing Deceptive Arguments

People who feel strongly about an issue use many techniques to persuade others to agree with them. Some of these techniques appeal to the intellect, some to the emotions. Many of them distract the reader or listener from the real issues.

A few common examples of argumentation tactics are listed below. Most of them can be used either to advance an argument in an honest, reasonable way or to deceive or distract from the real issues. It is important for a critical reader to recognize these tactics in order to rationally evaluate an author's ideas.

    a. *deductive reasoning*—the idea that since a and b are true, c is also true
    b. *categorical statements*—stating something in a way that implies there can be no argument
    c. *scare tactic*—threatening that if you don't do or believe this, something terrible will happen
    d. *slanter*—attempting to persuade through inflammatory and exaggerated language instead of through reason
    e. *strawperson*—distorting or exaggerating an opponent's ideas to make one's own seem stronger

The following activity can help you sharpen your skills in recognizing deceptive reasoning. The statements below are derived from the viewpoints in this book. *Beside each one, mark the letter of the type of deceptive appeal being used. More than one type of tactic may be applicable. If you believe the statement is not any of the listed appeals, write N.*

1. Because three-fourths of Americans disapprove of yelling or swearing at children, it can be assumed that most American parents do not yell at their children.

2. Child abuse prevention programs are useless.

3. It is far too easy for a helpless, neglected child to fall into the black hole of the cold, uncaring, bureaucratic child welfare system.

4. Abuse prevention programs cause children to have nightmares and irrational fears.

5. Child abuse can be sexual, physical, or emotional.

6. Since almost all parents spank their children at one time or another, spanking cannot be considered child abuse.

7. The devious, depraved, predatory pedophile is as harmful to society as cancer is to the body.

8. Proponents of child welfare programs want to stand on street corners and hand out the taxpayers' money to any family willing to take it.

9. Preschool education helps children.

10. A pedophile is an individual with intense, recurrent sexual fantasies involving children.

11. Neglected children must be helped immediately. If they are not, they will grow up to become angry, violent adults terrorizing American streets.

12. Because foster parenting is such a difficult job with few rewards, it can be assumed that all foster parents are altruistic, caring people.

13. Some so-called experts on child abuse believe that pedophiles are mentally ill and need rehabilitation. These experts would free abusers, permitting them to attack again.

Periodical Bibliography

The following articles have been selected to supplement the diverse views presented in this chapter.

Douglas J. Besharov	"Protecting the Innocent," *National Review*, February 19, 1990.
John N. Briere	"Molested Victims' Pain Persists," *USA Today*, August 1990.
Paul Ciotti	"When Strangers Near," *Los Angeles Times*, March 31, 1989.
Alexander Cockburn	"Out of the Mouths of Babes: Child Abuse and the Abuse of Adults," *The Nation*, February 12, 1990.
David Gelman	"The Sex-Abuse Puzzle," *Newsweek*, November 13, 1989.
Linda Gordon	"The Politics of Child Sex Abuse," *Against the Current*, March/April 1989. Available from 7012 Michigan Ave., Detroit, MI 48210.
Robert Horowitz	"Tighten Standards for Termination of Parental Rights," *Children Today*, May/June 1989. Available from the U.S. Department of Health and Human Services, 200 Independence Ave. SW, Washington, DC 20201.
Brian H. McNeill	"Dramatic Rise in Child Abuse from Growing Economic Stress," *New Unionist*, April 1990. Available from New Union Party, 621 W. Lake St., Minneapolis, MN 55408.
Salvador Minuchin and Joel Elizur	"The Foster Care Crisis," *The Family Therapy Networker*, February 1990. Available from 7705 13th St. NW, Washington, DC 20012.
Pam Mitchell	"Child Sexual Abuse—Speaking Up for Children's Rights," *Resist*, January 1989. Available from One Summer St., Sommerville, MA 02143.
Dan Morris	"Families in Trouble: How to Know When to Get Help," *U.S. Catholic*, August 1989.
National Review	"Abusing Common Sense," May 28, 1990.
Dorothy Rabinowitz	"From the Mouths of Babes to a Jail Cell," *Harper's Magazine*, May 1990.
Andrew Vachss	"Today's Abused Child Could Be Tomorrow's Predator," *Parade*, June 3, 1990.
The World & I	"Child Abuse and Society's Response," special section on child abuse, June 1990.

CHAPTER 3

What Government Policies Would Help America's Poor Children?

Chapter Preface

The American government has made many attempts to aid impoverished children. Franklin Roosevelt's New Deal, for example, initiated the Aid to Families with Dependent Children program. The Head Start education program for impoverished preschoolers began as part of Lyndon Johnson's Great Society.

Marian Wright Edelman believes programs such as these must be expanded. Edelman is the founder of the Children's Defense Fund and author of *Families in Peril: An Agenda for Social Change.* She maintains that the whole nation benefits from investing in programs that feed, clothe, and educate America's estimated thirteen million poor children. The cost of making such an investment now is small compared to the cost of supporting uneducated and unhealthy adults in the future, Edelman asserts.

Not all Americans, however, support government programs for poor children. Some agree with noted pediatrician T. Berry Brazelton, who suggests that existing government poverty programs often encourage dependency. He writes, "To qualify for help, a family must first identify itself as a failure. The labels stick. Treated as such, people will feel and act like failures. Despite the huge amounts spent on welfare, the efforts are generally counterproductive."

While experts agree that the high rate of childhood poverty is a problem, they often have different views on how to ease it. The authors in the following chapter debate the government's role in helping poor children.

"We can pay a little now to try to prevent blighted childhoods or we can pay a lot later for the consequences."

Increased Government Spending Would Help Poor Children

Ford Foundation Project on Social Welfare and the American Future

The Ford Foundation, one of the world's largest philanthropic institutions, establishes and supports programs that promote world peace, democratic government, economic well-being, education, and the scientific study of humankind. The foundation's Project on Social Welfare and the American Future was established in 1985 to analyze America's social welfare system and suggest changes to improve the system. In the following viewpoint, the members of the project's executive panel argue that poor children can best be helped by increased government spending on programs that promote better prenatal and infant care, early childhood education, and health care.

As you read, consider the following questions:

1. What age group of Americans is most likely to live in poverty, according to the authors?
2. In the panel's opinion, how does childhood poverty, inadequate health care, and poor education affect America's economic competitiveness?
3. How much new government spending do the authors believe is needed to help poor children?

Excerpted, with permission, from *The Common Good: Social Welfare and the American Future* by the Ford Foundation Project on Social Welfare and the American Future, © 1989 Ford Foundation.

There is no more important contradiction in social policy than this: From child-development research we now know that the first few years of life play a crucial role in shaping a person's lifelong mental, emotional, and physical abilities. And yet it is for this stage of life that we seem to make our social investments most grudgingly and tolerate the greatest deprivation. To illustrate:

- About one in five children lives in poverty.
- More than 12 million American children—the equivalent of a medium-sized country—are now poor.
- Some 3.3 million children are now living with their teenage mothers; the proportion of out-of-wedlock births to teenagers has soared during the past twenty years.
- Child abuse and neglect are growing; more than 2 million cases are reported each year, about 900,000 of which are verified.

Although scientific knowledge about early childhood years has mushroomed, it is during these years that Americans are most likely to live in poverty. Simply put, our knowledge is not being applied.

The Fortunate and the Unlucky

As parents, grandparents, aunts, uncles, and friends, most of us have peered through the glass of a hospital nursery at rows of infants wrapped in blankets—so vulnerable yet so full of promise. If we could somehow look through that window to view all the nation's children, the spectacle would be alarming. In a typical recent year we would see one-quarter of a million babies born undersized (i.e., weighing $5^1/_2$ pounds or less), often afflicted by illness and handicaps. Some will die. In some inner-city hospitals more than one in ten babies are born drug-addicted. Forty-two percent of the white babies will live with a single mother by age eight, and most of these infants will experience a major spell of poverty during that time. Eighty-six percent of the black babies will live with a single mother by age eight, and most will be poor during most of that time. Many will grow up in an urban environment devoid of opportunity and full of danger. If current trends continue, more than 40 percent of the Hispanic children will experience poverty before age eighteen. Although many will also live in households headed by women, a growing proportion of poor Hispanic children will live in two-parent families.

To summarize, we could look through the nation's nursery windows and separate the fortunate babies born to hope and safety from the unlucky babies—perhaps one in four—born threatened and suffering. The fortunate majority of infants can look forward to a long life span and a good standard of living. They will be well fed and decently housed, see a pediatrician regularly and receive all of the appropriate immunizations, attend good schools, never suffer child abuse or neglect, and be raised in relatively safe neighborhoods. The large number of unlucky babies will experience a childhood lacking in the essential requirements for good health, physical safety, and proper mental and social development. By the time they reach kindergarten, they will already be falling behind through no fault of their own. Anyone looking at the rows of infants in a hospital nursery and consciously advocating policies that deliberately produce such outcomes would rightly be branded a monster. Yet such is the effect of our current policies.

It is easy to generate sympathy, if not tax dollars, for infants born burdened and suffering through no fault of their own. A more hard-nosed case for increasing our investments in young children can be made by calculating the long-range benefits from the point of view of pure self-interest. We can pay a little now to try to prevent blighted childhoods or we can pay a lot later for the consequences. In other words, money for decent prenatal care, or more than three times as much to deal with low-birthweight infants; several thousand dollars for a good preschool program to open the mind of a ghetto three-year-old, or tens of thousands of dollars to cope with a hardened teenage criminal. At the same time, we in today's work force will eventually depend on the abilities and economic productivity of the infants being born today. In 1950 there were seventeen workers to support each older retired person; today there are 3.5 workers, and by the next century there will be only about two workers for each retiree. Finally, wasted childhoods will produce inadequate workers at a time when we can ill afford it, when growing competition in the world economy is increasingly forcing the United States to specialize in goods and services that require a highly skilled, adaptable work force.

Beyond the nation's economic competitiveness or the future security of retirees, crime, disorder, and other social pathologies are being set in motion now by what is happening to too many children. Today's infants are literally the nation's future. Whatever America can or will be is taking shape today in the nation's nurseries. The underlying challenge is clear enough, and so too are the social costs. The question of how to provide opportunity and social protection to children is complex, for the well-being of all young children must be a societal as well as a parental concern. Parents have primary responsibility for their children, but we all have an interest in healthy babies and in children's adequate nutrition and cognitive development. . . .

The Cost of Caring

Two Federal programs geared to infants and children—WIC [Special Supplemental Food Program for Women, Infants, and Children] and Head Start—should be extended to a much broader group of children in need of help. In fiscal year 1988 Federal outlays for the WIC program totaled about $1.8 billion, and the program served 3.4 million people. The maximum potential number of people who could qualify for the program has been estimated at 6.5 million to 7.5 million, or about twice the number served today. If WIC were made an entitlement program, and all of the people eligible on income grounds actually qualified and participated, its cost would increase by $1.5 billion to $2 billion a year.

WIC. Households are eligible for WIC if they qualify as nutritionally at risk and have incomes up to 185 percent of the Federal poverty line. It is probable that in practice the population that participated would be limited by the nutritional-risk requirement and the likelihood that some who are eligible would not participate. Thus, the actual additional cost of making WIC an entitlement program would likely be less than the amounts noted above. To be on the safe side, however, we will assume

125

that current costs double, and allocate an additional $1.7 billion for WIC outlays.

Head Start. The Head Start program serves about one in five children aged three to five years old who are living in poverty, and only about one-fifth of those served are in full-day programs. Additional funding for the Head Start program could be used to cover more children, increase the proportion of children receiving full-day services, and extend coverage to children under three years old.

A report by the Congressional Budget Office suggested that the long-range impact of Head Start on such goals as increasing basic skills, avoiding crime, and finding employment is unclear as a result of the difficulty of finding adequate control groups. But the report pointed out that Head Start potentially could serve a number of more immediate purposes, including providing high-quality child care to children of working parents; increasing access to health screening, immunization, and a variety of social services; providing helpful cognitive stimulation to the children; offering employment and training to low-income adults; and making it possible for two parents to work.

Serving More Children

Expanding Head Start will be more expensive than expanding WIC. The annual cost per child served under Head Start has been estimated at $2,400, compared with a little less than $500 for WIC. Serving as many needy children as possible through Head Start involves scaling up the program to serve the 80 percent not being served now, as well as having more children in full-day programs.

It is difficult to put a precise price tag on this effort at scaling up. Clearly, some parents of eligible children may choose not to enroll them in Head Start programs. Other eligible children may already participate in state and local programs or may have started kindergarten. A realistic goal for the early 1990s is to serve half of the eligible population that is not being served now. We estimate that it will cost $2 billion to meet that goal.

Health. Ultimately, all children and pregnant women in families below the poverty line ought to be covered by either Medicaid or a private health insurance policy. We are reluctant to advocate expanding Medicaid to the entire poverty population, which includes many families headed by a worker whom we hope to see covered under private health insurance.

The Medicare catastrophic illness legislation passed by Congress in 1988 includes provisions that make more low-income pregnant women and children under one year of age eligible for Medicaid. This is a useful first step, but we need to go much further. There are approximately 12 million to 13 million people living below the poverty line without health insurance. About 4

million of these are children under eighteen years of age. An estimated one-half of these children would qualify for the type of
mandatory private coverage that we advocate below. The cost of
providing Medicaid coverage to the remaining group of low-income uninsured children is approximately $1 billion. It is im-
portant to note that this new coverage is "Medicaid only." It is
not an extension of Aid to Families with Dependent Children
(AFDC). We do believe that AFDC eligibility requirements should
be updated. But we do not believe that an extension of
Medicaid should be tied to AFDC.

Health Coverage for All

Ideally, both Medicaid and employer-sponsored group health
insurance ought to be broadened to assure health coverage for
all Americans. It is important to put some restrictions on cash
welfare assistance in order to maintain the incentive to work,
though this goal can be met with higher cash assistance benefits
than now exist in some states. But health coverage for the poor
ought not to be held hostage to these necessary restrictions on
cash assistance.

A National Necessity

Preventive investment in children and families is neither a luxury nor a choice. It is a national necessity. Investing in the young
must become the cornerstone of national domestic policy in the
coming political era if we are going to be economically competitive in the global arena. This commitment must go beyond political rhetoric, slogans and cosmetic solutions and be bolstered by a
comprehensive, well-conceived continuum of investment in specific, cost-effective, successful programs for children beginning at
birth and sustained until their transition to adulthood.

Marian Wright Edelman, *Human Rights,* Summer 1989.

Chapter I. Chapter 1 of the Education Consolidation and Improvement Act of 1981 funds compensatory education programs
for low-income and educationally deprived students.
Evaluations of the Chapter 1 program have shown positive
short-term effects on student performance, and some evidence
suggests a favorable longer-term impact.

The real level of outlays per poor child for this program has
fallen in recent years, as slight absolute increases in funding
have not kept pace with the combination of inflation and the
higher number of children living in poverty. The proportion of
poor children served by Chapter 1 fell from 75 percent in 1980
to 54 percent in 1985. Outlay increases of $1.5 billion per year

would make up most of the erosion in real benefits per poor child associated with inflation, and enable many school districts either to extend services to some newly poor children or maintain services for a longer part of some children's schooling. That might help avoid the erosion of shorter-term gains that has been found in some evaluations.

Future Benefits

Neither we nor any other group have solutions for all the profound problems of social welfare that shape the earliest stages of life in America. The amount of new government spending that we have recommended to help children in need—$6.2 billion—would go a long way toward meeting the needs of disadvantaged children. It is worth noting, however, that the recommended budget would not extend help to each and every child in need—a reflection of current budget realities and the value of learning as we go. We believe this investment in better opportunities for American children will produce great future benefits for our whole society.

"Increased governmental public aid programs were associated with rising, not falling, rates of child poverty. "

Increased Government Spending Would Not Help Poor Children

Richard Vedder and Lowell Gallaway

Government programs aimed at helping poor children are wasteful and ineffective, Richard Vedder and Lowell Gallaway contend in the following viewpoint. Vedder and Gallaway state that even though government spending for poor children has more than doubled since 1970, childhood poverty has risen by one-third. The authors believe that, instead of increasing spending, the government should encourage poor parents to work instead of relying on welfare. Vedder and Gallaway are both professors of economics at the Contemporary History Institute at Ohio University in Athens.

As you read, consider the following questions:

1. What factor do the authors believe is associated with the rise in childhood poverty?
2. Why do Vedder and Gallaway think increased government aid programs caused an increase in child poverty rates?
3. What comparison do the authors make between elderly Americans and children in America?

Richard Vedder and Lowell Gallaway, "Youthanasia: The Plight of the Rising Generation," *The Family in America,* July 1990. Reprinted with permission of The Rockford Institute.

Americans treat their young people very badly. This might sound like an outrageous assertion considering the billions of dollars and hours we spend annually on educating our youth and "enriching" children's lives through participation in summer camps, after-school sports, music activities and the like. Parents support their children financially longer and more generously than at any other time in our history.

Consider, however, the following ten stylized facts:

• Americans avoid bearing children more than ever, with birth rates at historic lows;

• The proportion of children in poverty today is much higher than 20 years ago. We are in a remarkable situation now in that a much larger proportion of our children are classified as poor than of our elderly population;

• American adults spend less time with their children than at any time in American history, despite evidence that familial nurturing is important to the economic, social, and intellectual well-being of our progeny;

• A record proportion of children suffer emotionally and often economically from illegitimacy and broken marriages;

• The knowledge of the world that we pass on to our children may be declining and is probably less than that taught to children in many other poorer nations;

• The proportion of our income that we set aside through savings for new investment is below that of many other nations, so our capital stock is growing relatively slowly, imperiling the economic advantages of life for future Americans;

• Amidst generally stable suicide rates, teenage suicide rates in America have risen dramatically and are high relative to other nations;

• America is borrowing unprecedented sums of money, reflected in the twin budget and trade deficits which some believe are "mortgaging the future" of our youth;

• Through our Social Security System, we are making commitments to adult Americans that will significantly burden the generation born after 1970;

• A moral relativism inculcated in our children has contributed to high rates of antisocial behavior, evident in a high incidence of crime and drug usage among our young. . . .

The Child Poverty Scandal

The relatively few children born face an uncertain economic future during their formative years. Whereas the incidence of poverty in general in the United States has changed little over the past two decades, this fact disguises a remarkable increase in child poverty rates and an extraordinary decline in poverty among senior citizens. Whereas in 1970, the poverty rate for

130

Americans over 65 was 70 percent greater than for children under 18, by 1988 the poverty rate among senior citizens was nearly 40 percent *lower* than for children. In the 1970-88 period, the poverty rate fell for adults while it rose substantially for children. In 1988, one of five children lived in poverty, according to the official government definition of poverty.

Perpetuating Dependency

The trend toward the failure of families to form accelerated during the period when the nation was committing an increased portion of its national wealth to helping the most disadvantaged. In 1959, 23 percent of poor families were headed by females. By 1982, this figure was 48 percent. This represents an unprecedented destruction of families. As a nation, we remain committed both to helping the poor and to ending their dependency wherever possible. Those two goals go hand in hand. If "helping" merely perpetuates dependency, then it is worse than no help at all.

White House Working Group on the Family, *Report to the President*, 1988.

The rise in poverty among children is closely associated with the disintegration of traditional families with two parents present. Some 64 percent of children classified as poor in 1988 lived outside traditional two-parent families. The poverty rate in two-parent families with children was a low 7.2 percent, one-sixth the extraordinarily high 44.7 percent poverty rate among children in households where the father was absent. . . .

Why are we allowing these obviously destructive things to happen to young Americans? We believe that some of what has happened has been totally unintentional. Youth have suffered from the unintended consequences of policies, some of which were deliberately designed to help them. Charles Murray's "Law of Unintended Consequences" has been at work.

Take child poverty. Most advocates of Aid to Families with Dependent Children (AFDC), Women, Infant, and Child (WIC) programs, food stamps, Head Start, and other programs sincerely believe that those programs do aid poor Americans, especially children. Yet the evidence suggests otherwise. Governmental transfer payments designed to aid lower-income Americans have grown dramatically over the past generation, yet child poverty has remained high and has been growing both absolutely and relatively.

Consider this fact: in 1970, federal, state and local governments spent $42.5 billion (expressed in 1982-84 dollars) on what the Social Security Administration calls "public aid." Included in the definition are spending for public assistance (e.g., AFDC and general relief), Medicaid, Supplemental Security income, food stamps, refugee assistance, surplus food for the needy, low-income energy assistance, etc. By 1986, that spending had more than doubled to $94.1 billion. In real per capita terms, the increase was an impressive 87.8 percent—a compounded annual rate of growth exceeding 4 percent a year in real terms. What happened to the child poverty rate? It *rose* by nearly one-third, going from 14.9 to 19.7 percent of children. Increased governmental public aid programs were associated with rising, not falling, rates of child poverty.

Lack of Incentives

Why? While whole volumes have been written about it, one key explanatory word has to be "incentives." Our public-assistance policies have unintentionally, but markedly, reduced incentives of poor individuals to work and at the same time increased incentives for the adult poor to raise children outside the traditional family. In radio talk shows across the country dealing with welfare, poor persons have told us time and time again what the sophisticated econometric evidence confirms: that many poor people cannot "afford" to work and, thus, cannot begin to rise the occupational ladder out of poverty.

It is not uncommon for a poor person who gets a job paying, say, $200 a week to have to give up $170 in benefits, including Medicaid. That person has an increase of $30 in income out of the $200 earned. She or he pays an 85 percent "tax" (in the form of foregone welfare benefits) on work earnings. For that $30, she or he has to pay transportation, buy clothes, and arrange for child care. There is little or even no financial incentive to work. Yet by working and succeeding, the individual in time might advance to a better job, say one paying $300 a week, in the process escaping poverty. While welfare income is fixed, work income can grow with experience and job success. The poor person has little incentive to go to work, yet failure to work consigns him or her to long-term poverty. About half of welfare payments go to support "long-term" welfare recipients, consistent with the "welfare dependency" thesis outlined above.

Take another phenomenon that has worked to disadvantage children, the rise in female labor force participation. Public policy has had the largely unintended impact of taking children away from their mothers. Governments have actively encouraged women to work outside the home in a variety of ways. Special income-tax credits are granted at both the federal and state level either for child care or, in some states, for just working. The federal government and increasingly state and local governments have gone into the babysitting business through subsidized child care and through providing for preschool education programs. The government is subsidizing institutionalized child care at the expense of traditional parental care for children.

The income tax has carried a "marriage penalty" that favors cohabiting single persons over married couples. The dependency allowance in the federal income tax, raised in 1986, has still fallen substantially relative to income levels over time. The Department of Labor has enforced outmoded laws against home working in an era when computer-based occupational opportunities could allow a return to the earlier pattern of using the home as a workplace, so permitting parents to spend more time with children. Indeed, as modern home conveniences like microwaves, disposable diapers, dishwashers, and frozen foods make housekeeping easier, the modern housewife often can perform occupational work in the home for several hours a day without neglecting traditional "housework" and without imposing any disadvantage upon her children. Yet the government sponsors no programs to promote home work. . . .

Children Are Powerless

For the past two decades, welfare-rights activists and others have cried about the need for more "public assistance to help our needy children," even while the poverty rate for children has risen amidst rapidly increased spending. The money for children has largely been siphoned off by adults who earn their living off children, either their own or other people's.

Welfare Harms Families

Welfare policy over the past 25 years has worked to expel male role-models and providers from the nest. As government handouts have increased, so the necessity of the father's presence in the household has diminished. This is why more than half of black children under 18 live today in mom-headed households, versus only 30 percent in 1970. The black family, though far from destroyed, is infinitely weaker as an institution than it was a generation ago.

William Murchison, *Conservative Chronicle*, November 1, 1989.

Children have suffered politically partly because children are unique in that they are defenseless. Their intellectual and emotional immaturity prevents them from being able to expose the travesties perpetrated against them. Worse, they cannot vote. Other groups that are disadvantaged can use their voting power to challenge obvious injustices, but children are politically powerless. They cannot vote, they cannot support Political Action Committees that buy votes from politicians, they can not inflict

133

political retribution on those adults who cynically use them to support their own economic self-interest.

In this regard, it is interesting to contrast the status of the elderly with that of our youth. By most accounts, our elderly never had it so good. Poverty among them is lower than among the general population. Huge increases in public-health support means few have severe worries about paying for health care. They live longer than ever. While many suffer from neglect from their children and families (a neglect partly caused by our social-insurance system), on balance their status is good. By contrast, children have suffered a relative economic decline, while schools and other public institutions are serving them poorly. There is one big difference between the two groups: the elderly vote, and children do not. The elderly have powerful lobbies such as the American Association of Retired Persons, which protect them against predatory practices by politicians.

Public Policy

Whether it be by accident or design, American children have been poorly served by the older generations that run their country. It is true that the problems of children go beyond deficiencies of public policy—the decline of religion in American life is but one example of a non-governmental cause of the decline in the position of children in society. Yet public policy is something that we collectively as a people control, and it has clearly imposed disadvantages on our most precious asset.

"Head Start proves that programs designed to fight poverty can not only succeed but thrive."

Expanding Head Start Programs Would Help Poor Children

Liza Mundy

Head Start is a government preschool program for poor children. Evidence shows that Head Start prepares poor children for school and helps them succeed, Liza Mundy asserts in the following viewpoint. Mundy, a reporter for States News Service and a contributor to the magazine *The Washington Monthly*, believes that many poor children fail in school because they are never taught basic social and learning skills. Head Start teaches them these skills, she argues. By expanding Head Start, Mundy contends that America's poor children will have a better chance of succeeding in school and in life.

As you read, consider the following questions:

1. What does the author mean when she says that Head Start has sometimes been a "vehicle for empowerment"?
2. Why have some public schools and teachers had difficulty working with Head Start children, according to Mundy?
3. Why does the author support an expansion of the Head Start program?

Liza Mundy, "The Success Story of the War on Poverty," *The Washington Monthly*, December 1989. Reprinted with permission from *The Washington Monthly*. Copyright by The Washington Monthly Company, 1611 Connecticut Ave. NW, Washington, DC 20009, (202) 462-0128.

They never would have filmed "Leave It to Beaver"—or even "Sesame Street"—near the intersection of Florida Avenue and Benning Road, in southeast Washington. Once-elegant townhouses are battered and boarded up. Groups of men hang out at a bus shelter waiting for something to come along. On the sidewalk nearby, a small girl, maybe four years old, stands by herself in a bright pink jacket, watching the traffic. Some tenants of a large housing project have hung plants in their windows and put patio furniture on their porches, but it's hard to imagine a barbecue in this neighborhood, where drug dealers are battling for turf vacated by the arrest of Rayful Edmond III, allegedly Washington's foremost drug entrepreneur. To an adult, the scene is hostile enough; to a child, it testifies grimly to what life holds in store. On a cold September morning in this neighborhood, 13 kids gather in a warm, spacious basement room—all of them from poor families, all of them about four years old, all of them here for a Head Start preschool program that offers a half-day of sanctuary from the life outside.

It's the beginning of the school year, so most of the children are just getting the hang of things. Their teacher, a young black woman named Joann Ramsuer, sits cross-legged on the carpet handing each child a "personal symbol," a construction-paper square, triangle, or half-moon that makes the child feel special while he learns about colors and shapes. On receiving his symbol, each child names the area he's chosen to play in for the next half-hour (one rule of Head Start is that children make their own decisions, however small). After some bewildered standing around, most of the kids head for "waterplay," a large sink filled with green water and different sized household containers which, as the children pour water back and forth, help them grasp the notion of quantity. At Head Start, no activity is without a purpose.

Boosting Self-Esteem

As the morning passes, the kids warm to their environment—so much so that some begin to bicker and cry. Whenever things heat up Ramsuer or the program director, Mattie Jackson, tells them to "use your words" instead. Head Start kids are not as used to articulating their feelings as other children, so teachers try to coax these skills along. The same goes for self-esteem. As she circulates around the room, Jackson makes a point of telling children, "I like the way you're waiting for your food," or "I like the way you stand in line."

Inside, the kids hone their "fine motor skills"; outside, during a play period, they exercise their "gross motor skills" on a jungle gym. At lunchtime they work again at self-reliance, setting their own places, struggling to slice and butter a corn muffin, lining up afterward to scrape their plates. While the kids brush their teeth, a social worker comes in with a mother and child she has pulled off the street, to show them the center and put the child on a waiting list. The kids fetch blankets and bed down for a nap.

Helping More Children

We no longer need to ask, "Does Head Start work?" Rather, the challenge over the next quarter of a century will be to extend Head Start's success to even more eligible children and families.

Wade F. Horn, *Children Today,* May/June 1990.

This is pretty much how Head Start works in all 1,287 centers, in churches and cast-off elementary schools, cities and rural communities. Its aim is to prepare disadvantaged children for school by teaching them basic concepts that most kids have absorbed by first grade. It gets them accustomed to a social environment and persuades them to look at learning as something fun—and in the process checks their teeth and eyes, inoculates and feeds them. Teachers come from the childrens' world, often from their own neighborhood, and understand their needs in a way middle-class social workers can't.

While some parents undoubtedly use Head Start as an opportunity to watch more television, few get off scot-free. Head Start staff visit the children's homes several times a year to discuss each child's progress. They ask parents to work as aides in the classroom, serve on center planning boards, and assist with field trips and their children's "homework"—making colored slips, say, to help them practice distinguishing red from orange. Some centers offer parents classes in child care, English, health, and nutrition.

A Success Story

No preschool can single-handedly turn a crack baby into a college graduate, but there are plenty of things it *can* do. A recent study has offered some evidence that in the long run, preschool training can reduce welfare dependency, teenage pregnancy, and delinquency, while boosting a child's chances of graduating from high school and going on to college or vocational school. In the short run—charts and statistics aside—it teaches kids to tie their shoes and gives them some room to play and a little extra affection. Today, Head Start has become a fixture in low-income neighborhoods—so much so that many people take it for granted. Many have also forgotten how the program began, calling Lyndon Johnson's War on Poverty a complete failure and Head

Start a success in the same breath. In its modest way, Head Start proves that programs designed to fight poverty can not only succeed but thrive—that the War on Poverty "failed" because individual programs were bad or inadequate, not because government can't assist the poor. . . .

Head Start has been dogged throughout its history not just by external resistance but by disputes among its backers. Some poverty warriors felt a little, well, embarrassed by Head Start. Primed for revolution, the more radical community action leaders weren't overjoyed to learn they'd be fighting a war with crayons and colored paper. They saw the aim of providing "services" to poor children as too moderate, too middle-class, too square. Other divisions began to appear in the poverty camp. Community action staff members viewed Head Start as a competitor for OEO [Office of Economic Opportunity] funds. And Head Start generally enjoyed greater public support than other community action programs, which targeted older (and therefore less clearly benign) groups.

But probably most divisive was the question of whether Head Start was an education program or a vehicle for "empowerment." Jargon aside, it's always been both. From the beginning a central tenet of Head Start has been "up and out"—meaning that a parent might start as a volunteer, then become a paid teacher's aide, a teacher, or even return to college, and ultimately enter the middle class. While up and out didn't work for everybody, Head Start's archives are full of success stories like Maxine Waters, a former welfare mother who is now a California assemblywoman and activist for the poor. This goal of empowerment was noble, but it introduced the constant (and still present) danger that Head Start could devolve into a jobs program. And in fact, that has often happened when CAP [Community Action Program] administrators failed to make teaching a priority in assigning Head Start jobs.

Disappointing Study

None of these internecine quarrels helped much when the first blow fell in 1969, in the form of a study conducted by the Westinghouse Learning Corporation. All along, Sargent Shriver had been adamant about tracking the program with studies, and at one point asked Jule Sugarman to design a test that could show him the IQ gains he was getting per dollar. But Westinghouse didn't produce what Shriver wanted; it concluded that any IQ gains among Head Start children dissipated by third grade. The press scooped up these findings, and suddenly the word was out that Head Start was a "failure.". . .

You'd think it wouldn't take a rocket scientist to figure out that if kids leave Head Start doing well and then begin doing poorly in elementary school, the schools probably aren't pulling their weight. Unfailingly, though, Head Start has taken the rap from policymakers for a public school system that's indifferent to the children of the underclass. . . .

An Equal Start

Give any American kid an equal place at the starting line and just watch what that kid can do. Head Start helps kids get that equal place.

George Bush, speech, Fall 1988.

This lack of follow-up attention meant that Head Start kids usually had only one or two years of learning through play-oriented activities under the care of sympathetic teachers. After that, they entered a public school system that catered to neat, well-behaved, highly motivated kids. The preschoolers had gotten a head start, but that didn't mean they'd caught up. Moreover, Head Start training didn't always go down well with public school teachers, who were used to docility and subservience in class.

Dr. Martin Deutsch, who pioneered a program similar to Head Start in the 1950s, found in his follow-up studies that teachers were often annoyed by the curiosity his program fostered, responding to the children's questions with hostility. Deutsch found this attitude had a "depressing impact" on the kids and their test scores. Dr. Irving Lazar, who directed a series of long-term studies of Head Start published in the 1970s, came to the same conclusion. "Many teachers really didn't like those Head Start kids. They were noisy and demanding and asked questions—they didn't come in terrified and sit down quietly. Head Start programs are relatively free places where kids have a lot of choice. A lot of public school teachers really felt those kids were awful, and complained about them."

Besides uppity kids, schools were faced with the new and unsettling phenomenon of uppity parents. Many poor parents had themselves been unhappy in public school, so their instinct was to avoid it as adults. Head Start, in contrast, gave these parents the exciting and novel idea that they could assist in their child's education—something that schools, accustomed to keeping parents at bay with a couple of inconveniently scheduled PTA [Parent Teacher Association] meetings per year, have always fought. "We tended to talk to the parents on the basis of informing them," said Sam Sava, executive director of the National Association of Elementary School Principals, "but Head Start made an all-out attempt to use the parent as part of the teaching process."

Sister Geraldine O'Brian, who runs a Head Start program for migrant families up and down the East Coast, described the case of a little girl who returned to Florida after the Virginia apple harvest and enrolled in first grade at a new school. She was summarily dumped back into kindergarten. When the girl came home and explained what happened, her mother fished out the developmental chart Head Start prepares for each child, then summoned her courage to visit the school. O'Brian said the teacher explained, "We know migrant children don't do well." Whereupon the mother asked to know whether her child's chart had been reviewed. The teacher said it hadn't been. The girl returned to first grade. . . .

Children make up the largest group of Americans in poverty, but Head Start reaches only one in five. (In contrast, the Children's Defense Fund estimates that two out of three four-year-olds whose families have annual incomes over $35,000 attend preschool.) Recently, though, Head Start has gotten a boost from the publication of *Changed Lives*, a study done on the Perry Preschool Program in Ypsilanti, Michigan, a particularly high-quality preschool for disadvantaged black children.

Like doctors who argue that providing good prenatal care is cheaper than caring for premature babies, the authors of this 1984 report claimed that in the long run, preschool can save the government a bundle in social costs. Although some of its results were unremarkable, the report did show that a well-funded preschool can have lasting effects: Compared to adults from a similar background, graduates of the Perry Preschool were more likely to have finished high school and gone on to college or vocational training, more likely to be self-supporting, and less likely to have been detained or arrested. Among former preschoolers, the rate of teenage pregnancy was half that of the control group—a potentially far-reaching benefit, since teen pregnancy often traps women in the cycle of poverty. According to a cost-benefit study, each dollar spent on this sophisticated preschool saved six that would have gone for special education, court and prison costs, and social services.

In large part it was Perry Preschool—combined with other studies that found Head Start kids less likely to flunk or to wind up in special education classes—that persuaded the Reagan and Bush administrations to get behind the program. . . . Head Start will get *some* more money (it got an increase of just $28 million in 1989) and seems to enjoy both conservative and liberal support. . . .

Head Start Needs Support

Head Start needs this boost and more: more slots, higher salaries, and an expansion of its mission to serve not just the poor but also the working poor. In addition to coming up with more money, Congress should create a national volunteer corps of young people committed to working for two or three years in programs like this. Most important, Head Start kids need follow through, something that seems to have gotten lost in the debate. You can do all you want to improve the quality and quantity of Head Start, but without competent and sympathetic teachers in the public schools, the early benefits will quickly fade—which may be why a third of the Perry Preschoolers still wound up as dropouts. We've always known that a stitch in time saves nine. What we're seeing in the battle between Head Start and the school system is that a stitch in time can also unravel.

"There is no measurable. . .benefit from Head Start."

Expanding Head Start Programs Would Not Help Poor Children

Kate Walsh O'Beirne

In the following viewpoint, Kate Walsh O'Beirne argues that Head Start does not help poor children and is a waste of money. Studies have shown that early education programs such as Head Start have no benefits for poor children, O'Beirne contends, and she believes that statistics showing benefits from such programs are misleading. She maintains that Head Start needs to be reformed, not expanded. O'Beirne is a visiting fellow at The Heritage Foundation's Thomas A. Roe Institute for Economic Policy Studies in Washington, D.C. The Heritage Foundation is a conservative think tank.

As you read, consider the following questions:

1. Why does O'Beirne think the results of the Perry Preschool study are not valid?
2. What are the risks of exposing children to formal education too early, according to the author?
3. What reforms of Head Start does the author suggest?

Almost 90 percent of American five-year-olds now attend kindergarten, although such schooling is compulsory in only a handful of states. In recent years there has been increased interest by states in providing formal education for four-year-olds. Twenty-eight states now fund pre-kindergarten programs, the majority focusing on compensatory programs for disadvantaged children. Some states have established special programs, while others, like California, provide services by adding state funds to the federal Head Start program.

The enthusiasm for early education programs for poor children stems from a belief that these programs have been proven to yield long-term benefits which more than repay the taxpayers' investment. Lawmakers are invariably, but incorrectly, told by program boosters that a dollar invested in preschool education saves as much as $6 in the future costs of special education, teen pregnancy, welfare, and crime. This impressive financial equation, regrettably, is not supported by research on the benefits of early compensatory education programs.

Disappointing Results

About 460,000 children, of whom 80 percent come from families below the poverty line, attend Project Head Start, the federally funded compensatory preschool program. This program provides health, nutrition, and education services to youngsters aged three and four. In 1985, exactly two decades after the program's inception, results of the most comprehensive study ever undertaken on the effects of Head Start were released. The chief findings: Although children show significant immediate gains as a result of Head Start participation, "[B]y the end of the second year [of elementary school] there are no educationally meaningful differences on any of the measures." Besides short-lived educational improvements, the study found only short-term gains with respect to tests of self-esteem, achievement motivation, and social behavior. The meaning of this comprehensive study: There is no measurable mid-term or long-term benefit from Head Start.

This conclusive finding is disputed mainly by a 1985 study of a single program—and the results of the study never have been replicated. This study of the Perry Preschool Program in Ypsilanti, Michigan, tracked 123 black youths into young adulthood and concluded that the 58 students who had attended the high-quality preschool program at ages 3 and 4 incurred half the rate of teen-age pregnancy shown by their non-preschool counterparts, had a much lower rate of arrests and juvenile delinquency, and were half as likely to become dependent on welfare.

This study of the experiences of only 58 graduates of one ex-

143

perimental preschool program stands in stark contrast to studies that have examined the records of millions of children and found that they have enjoyed no such long-term success after their Head Start experience. Yet the Perry Preschool study is widely quoted as "proof" that the American taxpayer can expect to save millions of dollars by investing in early education. Senator Edward Kennedy [D-Mass.], for instance, cites the Perry Preschool Project in support of his "Smart Start" legislation, arguing that this federal schooling of four-year-olds is ". . .a dropout prevention program, a teenage-pregnancy prevention program, and a crime prevention program." Kennedy's reliance on the Perry Preschool study ignores the warnings of experts that the Perry Preschool study should not be used to justify major new expenditures.

Unsupported Claims

The considerable research literature on preschool education will not support the claim that a program of national scope would yield lasting impacts on children's school performance nor substantial returns on the investment of public dollars.

Ron Haskins, *American Psychologist,* February 1989.

There are good reasons why the experts are very skeptical of Perry as a guide to the likely results of "Smart Start." For one thing, the sample at Perry was small. For another, the excellent results at Perry have not been seen elsewhere. After an extensive review of the research on both model preschool programs and Head Start, Ron Haskins, a developmental psychologist and a senior staff member of the House Ways and Means Committee, concludes in *American Psychologist:*

The considerable research literature on preschool education will not support the claim that a program of national scope would yield lasting impacts on children's school performance nor substantial returns on the investment of public dollars.

A probable reason for the heartening results at Perry is that the level of parental involvement in the program was intense. Example: Perry teachers visited each home weekly throughout the school year. Indeed, studies of compensatory preschool education find repeatedly that increased parental involvement in the education of their children appears to be the key to long-term gains for poor youngsters. The Perry program's home visits guaranteed involvement by every parent. But the national Head Start program [does not] provide for a similar level of participation by parents. Kennedy's "Smart Start" would make things even worse, sending four-year-olds out of the home and off for formal schooling by professionals.

To date, federal and state efforts in early childhood education have focused on disadvantaged children, seeing the purpose of government programs as compensating for shortcomings in poor families. . . .The assumption is that the earlier children receive formal education the better.

Formal Schooling

Many experts warn, however, that such formal schooling for four-year-olds could be damaging. David Elkind, author of *The Hurried Child* and *The Miseducation of Children: Superkids at Risk*, is dismayed at the current enthusiasm for schooling of very young children and accuses its proponents of ". . .blatantly ignoring the facts, the research, and the consensus of experts about how young children learn and how best to teach them." He tells of the harm of exposing children to formal instruction too early:

> We miseducate children whenever we put them at risk for no purpose. The risks of miseducating young children are both short- and long-term. The short-term risks derive from the stress, with all its attendant symptoms, that formal instruction places on children; the long-term risks are of at least three kinds: motivational, intellectual, and social. In each case, the potential psychological risks of early intervention far outweigh any potential educational gain.

Edward Zigler, director of the Bush Center in Child Development and Social Policy at Yale University and the architect of Head Start in the 1960s, also criticizes universal preschool education as a "misguided enterprise" that does not improve the quality of education. Such proposals, says Zigler, reflect "insensitivity" to the different needs of children and their families. When parents do not both work full-time, preschool education would "needlessly deprive parents and children of valuable time they could spend together." Although a proponent of compensatory education with comprehensive health and family services for poor youngsters, Zigler believes it is a "fundamental error" to advocate the educational component for middle-class students. The gains enjoyed by poor preschoolers generally are a result of medical and social services provided by a comprehensive program—not the formal schooling advocated by "Smart Start." "Those who argue in favor of universal preschool education," says Zigler, "ignore evidence that indicates early schooling is inappropriate for many four-year olds and that it may even be harmful to their development.". . .

Professor Zigler highlights the benefits that young children enjoy by remaining at home until kindergarten.

Decision makers must be sensitive to the individual needs of children and parents and recognize that, wherever the family situation permits it, the best place for a preschool child is often at home. . . . [M]any competent, caring parents who are at home resent school administrators' proposals to keep their preschool children in a full-day, early education program. In fact, recent work by [researchers] has demonstrated that the conversations children carry on at home may be the richest source of linguistic and cognitive enrichment for children from all but the most deprived backgrounds. This body of work highlights the vast scope of information and ideas that are transmitted at home, as opposed to the circumscribed agenda of the school.

In light of the well-documented, disappointing short-term benefits of Head Start, and the lack of any measurable longer-term benefits, policy makers should be focusing on ways to strengthen that program for disadvantaged youngsters, rather than spending vast new funds to expand the program to the middle class. It would be wasteful and poor policy to create new programs that resemble Head Start, but ignore the evidence of the program's strengths and weaknesses. Integrating Head Start programs into the public school system, moreover, would destroy the unique role Head Start plays in the community, and inevitably would lead to less parental influence and involvement over the program's operation and design. Such a state-run, formalized program could never provide the comprehensive services, or enjoy the local support, of independent Head Start projects. The National Black Child Development Institute, a nonprofit policy research organization in Washington, D.C., focusing on the needs of black children, is concerned that new preschool programs would adopt the methods of elementary education which often have segregated black children, labeling them as "nonachievers," and which have not been responsive to the concerns of black parents.

Improve Head Start

Improving the existing Head Start programs thus should be the priority, not creating a universal preschool education program. Research suggests that increased parental involvement in the program is the key to benefitting children permanently. The Bush Administration has proposed a $250 million increase in Head Start's $1.2 billion budget, and this new funding should be used to experiment with ways to ensure that all parents become full partners in the education of their youngsters. Children would certainly benefit if this parental activism continued as children began formal schooling.

Policymakers also must recognize that no preschool program can hope to compensate for the staggering deficiencies of the American public school system—shortcomings which are most damaging in the case of minority students. Providing education programs at an earlier age is no substitute for improving the quality of public education.

In addition, Congress and the governors must realize that disadvantaged children cannot be assisted effectively if their family situation is ignored. Almost half of all Head Start children come from families on welfare. The 1,300 local Head Start projects thus should be coordinating their activities closely with local welfare agencies, with the shared goal of helping families achieve self-sufficiency. Many parents of children in Head Start are employed by the program, and Head Start centers often do service as a focus for community efforts to deal with social problems and to provide parents with better information on available social services. However, the emphasis placed on this help for the families of children in the program depends on the local center. Head Start's role as a ladder for the family on welfare should be expanded.

The Risks of Early Education

We miseducate children whenever we put them at risk for no purpose. The risks of miseducating young children are both short- and long-term. The short-term risks derive from the stress, with all its attendant symptoms, that formal instruction places on children; the long-term risks are of at least three kinds: motivational, intellectual, and social. In each case, the potential psychological risks of early intervention far outweigh any potential educational gain.

David Elkind, *Phi Delta Kappan*, May 1986.

The welfare reform legislation passed in 1988 offers an opportunity for strengthening Head Start's impact on the families of disadvantaged children. The work, training, and education programs in the welfare reform act will affect thousands of parents on welfare. Mothers with children under the age of six will have to participate in these programs. Head Start centers should reserve spaces for children whose parents are participating in these new work and training programs. If Head Start were to treat these families as a priority, the preschool program could help secure independence from welfare—the first and vital step in ensuring a bright future for poor children.

Both Head Start's increased funding and the monies available to the states under the new welfare law should be used to enroll these children, and to expand the program's hours to meet the needs of welfare parents in training programs. The aim, in other words, should be to provide a better range of services to poor families, not to expand Head Start's educational component to middle-class children.

Some argue that if the Head Start program were expanded to include a far larger number of middle-class children, disadvantaged children would somehow benefit from this association. However, even those experts, such as Yale's Edward Zigler, who agree that the mixing of middle-class children into Head Start could benefit underprivileged children caution that the harm from preschool education to middle-class children will outweigh the benefits to poorer children.

A Panacea for Education's Ills

Universal preschool education is the latest in a series of panaceas offered to cure America's education ills. Like so many other putative panaceas, the proposals to create a federal program are based on highly selective and misleading data.

Professor Elkind writes:

> There is really no evidence that early formal instruction has any lasting or permanent benefits for children. By contrast, the risks to the child's motivation, intellectual growth and self-esteem could well do serious damage to the child's emerging personality. It is reasonable to conclude that the early instruction of young children derives more from the needs and priorities of adults than from what we know of good pedagogy for young children.

Preschool education potentially may have significant benefits for disadvantaged children if parents became more closely involved with them and if they serve to rally community efforts to reduce welfare dependency. Thus federal policies to boost preschool education for poor children should focus on strengthening parental involvement in Head Start and in making the program more readily available to assist families in becoming independent of welfare. The program should remain targeted on the poverty population, and precious slots should not be allocated to middle-class youngsters who do not need Head Start's services.

There are plenty of private programs available for those middle-class parents who believe that preschool education is desirable. However, child development experts caution that such formal schooling can be damaging to young children. Federal and state governments would be irresponsible to encourage and subsidize any program for youngsters with the potential to do more harm than good.

"The costs of adolescent parenthood are enormous—for the teen parents, for their children, and for society. "

Reducing Teen Pregnancy Would Decrease Childhood Poverty

Marian Wright Edelman

Marian Wright Edelman, a well-known spokesperson for children's rights, is the founder and president of the Children's Defense Fund, a Washington, D.C. organization that promotes programs and policies for America's children. In the following viewpoint, Edelman states that teenage pregnancy is a major cause of childhood poverty and other social problems. Teenage mothers are less likely to graduate from school and more likely to raise their children in poverty, she maintains. She believes that reducing teenage pregnancy through sex education and other social reforms will decrease childhood poverty in America.

As you read, consider the following questions:

1. What does Edelman list as some of the social costs of teenage pregnancy?
2. Why does the author believe minority teens are disproportionately affected by the consequences of early parenthood?
3. What does Edelman state are some of the pitfalls society should avoid in its attempt to reduce teenage pregnancy?

Reprinted by permission of the publishers from *Families in Peril: An Agenda for Social Change* by Marian Wright Edelman, Cambridge, Mass.: Harvard University Press, copyright © 1987 by the President and Fellows of Harvard College.

In every child who is born, under no matter what circum-
stances and of no matter what parents, the potentiality of
the human race is born again and in him, too, once more
and of each of us, our terrific responsibility toward human
life: toward the utmost idea of goodness, of the horror of
terror, and of God.

—James Agee,
Let Us Now Praise Famous Men

Teen pregnancy is a serious problem. Indeed, it is epidemic among all races and classes of American youth today. It could happen to your daughter, your niece, your grandchild, your friend's child, unless all Americans begin to think of ways to help children avoid premature sexual activity, pregnancy, and parenthood.

Each day more than 3,000 girls get pregnant and 1,300 give birth. Twenty-six thirteen- and fourteen-year-olds have their first child, thirteen sixteen-year-olds have their second child. Each year, 1.1 million American teen girls—one in ten—become pregnant. That is more than the entire Massachusetts school enrollment. Over half a million teenage girls have babies, a number nearly equal to the total population of the city of Boston. More disturbing is the pregnancy increase among younger teens. Each year, 125,000 girls fifteen and under become pregnant.

According to data from the Alan Guttmacher Institute, the United States leads nearly all developed nations of the world in rates of teenage pregnancy, abortion, and child-bearing, even though it has roughly comparable rates of teen sexual activity. The data show that our top-ranked status does not result only from the high rates of pregnancy and parenthood among minority teens. The pregnancy rates for white teenagers are twice as high as those of Canada, France, and England. Moreover, the maximum difference in birth rates occurs among girls under the age of fifteen, the most vulnerable teenagers.

Costs to Society

The costs of adolescent parenthood are enormous—for the teen parents, for their children, and for society.

• Forty percent of teenage girls who drop out of school do so because of pregnancy or marriage. Only half of the teens who become parents before the age of eighteen graduate from high school.

• A teen parent earns half the lifetime earnings of a woman who waits until age twenty to have her first child.

• Teen mothers are twice as likely to be poor as are non-teen mothers. Babies born to single mothers are two and a half times more likely to be poor than those born to two-parent families.

150

- Only 54 percent of all teen mothers in 1983 began prenatal care in the first three months of pregnancy. Babies of mothers who receive late or no prenatal care are three times more likely to die in their first year of life than those who receive early care.
- Babies born to teens represented about 14 percent of all births in 1983, but 20 percent of all low-birth-weight births. Low-birth-weight babies are twenty times more likely to die in the first year of life and special hospital care for low-birth-weight babies averages $1,000 a day.
- Medicaid pays for 30 percent of all hospital deliveries involving pregnant teens, at an annual cost of about $200 million a year.
- In 1985 half a million babies were born to teenage girls. The public cost was 1.4 billion dollars.

Ed Gamble. Reprinted with permission.

The international data make it clear that these costs are not the inevitable outcomes of increased adolescent sexual activity, but of our inability as a society to deal in a preventive way with the implications of that increase: to provide early comprehensive sex and family-life education in our homes, schools, and other institutions and to give sexually active teens access to family-planning services and counseling. The United States laments its high numbers of teen pregnancies but winds up providing for large numbers of teen parents and their children because we do not encourage early parental and other appropriate adult communication with children about the consequences of too early sexual activity, and we refuse to give our teens the capacity to delay parenthood, while unsuccessfully imploring too many of them, too late, to delay sexual activity. These data demonstrate the bankruptcy of such a policy—or lack of it. Withholding sex education and family-planning services has *not* led to less teenage sexual activity in the United States. Conversely, the provision of this information and service in Europe and Canada has resulted not in increased sexual activity but in heightened sexual responsibility.

Open Communication Needed

Adopting the approach to pregnancy prevention taken by our European counterparts will help reduce the rates of teen pregnancy and parenthood. We need to encourage a national atmosphere, in a wide range of settings, of open parental and responsible adult communication with the young about sexuality. State mandates for family-life education and the development of decision-making skills in the schools should begin in early childhood and continue through the high school years. At present only a minority of students receive timely and comprehensive sex or family-life education in the schools. The norm in the United States is definitely too little too late. Fewer than one school district in five offers students in-depth discussion of such basic issues as the responsibilities of parenthood, the consequences of teen pregnancy, or how to resist peer pressure for sex, before the ninth grade. And four out of every ten sexually active teens who need contraceptive counseling and services are not receiving help from a clinic or private doctor. . . .

Teen pregnancy and parenthood is as old as teen sex. What has changed dramatically is the utility or nonutility to the culture of teen sex and child-bearing. As a result of socioeconomic change, we no longer want teens to give birth and have imposed a moralistic overlay. Adolescent parenthood is no longer a viable option for thriving and progressing in society. As recently as the turn of the century, as in earlier times, youth generally finished school around the time of the onset of physical maturity, entered the work force as adults while in their teens, and had families by their late teens. By the 1940s, however, the schooling process for the middle class was stretching into the early twenties. Today half of our young adults are still in school at the age of nineteen. Only half have entered the labor force as nonstudents at age twenty. Half are still unmarried at age twenty-four, and half of the women twenty-five years and under have not borne their first child. The educational and social maturation process, as a foundation for economic self-sufficiency, extends well into the twenties. But for too many youth, economic reality, particularly if accompanied by unintended pregnancy, grinds this process to a halt and makes economic success a distant dream.

Increased Chance of Poverty

A single parent under twenty-five is nine times as likely to be poor as a young woman living on her own without children. Three-quarters of all single mothers under that age live in poverty. With more than half of all teen mothers raising their children alone, and with those who are married facing higher rates of separation and divorce, the costs of teenage parenthood—to the parents, to the children, and to society in terms of money spent and productivity lost—are too great to ignore.

Teenage pregnancy is a problem because it very often precludes the completion of education, the securing of employment, and the creation of a stable relationship, and because it makes the completion of each of these transitional steps more difficult. It is a problem because we no longer live in an America in which eighteen- and nineteen-year-old men can earn enough to support a family, and because we have never had an America in which the average single woman with children could earn a decent wage at any age. Meanwhile, young men, especially young black men, are increasingly unable to fulfill a traditional role as breadwinner and are less willing to accept their responsibilities as fathers. In 1970 three teen births out of ten were to single mothers. In 1983 this number had increased to more than five out of ten.

In 1984, 65 percent of teen hourly workers and 29 percent of hourly workers in their early twenties could not make wages sufficient to raise an intact, one-income family with a child out of poverty. And that is the proportion of those who were employed. Among black males, only 59 percent were employed in January of 1986; among black teen males only 21 percent were employed.

Race and Teenage Pregnancy

Contrary to popular perception, the majority of teen parents (342,283 of 499,038 in 1983) are white. Poor and minority teens, however, have a disproportionate share of teen births and are disproportionately affected by the social and economic consequences of early parenthood. A black teen is twice as likely to become pregnant as a white teen. A black teen is five times as likely as a white teen to become an unwed parent. This is primarily, albeit not completely, correlated to higher poverty rates among black teens. Nor is teen pregnancy just an urban, big-city problem. The ten worst states for percentage of teen out-of-

153

wedlock births are overwhelmingly Southern states that are typically less urbanized.

Adolescent pregnancy is everybody's problem in every part of the United States. The black community knows it has a disproportionate problem and is taking steps to respond. The white community has to understand that it, too, has a problem, as white families are now beginning to reflect the patterns of black families twenty years ago. The white teen birth rate has increased slightly, while the black teen birth rate has decreased. . . .

Making a significant dent in any major social problem requires a lot of hard work and persistence over a long period of time; endless trial and error; constant testing, refining, and mixing of strategies; flexible responses to changing times, new needs and targets of opportunity; and systematic, step-by-step movement toward long-term goals.

These goals must be:

• to reduce the incidence of first teen pregnancies;

• to reduce the incidence of repeat teen pregnancies;

• to reduce the number of teen school dropouts as a result of pregnancy and parenting;

• to reduce the number of babies born to poor mothers who have not received comprehensive prenatal care. . . .

Pitfalls to Avoid

• *Moralizing*. Some of us point judgmental fingers at others or assume that one age group, class, or race has a corner on morality. Such attitudes obscure causes and effects and can lead to backlash rather than cooperation and change. Moralizing will not solve the teen pregnancy problem. But moral adult examples and efforts to provide constructive alternatives to young people can help.

• *Using teen pregnancy as another excuse to batter the poor*. Research by Mary Jo Bane and William Wilson indicates that welfare is not the cause of teenage pregnancy. Teen pregnancy rates are higher in states with the lowest welfare benefits and lowest in states with higher welfare benefits. Most teen pregnancies are unwanted or unplanned.

• *Quick fixes*. The media and too many politicians and citizens are looking for magic bullets or quick results to complex problems. Preventing teen pregnancy and alleviating the poverty of female-headed households are long-haul battles, which we must fight systematically and step by step.

• *Despair*. Our biggest initial task is to pierce the veil of despair, provide a glimmer of hope for young people going nowhere in our society, identify efforts that seem to be making a difference, and package them in ways that a majority of the American public can support.

• *Stereotyping*. At all costs we must resist a national inclination to define the complex problem of teen pregnancy as one peculiar to a black "underclass," and to act as if welfare is the main cause or consequence of this social phenomenon which affects many different target groups in different ways and which will respond to a range of outreach strategies and remedies. The families portrayed in the media too often are one slice of the black family crisis that must be addressed by the black community and by the nation. But there are other slices of black and white youth and family reality about whom we do not hear: the many millions of children in poor families who are not on welfare or who are coping despite teen pregnancy and other barriers of poverty; the many poor children who do not get pregnant at all; and the millions of middle-class teens, black and white, male and female, who need the same parental communication and value transfusion that poor children also need.

A Cycle of Poverty

There is little dispute that teenage pregnancy increases dramatically a woman's chances of living in poverty, which in turn increases the chance of her children becoming teenage parents and living in poverty. Welfare support and other public programs are necessary to help these young families, but studies have shown that if the pregnancies were delayed by just a few years the chance of a woman's depending on welfare goes down substantially.

Center for Population Options, *Teenage Pregnancy and Too-Early Childbearing: Public Costs, Personal Consequences,* September 1989.

• *Political carelessness.* Our goal must be to win for children and poor teenagers. In order to do this, we must emphasize the issues that unite rather than divide us. If there is more than one way to achieve a result, and one road has a lot of political traffic while another has less or none, take the latter road. Social reformers need to anticipate better the political opposition and figure out ways of going around it, wherever possible. But we should also be prepared to fight and to do the careful political organizing that ensures victory despite controversy. Too often we let a few noisy people scare us away from fighting for programs that children need. We can organize and fight as effectively as they can if all of us are willing to make the effort.
• *A lack of confidence and patience.* We must not fear testing a variety of approaches until we hit upon the combination that works. Social-reform strategies are not different from the scientific method; it is trial and error, trial and error. We must avoid unrealistic expectations for ourselves and others. Comprehensive, long-term efforts are essential to recapture the future for today's

youth. Few, if any, major social reforms, whether child labor protection or dismantling legally entrenched racial segregation, whether female suffrage or black voting rights, have accrued in the absence of a long and arduous struggle, usually lasting decades.

A Long Struggle

The pace of American life has quickened, and perhaps social problems develop more quickly than they used to. Certainly public attention is more ephemeral than it used to be. But strengthening families and preventing teen pregnancy requires the same concerted effort over the long term as did earlier struggles for social progress. A setback this month, this year, means little. The struggle will take many years. Nothing less will make a real difference.

"Teenage pregnancy per se is not the precipitator of social problems."

Reducing Teen Pregnancy Would Not Decrease Childhood Poverty

Charlotte Low Allen

Teenage pregnancy is not the social problem that many people claim it is, Charlotte Low Allen maintains in the following viewpoint. Allen states that new research shows that a teenage mother does not have an increased chance of living in poverty or of dropping out of school. Society should create policies that support the family rather than policies that discourage teen pregnancy, she believes. Allen is the senior law editor for the weekly newsmagazine *Insight on the News,* published by *The Washington Times* newspaper.

As you read, consider the following questions:

1. What statistics does Allen cite to support her claim that teenage pregnancy is decreasing?
2. Why does the author believe teaching birth control to high school students is not the way to deal with teenage pregnancy?
3. How do the goals of poor teenagers differ from those of middle-class teenagers, according to Allen?

The girl who has an illegitimate child at the age of 16 suddenly has 90 percent of her life's script written for her. She will probably drop out of school; even if someone else in her family helps to take care of the baby, she will probably not be able to find a steady job that pays enough to provide for herself and her child; she may feel impelled to marry someone she might not otherwise have chosen. Her life choices are few, and most of them are bad.

These three sentences, from a 1968 article by sociologist Arthur A. Campbell, are the most famous words ever written about teenage pregnancy. Widely disseminated, they formed the philosophical basis for more than two decades of efforts of education, subsidization, exhortation and persuasion to get teenage girls not to have babies.

A massive 1987 report by the National Research Council, "Risking the Future: Adolescent Sexuality, Pregnancy and Childbearing," listed a litany of the "personal and public costs" of adolescent pregnancy; they included "discontinued education," "reduced employment opportunities," "unstable marriages," "low income," "frustration" and "hopelessness." The report called for intensifying a variety of preventive strategies, from promotion of contraceptives to the now-popular concept of "life options" or self-esteem programs designed to encourage teenagers to delay sex. Other reports appear periodically that try to calculate the cost to taxpayers of adolescent childbearing in terms of welfare and Medicaid benefits. . . .

False Assumptions

There is only one problem, a number of scholars have argued: None of these commonly held assumptions is exactly true. Just for starters, the peak year for teenage childbearing was not in the 1960s or 1970s. It was in 1957. That year, the fertility rate was 97.3 births per 1,000 females 19 or younger. By 1977, it had fallen to 52.8 births, and to 51.1 births in 1987—a fertility decline of almost 50 percent over 30 years. The gross number of such births has also shrunk each year as the number of teenagers has declined with the passing of the baby boom. In 1987, 462,312 teenagers gave birth, and by 1992, the U.S. Census Bureau estimates, there will be 420,000 births to teens if the fertility rate continues at present levels. About 10 percent of girls get pregnant at some time between age 13 and 19; half give birth, 40 percent have abortions and the rest miscarry. This has coincided with a general decline in fertility for all age groups and races. (The teen fertility rate for blacks in particular has also declined, though far more slowly than for whites, and it remains, at 89.7, twice as high as that for whites.) At the current fertility rate, a woman can expect to have 1.9 children, which is lower than the population replacement level of 2.1.

158

Of the births to younger teenagers, only 10,000 each year are to girls younger than 15, a number that has stayed constant for about a decade. Research shows that these births reflect a significant number of pregnancies brought about by rape or incest. All 462,312 adolescent births in 1987 represented just 12 percent of the total number of births in the United States that year (in 1973, 20 percent of births were to teens).

Teenage Pregnancy Is Not Harmful

I would like to go on the record in opposition to the view that teen childbearing is self-destructive, irrational or anti-social. Stopping teen pregnancies buys them nothing. In fact, it may even harm them.

Arline Geronimus, address before the American Association for the Advancement of Science, February 1990.

The other demographic fact is that two-thirds of all teenage births are to young women age 18 and 19, women who have graduated from high school (or dropped out), are old enough to vote and are legally adults. Half of all teenagers who give birth are married; in rural areas and among Hispanics, youthful marriages are common. Those marriages can be fragile, but a 1986 study showed that after 10 years, three-fourths of teenage marriages with legitimate babies were intact among whites and half among blacks.

And, it is likely that almost every American had a mother, grandmother or great-grandmother who first gave birth as a teenager and turned out just fine. During the 1920s, the adolescent childbearing rate was exactly what it is today, and few teenage mothers finished high school; no one worried about them. Rosalynn Carter was 18 when she bore her first child.

Out-of-Wedlock Births

The reason teenage childbearing today looks like an "epidemic" and a major social problem but did not in 1957 or 1937 may be due to one crucial difference: the fact that nearly all teenage births 30 years ago took place in marriage. Of babies born out of wedlock, 50 percent were relinquished for adoption in 1970; now, 90 percent of unmarried mothers raise their babies.

There is very little research correlating a mother's marital status to social and medical problems for her children such as poor nutrition, low school attainment, delinquency and crime. One scholar who has looked at the numbers, Nick Eberstadt of the American Enterprise Institute, says birth out of wedlock is the key predictor for later trouble, whether the mother is in her teens, her early 20s—the peak fertility years in which childbearing occurs—or even older.

"It doesn't matter what the mother's socioeconomic status is or her race," says Eberstadt. Ninety percent of teenage births to blacks now take place out of wedlock (compared with 47 percent 20 years ago). But the fastest rise in out-of-wedlock births has been among whites. In general, illegitimate births rose 40 percent from 1980 to 1987, accompanied by a decline in the marriage rate during the same period; the number of cohabiting unmarried couples quintupled as a proportion of all couples in 1970–88. Furthermore, a number of sociological studies have shown Campbell's deterministic assumptions—that having a baby as a teenager automatically ruins a woman's life—to be far from the mark.

The most famous work of scholarship on teen pregnancy is an ongoing longitudinal study of 400 teenage mothers in Baltimore from the late 1960s to date by Frank F. Furstenberg Jr., a sociology professor at the University of Pennsylvania. Although he described adolescent pregnancy as "a social problem," he also found that most of the mothers adapted successfully to motherhood and that 70 percent were married five years later. Their children lagged in school, but Furstenberg suggested that might be due to economic disadvantage. He also found relatively low rates of long-term welfare dependency among teenage mothers. Only one-fourth were on welfare when their children were born, and most were back in the work force by the time their youngest child was 3. Furthermore, Furstenberg found that only one-third of the daughters of women who bore their first child as teens became teenage mothers.

Pregnancy Is Not the Problem

More recent studies further bolster the notion that teenage pregnancy per se is not the precipitator of social problems. Dawn M. Upchurch, a health policy professor at Johns Hopkins University, and James McCarthy, a public health professor at Columbia University, issued a paper concluding that teenage mothers are no more likely to drop out of school than teens who did not have babies, although girls who bore a child after dropping out of school were less likely to return than their childless peers. Steven D. McLaughlin, a researcher at the Battelle Human Affairs Research Centers in Seattle, issued results of a longitudinal study showing that the self-esteem of adolescent mothers who kept their babies was about the same as that of teens who relinquished their infants for adoption (the mothers who relinquished did somewhat better financially and educationally, however).

In March 1990, two University of Washington researchers, Shelly Lundberg and Robert D. Plotnick, delivered a paper to a

Health and Human Services Department-sponsored forum on the underclass reporting that for black women, having a child before age 19 has no effect on earning potential. In fact, black women, married or not, who start having children in adolescence can expect to earn 14 percent more during their 20s than black women who postpone childbirth until that decade. For disadvantaged black women, the earnings gap is 21 percent if the child is out of wedlock, 29 percent if the woman is married when she has her first child. "Our study is still ongoing, and it's still too early to say why this is," says Lundberg. For whites, bearing a child out of wedlock during adolescence does carry an earnings penalty—but a low 14 percent.

On February 16, 1990, a grenade landed in the debate. A 33-year-old assistant professor of public health policy at the University of Michigan, Arline T. Geronimus, made a three-hour presentation to the American Association for the Advancement of Science. Her findings reflected research on the health of adolescent mothers and their infants that she had already published in two papers and expects to publish in more. She declared that because poor women, especially poor black women, are healthier in their adolescence than they are during their 20s and very poor women have little to lose by having babies early—indeed, might have a network of kinfolk to help them—teenage childbearing makes adaptive sense for the impoverished, just as it does in poor countries where life expectancy is short (in Bangladesh, more than 85 percent of women bear their first child while in their teens).

"I would like to go on the record today in opposition to the view that teen childbearing is self-destructive, irrational or antisocial," Geronimus declared. "Stopping teen pregnancies buys them nothing. In fact, it may even harm them."

Angry Responses

Her presentation drew quick and hostile responses from the advocacy establishment. "Her facts are misrepresentative, her premise is wrong and the policy implications of her arguments are perverse," Karen Pittman of the Children's Defense Fund told *The New York Times*. "She might be right from the teenager's point of view, but the public costs are still there," says researcher Martha Burt of the Urban Institute. In a letter to *The Washington Post*, Rosann Wisman, executive director of Planned Parenthood's District of Columbia office, accused Geronimus of ignoring "uncontradicted data" showing that "for most adolescent families, becoming a parent is detrimental to the health and welfare of both the teenage mother and her child."

"We have an almost ideological disapproval of teen childbirth," says Geronimus. "We don't as a society have a meaningful role for young people to play. We think that the meaningful role for them is to be in college, but for poor women, college is not a meaningful option. They talk about having children in very positive terms. I've found from talking to them that they find raising children to be very meaningful work. They have grown up having to care for younger children, and they know how to take care of babies."

Teenage Pregnancy Is Not a Crime

The media are hammering into our minds that teenage pregnancy is a terrible problem, so that we finally no longer ask ourselves what the problem consists of, or whose problem it is. We simply accept that it is somehow similar to being a criminal.

We immediately recognize how perverse this is when we think about how other times and cultures have treated their young women. In most societies, somewhere between 16 and 18 years was considered a good age for a woman to start having children.

Alfred Kracher, *National Catholic Reporter*, September 22, 1989.

What Geronimus is saying is that adolescent childbearing is a phenomenon of the poor and the very poor, of young women who grow up early and look their best when they are young, have little interest in higher education, do not see themselves as having careers and live in communities where health starts deteriorating quickly. The "opportunity costs"—forgone earnings potential—of having a child early are close to nil, and life expectancy is short.

Teenage girls with college and career aspirations typically choose abortion—or their mothers choose it for them—when they get pregnant, and they are from the same highly motivated socioeconomic group that uses contraception faithfully. If the United States had the same social homogeneity as, say, Canada, it is likely the nation would have the same teenage fertility rate as well, which is one-half that of the United States.

Poverty and Childbearing

If Geronimus and others such as Upchurch, McCarthy and Lundberg are right, teenage childbearing does not so much cause poverty as grow out of poverty. The rate for blacks is twice that for whites because blacks constitute the highest proportion of the urban underclass. And if early childbearing is associated with such negative consequences as drugs and low-birth-weight infants, it is because such things are endemic in poverty as well. In fact, the difference in the neonatal death rate—the rate of babies who die between birth and four weeks—for infants born to teenage mothers and to mothers age 25 to 29 disappears when the numbers are adjusted for socioeconomic status, Geronimus says.

If this research is correct, a public policy overwhelmingly oriented toward teaching high school students how to use birth control—viewing teen pregnancy as a problem of ignorance that information can solve—may be on the wrong track. A series of research papers in the mid-1980s by Douglas Kirby of the Washington-based Center for Population Options concluded that sex education in school had no effect on adolescent contraceptive use, and a report by Kirby on school-based clinics showed similar findings. Only one experiment, by Johns Hopkins University demographer Laurie Schwab Zabin, indicated that an off-the-premises clinic for high school and junior high school students produced dramatic decreases in pregnancy. But Zabin's research has been faulted as using a hit-or-miss approach that did not follow through on specific populations.

Even at the New York City-based Guttmacher Institute, a leading proponent of education and contraception as the way to reduce adolescent pregnancy, there has been some rethinking. "Most of the programs we have had have been preaching sex education," says Jeannie I. Rosoff, the institute's president. "We now know that increasing knowledge does not necessarily affect behavior. But sex education is something we know how to do."

Strengthen Families

A better approach, some scholars say, would be to focus on policies to strengthen young families. One theory, by Maris Vinovskis, a University of Michigan professor and adolescent-pregnancy consultant during the Carter and Reagan years, is not to discourage pregnant teens from getting married (now, the prevailing wisdom is against youthful marriages on the theory that they will not last). "It's too easy to give up on fathers and say, 'What's the use?'" says P. Lindsay Chase-Lansdale, a researcher at the University of Chicago's Chapin Hall Center for Children, who collaborated with Vinovskis on a policy paper encouraging stronger efforts to collect child support from young fathers (1988 welfare reforms went in this direction).

The boys who father children with teens tend to be a few years older than the girls—and thus higher earners. Most are in their 20s, with an average earning capacity that is above the poverty level and steadily rises, according to a study by Robert Lerman, a sociologist at American University.

Preaching "morality" at teenagers as a way to reduce pregnancy is also frowned upon in these nonjudgmental days; young people are supposed to find the very idea of morality laughable. But the best indicator these days for not getting pregnant as a teenager is membership in a fundamentalist Protestant church that teaches in no-nonsense fashion that sex outside marriage is a sin. A study by Sandra Hofferth, an Urban Institute researcher, shows a direct correlation between weekly attendance at religious services and delayed sexual activity.

Finally, says Lerman, making a place for teens as productive members of society—perhaps via apprenticeships—would encourage them to think of themselves more maturely. After all, the 19th century sculptor Vinnie Ream was 18 when she chiseled a statue of Abraham Lincoln for the U.S. Capitol, and Joan of Arc was burned at the stake at 19. But today, many middle-class young people do not consider themselves grown-up and ready for adult responsibilities until they reach 30 or so. "I read a study that described a 25-year-old as an adolescent," says Joseph Adelson, a University of Michigan psychologist. That leaves lower-income teenagers without anything at all that is socially acceptable to do.

Postponing Childbearing

"People project on poor teenagers what a middle-class teenager would want—going to the senior prom, getting into the best college," says Geronimus. "We have sort of assumed that no teenager would ever want to have a child. In fact, most teenagers at this point in history don't want to become mothers, and for those teens, sex education and contraception may be the best approach. But bear in mind that poor men die much younger—I think the life expectancy in Harlem is lower than it is in Bangladesh—and there are high rates of joblessness. You just can't postpone forever the bearing of children.

"I think that people ought to stop focusing on teen childbearing as the cause of all the problems of the underclass," she says. "These are young women who are trying to do the best they can under adverse hardships in a dangerous community. We can't just sit back and say to them that it's their fault for having babies young."

a critical thinking activity

Recognizing Stereotypes

A stereotype is an oversimplified or exaggerated description of people or things. Stereotyping can be favorable. Most stereotyping, however, tends to be highly uncomplimentary, and, at times, degrading.

Stereotyping grows out of our prejudices. When we stereotype someone, we are prejudging him or her. Consider the following example: Mr. Smith believes all poor people are lazy and irresponsible. Whenever he sees a poor family, he assumes the parents have done something to cause the family's poverty: they are lazy, ignorant, or have no desire to work or study. He disregards the possibility that the parents are working but are still unable to make ends meet, or that circumstances beyond their control have forced them into poverty. Instead, he assumes that if they really wanted to get out of poverty, they could. Why? He has prejudged all poor people and will keep his stereotype consistent with his prejudice.

Part I

The following statements relate to the subject matter in this chapter. Consider each statement carefully. *Mark S for any statement that is an example of stereotyping. Mark N for any statement that is not an example of stereotyping. Mark U if you are undecided about any statement.*

S = *stereotype*
N = *not a stereotype*
U = *undecided*

165

1. Most poor women prefer to live on welfare than to work.

2. Head Start teachers are very altruistic.

3. Each year, 1.1 million American teen girls become pregnant.

4. Wealthy Americans are unconcerned about the plight of the poor.

5. The rise of women in the labor force has disadvantaged children.

6. The poor are less materialistic than the rich.

7. Many American parents are reluctant to discuss sex with their children.

8. Children are defenseless.

9. Poor children cannot do as well in school as children of more affluent parents.

10. Head Start students often do well in first grade.

11. A black teen is twice as likely to become pregnant as a white teen.

12. The stresses caused by poverty make it difficult for poor people to stay employed.

13. Black teenagers have so many babies because they are ignorant about birth control.

14. Head Start does not help poor children.

15. Many poor people are too proud to accept a handout from the government.

16. In 1982, 48 percent of poor families were headed by single mothers.

17. Many poor teenagers want to have babies.

18. The government is subsidizing institutionalized care at the expense of traditional parental care for children.

Part II

Based on the insights you have gained from this activity, discuss these questions in class:

1. Why do people stereotype one another?

2. What are some examples of positive stereotypes?

3. What harm can stereotypes cause?

4. What stereotypes currently affect members of your class?

Periodical Bibliography

The following articles have been selected to supplement the diverse views presented in this chapter.

Mary Jo Bane and David T. Ellwood — "One-Fifth of the Nation's Children: Why Are They Poor?" *Science*, September 8, 1989.

T. Berry Brazelton — "Why Is America Failing Its Children?" *The New York Times Magazine*, September 9, 1990.

Linda L. Creighton — "Challenging the Myths: The Case for Orphanages," *U.S. News & World Report*, October 8, 1990.

Leon Dash — "When Children Want Children," *Society*, July/August 1990.

William A. Donohue — "Failed Formulas: Teen Pregnancy and the 'New Freedom,'" *The Family in America*, September 1989. Available from The Rockford Institute, 934 N. Main St., Rockford, IL 61103-7061.

Nancy Gibbs — "Shameful Bequests to the Next Generation," *Time*, October 8, 1990.

Jonathan Kozol — "The New Untouchables," *Newsweek*, special issue, Winter/Spring 1990.

Susan E. Mayer and Christopher Jencks — "Growing Up in Poor Neighborhoods: How Much Does It Matter?" *Science*, March 17, 1989.

Sally Reed and R. Craig Sautter — "Children of Poverty," *Phi Delta Kappan*, June 1990.

Lisbeth B. Schorr — "Let's Stop Recycling Poverty," *The Family Therapy Networker*, November/December 1989.

Lawrence J. Schweinhart and David P. Weikart — "A Fresh Start for Head Start?" *The New York Times*, May 13, 1990.

Timothy M. Smeeding — "Children and Poverty: How the U.S. Stands," *Forum for Applied Research and Public Policy*, Summer 1990. Available from The University of North Carolina Press, PO Box 2288, Chapel Hill, NC 27515-2288.

Society — Special issue on children, March/April 1987.

James R. Thompson — "Preventing Pregnancies Among Adolescents," *Society*, March/April 1989.

Laurie Udesky — "Welfare Reform and Its Victims," *The Nation*, September 24, 1990.

How Can the Health of America's Children Be Improved?

AMERICA'S
CHILDREN

Chapter Preface

A pregnant woman arrives at a hospital emergency room, ready to deliver her baby. It is her first visit to a doctor since her pregnancy began. The baby, born with syphilis, has cataracts, liver and heart problems, and rickets. Doctors work for a month and the hospital spends more than $70,000 working to save the baby's life. The anguish and the expense could all have been avoided if the mother had received a $20 penicillin shot early in the pregnancy.

This true case illustrates the paradox of America's child health-care system. While U.S. medical technology surpasses that of all other nations, the number of pregnant women receiving prenatal care is decreasing. American physicians can now save newborns who weigh as little as a pound and a half, but they have been unable to markedly decrease America's infant mortality rate. It remains the highest among twenty industrialized nations, according to a 1990 study by the U.S. Bureau of the Census. As Democratic representative George Miller, chairman of the House Committee on Children, Youth, and Families, states, "The U.S. is very good at saving very ill babies that would have died at birth in less developed countries," but it does "a terrible job of preventing infants from getting sick in the first place." Rae K. Grad, the executive director of the National Commission to Prevent Infant Mortality, estimates that for every dollar spent on prevention, more than three can be saved in newborn intensive care.

Many experts maintain, however, that improving access to prenatal care may not solve the problem. Even when the government provides prenatal care and child health care, many Americans do not use it. "You could put prenatal care on every street corner and make it free, and not get every pregnant woman to come in," says Kathy Sanders-Phillips, developmental psychologist at Martin Luther King Jr. General Hospital in Los Angeles. Many drug-addicted women, for example, are too afraid, unaware, or unconcerned to seek care. In 1988, 11 percent of all live births, or 375,000 babies, were born to mothers who used drugs while they were pregnant. Many of these babies required intensive care. Experts such as Florida prosecutor Jeff Deen, the first to successfully prosecute a woman for using drugs while pregnant, believe that children's health care will only improve if parents are held accountable for neglect, substance abuse, and other behaviors that harm children. Society must send a message to parents that it "cannot afford to have two or three cocaine babies from the same person," Deen states.

The authors in the following chapter discuss why many U.S. children are unhealthy and debate ways of improving the health care system for children.

"Early and adequate prenatal care is the single factor most likely to prevent infant deaths."

Increasing the Availability of Prenatal Care Can Improve Children's Health

Harmeet Dhillon Singh

In the following viewpoint, Harmeet Dhillon Singh argues that a lack of prenatal care for poor women has resulted in high U.S. infant mortality rates. Singh believes reforming Medicaid, reforming the insurance industry, and creating programs to counsel pregnant women will result in better and more available prenatal care. Singh is an assistant editor of the quarterly *Policy Review*, published by The Heritage Foundation, a conservative think tank in Washington, D.C.

As you read, consider the following questions:

1. What factors does the author state helped decrease infant mortality from 1918 to 1970?
2. Why is applying for Medicaid difficult for many women, according to Singh?
3. What insurance reforms does the author believe would help poor women?

Harmeet Dhillon Singh, "Stork Reality." Reprinted with permission from the Spring 1990 issue of *Policy Review*, the flagship publication of The Heritage Foundation, 214 Massachusetts Ave. NE, Washington, DC 20002.

The most important part of solving any problem is first defining it. Take the example of polio. We used to treat it by giving patients crutches, braces, and eventually, iron lungs. But once we isolated the virus, we were able to develop a vaccine. The problem with the way we approach infant mortality today is that we're trying to solve it with braces and crutches, using the same old approach we once used with polio. We haven't faced up to the real problem, which is fundamentally a social one.

—Dr. George Graham, Johns Hopkins University

A nation's rate of infant mortality is a barometer of its success in combating poverty, ignorance, and disease. It is therefore a tragedy and a source of embarrassment that the United States ranks below 18 other countries in infant mortality, lagging behind Singapore, Hong Kong, and Japan, as well as most of Western Europe. A black child born in the United States is less likely to survive his first year than a child born in Costa Rica or Bulgaria. A black infant born in the District of Columbia is more likely to die before the age of one than a baby born in North Korea. While other countries often use different methods and standards to count infant deaths, the U.S. rate is still unacceptably high.

A Remarkable Improvement

By historic standards, of course, the current infant mortality rate is a remarkable improvement. In 1918, when the U.S. infant mortality rate was sixth in the world, there were 77 deaths per 1,000 live births; 25 years later, the figure had dropped by half. By 1960, the rate was 26 per 1,000, and it declined steadily, leveling off during the '80s to its current rate of about 10 per 1,000.

Better sanitation, chlorinated water, victorious battles against infectious diseases such as tuberculosis, amoebic dysentery, cholera, and typhoid fever, and the advent of vitamin-enriched baby formula and foods all did their share in drastically cutting the rate over the past half-century. During the past quarter-century and especially during the early '70s, the development of respirators and the introduction of neonatal intensive care units and other life-saving technology for critically ill newborns reduced the rate even further. Now, however, it seems that both high technology and inroads against disease have reached their thresholds, and health care officials have begun to look elsewhere for answers. . . .

Federal programs for prenatal care—primarily Medicaid, the Special Supplemental Feeding Program for Women, Infants, and Children (WIC), and the Maternal and Child Health block grant —are unnecessarily fragmented and clogged with paperwork.

Second, particularly in rural areas in the South but also in other parts of the country, there are not enough public health clinics or private practitioners willing to serve low-income expectant mothers. Third, about a sixth of all expectant mothers lack private health insurance and are also ineligible for Medicaid, leading many of them to forgo routine prenatal care checkups, to say nothing of more specialized treatment. . . .

Infant Mortality Rates

Infant deaths per thousand births in 20 industrialized countries*

Country	Rate		Country	Rate
United States	10.4		Denmark	8.2
Austria	9.9		Canada	7.9
Australia	9.8		France	7.6
Belgium	9.7		Netherlands	7.6
German Democratic Republic	9.2		Hong Kong	7.5
United Kingdom	9.1		Singapore	7.4
Ireland	8.7		Switzerland	6.8
Federal Republic of Germany	8.6		Finland	6.3
Spain	8.5		Sweden	5.7
Norway	8.5		Japan	5.2

*Babies who die before one year of age.
NOTE: Figures are the last available from each country—they are from 1985, 1986 or 1987.
Source: United Nations Department of International Economic and Social Affairs, Statistical Office

Over 40,000 babies born in the United States will die before they celebrate their first birthdays. According to Assistant Secretary of Health and Human Services James O. Mason, "Another 400,000 infants born this year will live to their first birthday but may become statistics of another kind. These unfortunate children will be born with or develop chronic conditions that are disabling enough to deprive them of true independence." The preventability of many such statistics heightens their poignancy.

In the U.S., early and adequate prenatal care is the single factor most likely to prevent infant deaths. Women who do not obtain proper prenatal care are two to three times more likely than those who do to deliver low-birthweight babies. In a 1985 report, the National Governors' Association's Southern Regional Task Force on Infant Mortality found that low-birthweight babies (those under five and a half pounds) are 40 times more likely to die during the neonatal (first month after birth) period than normal babies. In fact, although low-birthweight babies comprise only 7 percent of all live births, they account for 60 percent of all infant deaths. Laboratory testing and medical evaluations designed for early identification of high-risk mothers, plus heeding the medical, dietary, and hygienic advice provided during prenatal care visits could have prevented many, if not most, of those deaths.

Not only is prenatal care crucial to a successful pregnancy, it is cost-effective as well. The cost of a prenatal and delivery care package ranges from $500 to $1,000. By contrast, according to the Office of Technology Assessment, the U.S. health care system spends between $14,000 and $30,000 per low-birthweight child—primarily for intensive care during the infant's first year. The lifelong cost of health care for illnesses and disabilities associated with low birthweight has been estimated at over $250,000 per child. A 1988 study by the Congress-appointed National Commission to Prevent Infant Mortality estimated that hospitalization and medical costs for low-birthweight babies alone total more than $2 billion a year. A widely cited 1985 study by the Institute of Medicine, a branch of the National Academy of Sciences, calculated that each dollar spent on prenatal care for low-income, under-educated women would result in first year savings of $3.38 due to a lower rate of low birthweight.

Medicaid's Red Tape

The federal government already spends $5.8 billion on prenatal care-related programs, matched by state contributions of $1.7 billion to these programs. The major federal programs include Medicaid ($2.9 billion), WIC ($2.1 billion), the Maternal and Child Health block grant, which supplements public health care clinics ($500 million), and a host of smaller programs such as Title X family planning, immunizations, community health centers, and migrant health centers. Despite these huge outlays, in most states fewer than half of all Medicaid recipients received adequate prenatal care, according to a 1987 General Accounting Office report. In some Alabama counties, as few as 18 percent of these women obtained the proper care. Some mothers failed to take advantage of services available to them because they lacked transportation, others because they did not know they were pregnant. But for many, the chief obstacle to prenatal care was the red tape and fragmentation associated with Medicaid. . . .

Applying for Medicaid often requires the patience of Job and the stamina of a marathon runner. Applications can run as long as 40 pages, and submitting all the required documents requires an average of two and sometimes three trips to the "processing center," a monumental task in itself for women who often don't own cars or live in areas without public transportation.

Bureaucratic Barriers

For each dollar spent on prenatal care, a savings of $3 results during the infant's first year of life. When prenatal care prevents a low-weight birth, the savings in hospitalization and long-term costs can be from $14,000 to $30,000.

But in our society, it frequently is difficult for a pregnant woman to get prenatal care. Some estimates indicate that more than 8 million women of childbearing age have no health insurance at all. Further, much private health insurance provides less-than-adequate prenatal benefits, and many Medicaid beneficiaries face almost insurmountable bureaucratic barriers to prenatal care.

American Medical News, October 19, 1990.

A Medicaid applicant usually waits from 30 to 60 days to find out if she is eligible. If she is denied, chances are it is because she failed to fill out the forms properly: the rejection rate for "failure to comply with procedural requirements" exceeds 70 percent in some states. Rejections for "excess income"—the most logical reason a person would be denied—account for only 20 percent. These tortuous eligibility procedures constitute *de facto* rationing of Medicaid, a gamble unfairly stacked against women least equipped to play this game.

Several states are trying to cut through the red tape, and in some cases the federal government has helped by relaxing certain eligibility requirements for Medicaid. One useful reform is continuous eligibility, which allows the state to keep a woman on the Medicaid rolls for the duration of her pregnancy and 60 days after delivery, instead of having to again complete the tiresome paperwork three and six months after becoming eligible. Thirty-eight states have opted for this reform.

Another important reform is presumptive eligibility, which allows a health care official to conditionally certify a woman eligible for Medicaid upon a verbal declaration of income, pending the completion and processing of a formal application. This option is especially useful to county health clinics providing same-day walk-in service because it ensures early care. To date, 20 states have taken advantage of this option.

In lieu of presumptive eligibility, or sometimes coinciding with it, some states have initiated guidelines for expediting the processing of Medicaid claims. In California, where the routine Medicaid processing period is 45 days, pregnancy is treated as a medical emergency, allowing processing to be completed in less than a week. Michigan has instituted a requirement that Medicaid applications from pregnant women be processed within 24 hours. Other states, including Florida, West Virginia, and Minnesota, have condensed their application forms, in some instances reducing them from 40 to three pages.

No Room at the Clinic

Once the woman becomes eligible for Medicaid, she can then make an appointment—but she might have a hard time finding a doctor. The crisis in obstetrician/gynecologist availability is being felt by all women in this country, but poor and rural populations have been the hardest hit. The main culprit in obstetrical care scarcity is skyrocketing malpractice insurance rates, which can add hundreds of dollars to prenatal care and delivery for each baby.

Because of extremely low reimbursement rates (averaging about 44 percent of what the doctor would make from a privately insured patient, but in some areas less than 20 percent of the going rate) and mountains of paperwork, about 40 percent of obstetricians will not treat Medicaid patients.

Thus, the woman is likely to turn to her local county health clinic. Since 1984, a large amount of the prenatal care burden has shifted from private providers to public clinics, increasing the clinics' load by 50 percent. The good news for the pregnant woman is that she is more likely to get comprehensive services at the health care clinic, including advice on proper nutrition, counseling, even referrals to nutritional programs or social services for those who are eligible. However, even in states where prenatal care is given high priority, such as North Carolina, the waiting list for treatment in many county clinics averages two months.

The number of clinics in rural areas, especially in the South, is an integral part of the availability crisis. Women may sometimes find themselves 50, even 100 miles away from the nearest county health clinic. A recent attempt to provide comprehensive prenatal care services for the small town of Slater, South Carolina, demonstrates the problem. While the publicly funded Slater-Marietta Health Care Services Clinic processes WIC, AFDC [Aid to Families with Dependent Children], and Medicaid claims and has part-time nurses who provide immunizations and other routine health services, the Medicaid-eligible pregnant woman still has to travel to the town of Greenville, nearly

20 miles away, to see a doctor there in the county clinic. Attempts to convince the state health department to provide a doctor at the Slater clinic on a part-time basis have proven unfruitful for lack of funding; Medicaid processing may be withdrawn from the site as well. However, the clinic's executive director, Karen Cottingham, has tried to have the town of 15,000 declared a Health Manpower Shortage area, which would entitle it to federal funds for medical personnel, which might include a nurse-practitioner plus a part-time doctor. . . .

Navigation Aids

Some states have begun to employ case managers to help women navigate the complex, fragmented system. In North Carolina, each woman entering the public prenatal care system is assigned a case manager, who acts as an advocate for the "client" by informing her of services that are available, helping her complete forms, and, if necessary, making sure that she gets transportation to her appointments and follows up on the recommendations of nurses and doctors at the clinics.

Saving Money and Lives

The cost of providing intensive care for infants in the United States topped $4 billion. Half of that could have been saved if all pregnant women had received prenatal care, according to the commission on infant mortality.

Prenatal care saves money as well as lives. In community health clinics, comprehensive care costs about $1,200. The average bill for a baby in intensive care is $19,000. For every dollar spent on prevention, more than three can be saved in newborn intensive care, and another six may be saved in lifetime care of permanently disabled children.

Jonathan Freedman, *Los Angeles Times*, May 15, 1990.

Another area of innovation is aggressive outreach, which includes everything from high-tech marketing in the form of advertising and public service announcements, to case-finding workers going door to door in rural and urban areas to find pregnant women. Yet health care workers are presented with a dilemma, as North Carolina's Marcia Roth observes: "Local workers do only as much outreach as they can handle. If you already have a large waiting list, you may be rather reluctant to go out and 'beat the bushes' for new women.". . .

While Medicaid reform would greatly improve the accessibility of prenatal care for poor women, it doesn't address the larger question of the uninsured. In 1985, 17 percent (9.5 million) of all women of childbearing age lacked insurance, according to the Alan Guttmacher Institute. Three-quarters of these were either women who worked or were dependent on working spouses, but did not have the benefits of employer-provided insurance. These women, who usually pay thousands of dollars in taxes to the federal government each year, often forgo prenatal care and deliver their babies in hospital emergency rooms, then default on their bills. Uninsured women are even more likely than the poor dependent on Medicaid to receive inadequate prenatal care.

Restructuring Health Insurance

The long-term solution to this problem is a fundamental restructuring of health insurance, making it more affordable to those just above the poverty line, and providing tax credits both for insurance premiums and for out-of-pocket health care expenses. Unfortunately, most of the debate about uninsured pregnant women has centered on the prospect of adding them to the Medicaid rolls, which merely introduces them to a quagmire of red tape and long lines without significantly improving the likelihood that they will obtain proper prenatal care.

While lack of insurance is a serious problem for hundreds of thousands of pregnant women each year, it need not be insurmountable. Mary's Center in Washington, D.C., is a case in point. The clinic, which treats mostly non-English-speaking immigrants (both legal and illegal), charges its patients on a sliding scale according to their incomes. The legally eligible can also apply Medicaid funds toward their bills.

The clinic also receives private foundation funding, and gets some help from the D.C. Health Service in the form of free vaccines and the part-time help of a pediatrician. Making extensive use of midwives (including a nun) and contracting with hospitals for delivery facilities, the center's expenses are low while its success rate is very high. Drawing on the Catholic Church, the public health system, private philanthropy, and fees from its patients, Mary's Center demonstrates that even illegal aliens, for whom lack of insurance may be the least of their problems, can get excellent prenatal care when local initiative overcomes institutional barriers.

"The promise of standard prenatal care as a dramatic cure for infant mortality was overrated."

Increasing the Availability of Prenatal Care Alone Cannot Improve Children's Health

Ann Hulbert

Ann Hulbert is a senior editor for *The New Republic*, a weekly magazine of political opinion. In the following viewpoint, Hulbert contends that more available prenatal care for poor women will not ease the problem of high infant mortality. Free prenatal care is already available, she maintains, but women do not take advantage of it. She argues that high infant mortality is caused by social problems such as drug use, teenage pregnancy, and inadequate education. Only when these problems are addressed, the author concludes, will the infant mortality rate decline.

As you read, consider the following questions:

1. Why does Hulbert believe America's infant mortality rate is so high?
2. What common characteristics are shared by women who bear low-birth-weight babies, according to the author?
3. Why does the author oppose imprisoning pregnant drug addicts?

Ann Hulbert, "Saving America's Babies," *The New Republic*, November 13, 1989. Reprinted by permission of *The New Republic*, © 1989, The New Republic Inc.

Marion Barry has called Washington's campaign against infant mortality "the most comprehensive anywhere in the country." The city has introduced free prenatal care and evening hours in public health clinics, a hotline, child care, appointments guaranteed within two weeks of a call. Yet in the first half of 1989 the infant mortality rate here, long among the highest in the country, approached Sri Lanka's. It surged from 23.2 in 1988 to 32.3—more than three times the national rate of ten. (That means ten babies out of 1,000 die before turning one.)

A New Approach

Dr. Reed Tuckson, the D.C. Public Health Commissioner, is frank about these results. Although visits to clinics rose by 22 percent in 1988, the crack epidemic, AIDS [Acquired Immune Deficiency Syndrome], and other problems among the poorest in the city have dwarfed the campaign's efforts. Keeping clinics open late in the worst neighborhoods has become increasingly dangerous; getting women to come to them has become more difficult. So the emphasis is on a newly aggressive approach, he said at a conference. It features the "MOM van, the Maternity Outreach Mobile," which collects women for prenatal appointments, drug treatment, and other help.

Until now a quiet problem, America's high infant mortality rate is suddenly front-page news. Across the country neonatal intensive care units report that their beds are crowded with tiny, unhealthy babies born to drug-abusing mothers. In an unhappy irony, these are precisely the kinds of stories that raise questions about the conventional medical solutions. Over the last half decade or so, children's advocates, health care experts, and politicians have been crusading for "access": to health insurance, to more and better prenatal care, to friendlier doctors and nurses in more convenient settings. The theory has been that as soon as barriers are lifted (one in four women of childbearing age isn't covered for maternity care), women will go to doctors earlier and more often and have healthier babies.

But this confidence in what might be called supply-side medical solutions has faltered lately. At last people are talking openly about the daunting social dimensions of the problem as well. America's infant mortality rate is as high as it is (it ranks 18th among developed countries) because the rates among the poor, especially blacks, are truly dismal. The black rate is 17.9, twice the white rate; in the poorest inner cities across the country, babies are dying almost as often as they do in Washington. As Tuckson said: "We are losing [the fight]. . .because [it]. . .is a fight against. . .a larger set of very complicated, very deeply rooted issues that are ingrained in the American experience; and, particularly. . .in the experience of people of color in this country."

179

Framing the issue this way is obviously unsettling. It raises doubt about the old faith in access. In the case of troubled women who need care most, Tuckson worried that even friendlier staffs in more convenient clinics would be left "twiddling [their] thumbs waiting. 'Hey, we are open. We have extended hours. Everything is here. Where is everybody?'" This new skepticism may sound like grounds for inaction, but is in fact an important step forward: an overoptimistic medical campaign is becoming a more sober social rescue effort. "Access" now includes MOM vans and other special efforts to seek out pregnant women. For those most likely to have low birthweight babies (under 5.5 pounds, 20 times more likely to die in their first year than bigger newborns), "prenatal care" now means drug treatment and other social support, not just regular obstetrical visits. It's good the campaign is coming out of the doctor's office, because the real crisis is elsewhere.

Joel Pett/*Lexington Herald-Leader.* Reprinted with permission.

Even before crack, the promise of standard prenatal care as a dramatic cure for infant mortality was overrated. Between the mid-1960s and early 1980s, the infant mortality rate dropped by half. But wider participation in prenatal care wasn't the cause of that success—even if it looked as though it was. The infant mortality rate was improving just when prenatal care was improving, thanks to an array of programs designed to help poor pregnant women, mothers, and children—Medicaid; the Title V Maternal and Child Health Block Grant; the Migrant and Rural Health Centers and Community Health Centers; and the Special Supplemental Food Program for Women, Infants, and Children (WIC). But a second look shows that the drop in infant mortality was *not* matched by a comparable decrease in the low birthweight rate, the goal of prenatal care. The impressive drop was due largely to better medical technology able to save smaller babies. As the technology reached limits, the infant mortality rate hit a plateau.

High-Risk Women

Ordinary, preventive obstetrical care alone—monitoring the progress of a pregnancy, and advising on nutrition, hygiene, and general health habits—can't solve the many problems that put the poorest women at risk of having low birthweight babies. In its report, the U.S. Public Health Service Expert Panel on the Content of Prenatal Care called for non-medical care for women at highest risk: they need additional help with "psychological or social problems." (At the same time, the old medical myopia was still in evidence in a sweeping new prescription—a "preconception visit" for all women, hardly useful for the riskiest group, whose pregnancies are rarely planned.)

Unfortunately, those in greatest need of extensive help are also the hardest to reach. The women most likely to bear low birthweight babies are disproportionately teenaged, poor, ill-educated, black, and unmarried (infant mortality correlates especially closely with illegitimacy)—and drug abusers. Pregnant women on drugs (most of whom use more than one, and drink alcohol too) are the most obvious case of elusive patients; some studies suggest that they account for a third of the pregnant women who get insufficient or no care. "A person who is addicted to drugs has another priority. The unborn child is not a priority," one social worker in D.C. explained to *The Washington Post.*

Teenagers and Infant Mortality

Teenagers, the other obvious focus of an aggressive campaign against infant mortality, often deny their pregnancies for months, have unhealthy eating and other habits, and are among the least conscientious patients. The less educated the mother, the less likely she is to think that prenatal care is important. In a survey of teenagers in Hartford, where prenatal care is free for residents, only a third saw doctors in their first trimester.

The question is no longer where to start in tackling infant mortality. The rallying cry has long been to expand insurance coverage, and now Congress has begun to respond, as have the states. Medicaid eligibility has been broadened over the past several years, an important step in dealing with the health care crisis in the United States (which, unlike most other developed countries, fails to provide universal coverage). Congress has separated Medicaid from AFDC [Aid to Families with Dependent Children] and required that states cover pregnant women and children up to 100 percent of the poverty line. It has also proposed other sensible reforms, such as simplifying the application process and instituting presumptive eligibility (which allows a pregnant woman to get care while her application is pending).

A Social Problem

Much of the decline in the infant mortality rate over the past fifteen years has been attributable to technology. But we are reaching the technological limitations of acute-care medicine for newborns.

From the social perspective, we must become aware of the relationship of drug use to infant mortality. In 1989, Dr. John Niles, the president-elect of the Medical Society of the District of Columbia, informed the Select Committee on Children, Youth, and Families that the infant mortality rate in D.C. had declined to 18 percent in 1983. But now the rate is nearly 30 percent. Dr. Niles blamed the increase solely on crack cocaine.

When examining the social variables which contribute to the infant mortality rate, we must also consider adolescent pregnancy and single parenthood. In many ways, infant mortality is as much a social problem as a medical one.

Thomas J. Bliley Jr., *The Heritage Lectures,* May 21, 1990.

But now it's clear that these changes by themselves aren't a cure-all, and the next steps are far less obvious. Further expansion (to cover the near poor, as Congress has suggested) won't do much for the poorest women with the riskiest pregnancies. Most of them are already eligible for Medicaid, and for the other maternal and child health programs in place since the 1960s. What's needed is some way to connect available programs with the women who need them most, and the trouble is that, as Ian Hill of the National Governors' Association observed, "Medicaid is not a service delivery program; it is a financing program." It is better to have Medicaid than not, but the record for care isn't great. Only 40 percent of Medicaid women got early prenatal attention, according to one study, compared with 85 percent of women with private insurance.

Having money for care clearly doesn't translate directly into getting care. The Alan Guttmacher Institute, which produced the most frequently cited report on financing maternity care in the United States, is about to issue a report on the availability of services across the country, and the findings are going to be discouraging. Thanks to soaring malpractice insurance rates and fewer obstetricians willing to take Medicaid patients (roughly four in ten won't), the pool of doctors has shrunk. And drug treatment programs have been a rarity all along.

Raise Medicaid Payments

One popular answer to the doctor shortage is to raise Medicaid payments to doctors. Unfortunately, that isn't likely to do much for the poorest women, at least in the inner cities. Most office-based doctors there already take Medicaid patients (often too many of them), and higher fees alone probably aren't enough to induce more private doctors to relocate in the ghettos. In any case, it's not clear that more private offices are what's needed. In those inner-city neighborhoods, and in rural areas, most women rely on community clinics, and such non-mainstream care makes sense. For 20 years the Community and Migrant Health Centers and other programs and clinics run by the state-administered Maternal and Child Health program have been trying to offer not merely medical attention but precisely the kind of nutritional, social, and psychological help that standard care doesn't aim to provide. . . .

Money doesn't automatically guarantee greater effectiveness. WIC, which has strong bipartisan support in Congress, was boosted $118 million to $2.13 billion. But in New York, where WIC was suddenly flush in 1986 (thanks to cost containment), the program has had trouble drawing more women and children to use that money; WIC reaches only about 40 percent of those eligible there. "We work hard to put them on the program," according to a WIC administrator in D.C., another city where the nutritional services are reaching fewer who need them, "but many women are not picking up their checks."

The Community and Migrant Health Centers have faced similar difficulties. Inadequate facilities are often the problem, especially in rural areas. But the issue sometimes isn't simply one of availability, as the Community Service Society suggested in a survey of 12 health center districts in New York with the worst birth statistics. "The reasons for the underutilization of prenatal care are not immediately evident," the report admitted, "since prenatal care is available in a variety of public and private health facilities in or close to most low-income districts in the city." A recent $20 million federal grant, part of an "infant mortality reduction initiative," has allowed the Community and Migrant Health Centers to emphasize more intensive "case management" to get women into care early and keep them. . . .

This marks a radical step beyond the old expectation that the

183

women most in need will simply come if the services are there. Inevitably, a paternalistic intrusiveness is an inherent part of the more comprehensive programs, which aim in effect to play the role of an ideal father of a woman's baby, or of a full and healthy family: to be a provider of all kinds of practical help, and a source of the "watchful concern/protection" that the Expert Panel on Prenatal Care defines as the heart of prenatal care. This paternalism may seem old-fashioned, but especially when it comes to teenagers and drug abusers, it isn't misplaced. Assertive guidance shouldn't be hard to justify for women so ill-equipped to protect their babies.

Emphasizing Individual Responsibility

Too often, however, it is. In its handbook on home visiting, the National Commission to Prevent Infant Mortality is lightly mocking about the style of home care in the 19th century, when "a healthy dose of moral counsel was given along with tangible relief such as food and clothing." But as Reed Tuckson emphasized, there has to be a moral goal. "Nothing we do in this room will work," he told the gathering of experts, "unless we get people to believe and understand their own individual responsibility.". . .

The Alan Guttmacher Institute closed its 1987 report, "Blessed Events and the Bottom Line: Financing Maternity Care in the United States," with an indignant call to action that sounds sadly irrelevant to the problem at hand: "Certainly, it is unconscionable that we as a society appear to care so little for the next generation that we cause couples to hesitate about having a baby for fear they can't afford proper medical care, and place obstacles in the way of pregnant women who seek and need such care." The real infant mortality problem lies elsewhere. We do want teenagers and women on drugs to hesitate about having a baby. And helping those who end up pregnant have healthier babies is more than a matter of removing obstacles. It takes stamina. "We'll bird-dog them daily if we have to," said an administrator at Constant Care, a community health center in the heart of Baltimore, whose patients get a hounding phone call if they break two appointments. The staff know who they're dealing with. "These women need nurture. We need to keep up our surveillance."

"Punishing [pregnant] women. . .for possession of cocaine and other illegal drugs might send a message that the state is firm in its resolve to prosecute those who break the law."

Imprisoning Pregnant Addicts Can Improve Children's Health

Suzanne Fields

The incidence of drug addiction among pregnant women is increasing dramatically, Suzanne Fields states in the following viewpoint. Fields maintains that, because education and social programs have done nothing to reduce drug use by pregnant women, such addicts should be imprisoned. While this may not be the best way to help addicts, she believes it may be the only way for society to protect unborn children from their mothers' addiction. The author is a nationally syndicated columnist for *The Washington Times* newspaper.

As you read, consider the following questions:

1. What comparison does Fields make between pregnant addicts and drunken drivers?
2. Why does the author think drug-education programs are not effective in reaching cocaine users?
3. What does Fields believe is the reason for the increase in laws punishing parents?

Suzanne Fields, "When Cocaine Babies Die," *The Washington Times*, June 1, 1989. Reprinted with permission.

185

Bianca, 2 days old, died of cocaine addiction. The oxygen she breathed couldn't reach her tiny brain.

A prosecuting attorney charged her mother with involuntary manslaughter for using cocaine while pregnant, but the grand jury in Rockford, Ill., refused to indict her. She could have gone to prison for five years.

The grand jury's refusal was hailed by women's rights groups, who said the charge was a breach of women's rights and that punishment would frighten women from seeking drug treatment or prenatal care.

They're probably right that the threat of punishment would frighten addicts, but it's difficult to see how such punishment would breach women's rights any more than punishing a male drunk driver for killing a pedestrian would breach the rights of men. . . .

Addicts Are Not Victims

No one—surely not many, anyway—wants the state policing pregnant women.

But neither is it helpful to define a cocaine mother as a "victim" herself, which is what her lawyer calls her.

"This is a general repudiation of the prosecution for trying to criminalize a pregnant woman who was herself a victim and who had already lost her child," Harvey Grossman, legal director of the ACLU [American Civil Liberties Union] in Chicago, representing the baby's mother, told *The New York Times*.

Bianca's short life is a tragedy, and like any tragedy, raises legitimate questions. Where does a mother's responsibility to her child begin? And where does it end?

If a woman knows that a certain substance will probably result in her baby's death, is she not responsible for the consequences? If her child lives, is she not responsible for caring for that child? If she doesn't care for the child, can she be charged with neglect, if not abuse?

What's shocking and frustrating, even to those who fear the establishment of what one woman calls a "prenatal police force," is the soaring number of women who have abandoned their responsibility to themselves and their children during their pregnancies, and afterward.

How did this happen?

Babies at Risk

Crack, a cheap form of cocaine, is, unlike heroin, popular with women. Use of this drug puts a generation of babies at risk. A study of 1,226 pregnant women in Boston's inner city found that one in five had used cocaine. In New York City between 1986 and 1988, the number of babies born with drugs in their system almost quadrupled, from 1,325 to 5,088.

Nor is this a big-city phenomenon. In little Bianca's hometown of Rockford, population 150,000, mothers of 27 infants took cocaine while pregnant. In Seaford, Del., population 5,500, crack has cut into the domestic tranquility of everyday life as drug-related murders and robberies increase along with the numbers of cocaine babies.

Education is hailed as the answer to the problem of addiction, but how do you educate women who are already self-destructive? With all the publicity attending the crack epidemic, it's difficult to believe that many of the cocaine babies were born to women who were unaware of the dangers to themselves and their offspring. They didn't care.

A Good Deterrence

Prenatal drug use, as distinguished from drug use by non-pregnant individuals, causes harm to the actor, harm to society, and harm to a fetus. The advantage to explicitly criminalizing prenatal drug use over and above illegal drug use in general is that this type of drug use is detectable by urinalysis testing on the newborn. The state can test the newborn but not the mother nor any other non-pregnant individual.

In this particular case, probable detection will be a good deterrence. Deterrence will be a weighty factor for pregnant women. They will know that they stand a greater chance of detection than the non-pregnant drug user. This risk alone will curb recreational users. In addition, ones who continue to use *will* be detected and *will be treated*. Most importantly, because of the pregnant woman's unique situation, *her* conduct causes suffering to all of us. Certainly, it is in the interest of society to criminalize this conduct, thereby discouraging prenatal drug abuse and encouraging maternal/fetal health and family order.

Kathryn Schierl, *The John Marshall Law Review*, Spring 1990.

"Caring enough" is not subject to legalisms affecting pregnancy. Somehow women who choose cocaine or crack as their destructive mechanism of choice don't care about anything but cocaine or crack. Punishing women like Bianca's mother for possession of cocaine and other illegal drugs might send a message that the state is firm in its resolve to prosecute those who break the law.

Responsibility as a legal term for parents has an ambiguous contemporary history. In Wisconsin, parents are held financially responsible for the babies of their unmarried teenage children.

In California, a mother was charged under a new law with "failing to exercise reasonable care, supervision, protection and control" of her child. Her son, 17, was a member of a gang and a suspect in a gang rape of a 12-year-old. The mother was said to have encouraged and supported other activities of the gang, including graffiti painting and the "celebration" of guns.

Frustration with Decadence

Such laws grow out of frustration with decadence and street crime that harm others, a stiffening of society's will to preserve itself. Can the law reinforce the notion that parents are responsible for the behavior of children for whom they are responsible for giving life?

Maybe, maybe not. Given the miserable givens, what else is there?

"There is a real danger that, faced with the possibility of incarceration, many pregnant women will not come in for prenatal care."

Imprisoning Pregnant Addicts Cannot Improve Children's Health

Douglas J. Besharov

Douglas J. Besharov, the first director of the National Center on Child Abuse, is a resident scholar at the American Enterprise Institute, a conservative think tank in Washington, D.C. In the following viewpoint, Besharov maintains that many American children are sick, abused, and neglected because of increased drug use by their parents. Imprisoning addicts will be ineffective, he believes, for it will only prevent addicts from seeking treatment and prenatal care. Besharov argues that the only way to protect children is to remove them from their drug-addicted parents.

As you read, consider the following questions:

1. Why does Besharov believe that providing free prenatal care to addicted mothers would not necessarily help their offspring?
2. How will increased drug education help the children of drug addicts, in the author's opinion?
3. How should the powers of hospitals be increased, according to Besharov?

Douglas J. Besharov, "Cracked-Up Kids—Right from the Start," *The Washington Post National Weekly Edition*, September 11-17, 1989.

In Washington, [D.C.] Greater Southeast Community Hospital released a 7-week-old baby to her homeless, drug-addicted mother even though the child was at severe risk of pulmonary arrest. The hospital's explanation: "Because [the mother] demanded that the baby be released."

The hospital provided the mother with an apnea monitor to warn her if the baby stopped breathing while asleep, and trained her in CPR [cardiopulmonary resuscitation]. But on the very first night, the mother went out drinking and left the child at a friend's house—without the monitor. Within seven hours, the baby was dead. Like Dooney Waters, the 6-year-old living in his mother's drug den, this child was all but abandoned by the authorities. . . .

Drugs and Child Abuse

Older children are often battered by their crack-crazed parents. In one highly publicized case, a 5-year-old girl was found dead in her parents' apartment with a broken neck, broken arm, large circular welts on her buttocks, and cuts and bruises on her mouth. Her 9-year-old brother was found the next day huddled in a closet. Both his legs were fractured. He had eight other broken bones, and bruises covered his body. Less dramatic but still hideous cases are far from uncommon.

Cases like these lead to proposals to expand treatment services for crack-addicted mothers. But at least for now, such services would probably make little difference. Crack addicts typically show little or no interest in prenatal care and are unlikely to seek it until very late in their pregnancy, if ever. Often they present themselves at the hospital only in time to give birth. Some new mothers abandon their sick babies in the hospital—not returning, even if the infant dies, to help bury it.

In fact, according to Dr. Elizabeth Brown of Boston City Hospital, "It is not extraordinary for a woman, bored and uncomfortable, to take crack purposely to induce labor."

Similarly, an expansion of drug-treatment services for women is long overdue but unlikely to produce quick or substantial results. Years of effort have yielded no widely applicable therapeutic program for treating heroin addicts. "Crack is new enough that no one has yet figured out an effective treatment," says Peter Reuter, a Rand Corp. specialist on drugs.

The other popularly debated alternative—"getting tough" with crack mothers—is equally unpromising. True, in the past few months there have been a number of criminal prosecutions of mothers: In Illinois, a jury refused to convict a mother whose daughter died of fetal exposure to cocaine. In Florida, a mother was convicted of delivering cocaine to her baby through the umbilical cord. In addition, some have suggested that pregnant drug addicts be placed in custody to make sure that they stop using drugs. District of Columbia judge Peter Wolf, for example, ordered a pregnant woman to remain in jail until she delivered her baby after she tested positive for cocaine use while awaiting trial on theft charges.

Treatment Needed, Not Prosecution

Policing pregnant women and jailing errant mothers will not solve the problem. Of course, the national crack epidemic is alarming and increasing drug use during pregnancy is one component for concern. Crack use during pregnancy threatens the health of the woman directly, threatens the course of the pregnancy and threatens the future of the child-to-be.

But these women need treatment, not prosecution, for their addiction. And yet, treatment is currently denied to most pregnant addicts. . . .

Most pregnant women, including addicted ones, want very much to do what's right for their future children. At a drug treatment program in New York City, 30 addicted women told me that they felt so guilty about using drugs while pregnant that they used more drugs to escape the feelings of self-loathing.

Pregnancy may indeed be a time when women can be motivated to get clean from drugs. But they need treatment, not punishment, in order to do so.

Wendy Chavkin, *The New York Times*, July 18, 1989.

But there are not enough prison cells for serious criminals, and what new ones are built will not go to drug mothers. Moreover, there is a real danger that, faced with the possibility of incarceration, many pregnant women will not come in for prenatal care. In any event, this approach provides no protection for the child once born, since its mother is only too likely to return to her addiction when released.

Stronger Anti-Drug Measures Needed

If neither punishment nor treatment for mothers is likely to improve things for the children of drug addicts, what can be done? One obvious step is for government and community leaders to expand their currently impoverished efforts to get out the message that drugs and parenthood do not mix. Hard as it may be to imagine, some young mothers do not believe that crack is bad for their babies. In this crisis, public-service ad campaigns such as "Beautiful Babies: Right From the Start," are no longer enough. The message needs to be blunt: "Using drugs while pregnant is wrong. It cripples and sometimes kills babies."

But sterner measures are also needed. To start with, hospitals should be given the legal power to care for drug babies until they are medically ready for discharge. About half the states have laws that allow hospitals to hold endangered children against parental wishes. These laws protect children when there is no time to apply for a court order or obtain police assistance. All states should have them. . . .

Public authorities must also face up to the fact that concern must not stop with a hospital discharge. The simple truth is that children should not be left with drug-addicted parents who cannot or will not care for them. Most children of addicts—even those living in dreadful conditions like Dooney's—are allowed by public authorities to remain at home where they suffer serious abuse and neglect. In 1987, of New York's child-abuse fatalities involving children previously known to the authorities, two-thirds were drug-related. . . .

We must face the implications of the mother's addiction—and our inability to break her habit. If parents cannot care for their children, the children should be removed from their care. This may require the overhaul of federal foster-care and adoption laws that have been wrongly interpreted to preclude early removal of these children. . . .

These are not total solutions—but they would do more to protect the children of addicts than wishful thinking about drug treatment or arguments about criminal prosecution. Each day that we fail to take decisive action means suffering, even death, for thousands of children.

*"[The] number of children with the AIDS virus
is. . .growing daily. "*

Devoting More Resources to Fighting AIDS Can Improve Children's Health

Alexandra Greeley

The AIDS epidemic is affecting more children every year,
Alexandra Greeley maintains in the following viewpoint. While
it is a common perception that only poor, inner-city children
contract AIDS, Greeley states that the disease is now spreading
to middle-class children in the suburbs. She contends that society must prepare to help care for the increased number of children with AIDS. Greeley is a free-lance health-care writer in
Reston, Virginia, and a contributor to *The World & I,* a monthly
magazine devoted to political, social, and cultural issues.

As you read, consider the following questions:

1. How do most children contract AIDS, according to the
   author?
2. Why does Greeley believe many middle-class Americans are
   not concerned about AIDS?
3. What does the author think society's response to AIDS
   victims will reveal about American civilization?

Alexandra Greeley, "Loving Kids with AIDS." This article appeared in the February 1988 issue and is reprinted with permission from *The World & I,* a publication of The Washington
Times Corporation, copyright © 1988.

AIDS. The disease inspires terror wherever it hits. Those infected with AIDS are often shunned because fear short-circuits logic and compassion. Yet sometimes the healthy react to a baby or child with AIDS more gently and lovingly. "Kids are kids," says Rev. Jerry Anderson, a minister with the Episcopal Caring Response to AIDS (ECRA) in Washington, D.C. "When dealing with kids, people don't get distracted by adult issues. Adults can be blamed, but with a child, there's no need to forgive or feel threatened. A child is a helpless victim," he says.

The public is confused about AIDS because information on it is often conflicting or fragmented. Doctors and health-care providers don't have all the answers either. Surgeon General C. Everett Koop sponsored a closed workshop on children with HIV [Human Immunodeficiency Virus] infection in the spring of 1987. He wanted health-care professionals to grasp the issues and make recommendations on how to deal with the pediatric AIDS crisis. At the time, Koop noted that most children with congenital AIDS became infected during an infected mother's pregnancy or at birth.

The Number of Children Diagnosed

The September 1987 figures from the Centers for Disease Control (CDC) show that a cumulative total of more than 575 children in the United States under the age of thirteen have been diagnosed with AIDS, most from black and Hispanic inner-city communities. About two-thirds have died.

The 575 figure represents only the children in the final stage of the disease, not those that test HIV positive or show symptoms of AIDS-Related Complex (ARC). "We don't have data on everyone with the virus," explains Dr. Martha Rogers of the CDC, although CDC guidelines are being expanded to cover all children.

Most experts believe that the more accurate number of children with the AIDS virus is closer to 2,000 and growing daily. According to the workshop report, there may be as many as 20,000 children with full-blown AIDS by 1991.

One of the confounding factors is that without routine screening of mothers and newborns and a good test for determining the presence of the virus, doctors cannot identify infants who are actually infected with the AIDS virus. Various studies of infected mothers have shown that though infants test positive for the antibody, they may not be infected with the virus. This is because the babies acquire the mothers' antibodies through what is known as passive transfer.

While adults rarely develop AIDS in less than two years after exposure to the virus, children often get the disease in the first year. Often the infected children come to light "by serendipity," says one Washington, D.C., AIDS expert. There is usually some symptom such as swollen lymph nodes or recurrent infections—earaches, diarrhea, respiratory problems—that lasts longer and is more severe than in normal children. Sometimes AIDS-infected children get meningitis or infections of the bloodstream. Often they require hospitalization. The central nervous system may be affected—often children with AIDS stop achieving developmental milestones, and sometimes they backslide. If they could walk and talk, they might lose those abilities. AIDS does not waste away a child's body as it does an adult's; instead, the child never gains any weight.

A Strategy Is Needed

When one thinks about acquired immunodeficiency syndrome (AIDS), a child usually does not come to mind. In part, this reflects the sheer magnitude of the disease in adults compared with children. As of July 1989, only slightly more than 1600 cases of AIDS in children had been reported to the Centers for Disease Control, representing less than 2% of the total number of cases of AIDS reported. However, the magnitude of the problem in pediatrics is likely to change, and some authorities project that as many as 10,000 to 20,000 children with AIDS will be detected during the next several years. The medical system must develop a strategy for the care and treatment of this growing population of children.

Philip A. Pizzo, *Journal of the American Medical Association*, October 13, 1989.

In most children, the course of AIDS is swift. The children can become symptomatic within 2 months after birth, and 70 percent die within 2 years.

AIDS is now moving out into the suburbs, notes Patricia Sealing, director of child health analysis for the National Association of Children's Hospitals and Related Institutions. The number of cases "is slowly moving toward the middle of the country," she says. "The association is surveying hospitals to get a fix on the magnitude of the problem, and also to try to assess the degree of underreporting. Many areas are now trying to develop respite and foster care programs so infected children are not just left in hospitals by sick mothers or families who cannot cope with any additional burdens."

Dorothy Ward Wimmer, an immunology clinical specialist at Children's Hospital, in Washington, D.C., notes that when she lectures to yuppie audiences about AIDS, they point to the fact that 80 percent of pediatric AIDS cases are black. "They figure that 'it can't happen to me, so why worry,' " says Wimmer.

Middle-class families fear the disease, yet they feel AIDS is not their problem. But they are wrong, says Chaplain Carol Bames-berger, founder of Interfaith AIDS in Dover, New Jersey—a community-based group that provides compassionate AIDS services. "White women have no fear yet, but that's a false sense of security." In 1987 in her middle-class community, only 20 people had AIDS. In 1988 over 90 cases were reported. It's an escalating phenomenon. . . .

The Impending Crisis

Dr. Jack Hutchings, associate director of the Department of Maternal and Child Health in Washington, D.C., and director of the spring 1987 AIDS workshop, says that local health departments should draw up policies following the surgeon general's guidelines. Welfare departments need to gear up for the impending crisis so they can give immediate authorization for money and family help. Community leaders and social workers should know how to minister to AIDS families.

Private individuals can help to care for children with AIDS through volunteer jobs. Bamesberger explains that people can become effective volunteers by educating themselves about AIDS and how it is transmitted. "After all," she says, "small kids are not into intravenous drugs and sex.". . .

Dr. Reed Tuckson, the health commissioner of Washington, D.C., thinks the way AIDS victims are treated may ultimately "characterize the quality of our civilization and provide a yardstick for evaluating the morality, ethics, and compassion of a society. It will be important to see if we can find enough persons with sensitivity, compassion, and decency to become foster parents or caretakers for these needy children."

VIEWPOINT

"*Illegitimacy is a direct hazard to the well-being of the young. . . .*"

Reducing Illegitimate Births Can Improve Children's Health

Nicholas Eberstadt

America's illegitimate births are to blame for its high infant mortality, Nicholas Eberstadt contends in the following viewpoint. Eberstadt asserts that it is not the poverty level of parents that determines a child's health, but rather their marital status. He maintains that social and health-care programs must be accompanied by increased moral behavior to decrease infant mortality. Eberstadt is a visiting fellow at the Harvard Center for Population Studies in Cambridge, Massachusetts, and a visiting scholar at the American Enterprise Institute, a conservative think tank in Washington, D.C.

As you read, consider the following questions:

1. Why does Eberstadt believe the poverty rate is an unreliable indicator of the health of America's children?
2. In what way does the author think illegitimacy and welfare are connected?
3. How have some social programs encouraged illegitimacy, in Eberstadt's opinion?

Nicholas Eberstadt, "Is Illegitimacy a Public-Health Hazard?" *National Review*, December 30, 1988, © 1988 by National Review, Inc., 150 E. 35th St., New York, NY 10016. Reprinted with permission.

In recent years, the well-being of America's children has become a topic of intense public discussion. Many authoritative commentators have concluded that childhood has become a time of significant, and increasing, risk in America. Considerable evidence, in fact, has been adduced to make the case that the material condition of America's children has seriously worsened over the past decade and a half.

The outlines of the problem, as typically presented, are by now familiar. By the reckoning of the U.S. Census Bureau, real per-capita income in the United States rose by more than 25 per cent between 1973 and 1986; yet over those same years the poverty rate for Americans under 18 years of age increased by nearly two-fifths: from just over 14 per cent to almost 20 per cent. While America had four million fewer children in 1986 than in 1973, almost three million more children were estimated to be living in poverty. Between 1973 and 1986, both the child-poverty rate and the absolute number of children in poverty rose in all the ethnic categories the Census Bureau delineated ("White," "Black," "Spanish origin"); relatively and absolutely, the greatest increase in measured poverty was among "White" children.

Placed in broader perspective, these figures and trends seem even more disheartening. Although the United States continues to enjoy virtually the highest per capita income in the world, a study published in *Science* magazine (and co-authored by the chief of the Census Bureau's Center for International Research) concludes that the rate of child poverty is higher in the United States than in Australia, Canada, Sweden, the United Kingdom, or West Germany—higher, indeed, than in any of the other industrialized countries for which calculations were presented. The assessment by Senator Daniel Patrick Moynihan, long one of America's foremost experts on social-welfare policy, is more distressing still. In the printed version of his 1985 Godkin lectures at Harvard, Moynihan writes: "It is fair to assume that the United States has become the first society in history in which a person is more likely to be poor if young rather than old."

The Deserving Poor

It is hardly surprising that these data and judgments should have attracted widespread attention and evoked deep concern. More interesting, perhaps, have been the particulars of the responses. For some, the issue of child welfare seems to have sounded reveille for a new era of social-policy initiatives. And indeed, it is in the circumstances of children that the strongest possible case for statist welfare policy is to be made. Innocent, vulnerable, imperiled through no fault or action of their own, children in distress might seem an almost crystalline representation of the idea of the "deserving poor"—those persons who can (and indeed should) be helped through public assistance without fear that they will succumb to the "moral hazards" that necessarily accompany such charity. . . .

CHARACTERISTICS OF FATHERS OF CHILDREN RECEIVING AFDC BENEFITS

Percentage of All AFDC Children

Year	Father Deceased	Father Incapacitated	Father Not Married to Mother
1937-38	48.4	22.8	2.8
1940-41	22.7	34.2	3.1
1948*	22.8	22.6	14.1
1961	6.9	21.4	18.2
1967	5.5	12.0	26.8
1975	3.7	7.7	31.0
1982	0.9	3.5	46.5
1986	1.9†	3.2†	48.9

*Data for 1948 refer to total AFDC families, not AFDC children.
†Either parent.

National Review, December 30, 1988.

The "poverty rate" is the statistic perhaps most commonly invoked in today's discussion about the condition of America's children. This is not the place for a detailed analysis of the technical and conceptual problems with that Census Bureau measure. Suffice it to say that the "poverty rate" is an ambiguous, and apparently increasingly unreliable, indicator of the actual well-being of American children. The poverty rate for children, for example, no longer tracks with the country's infant-mortality rate. Between 1973 and 1983, the incidence of child poverty in America is calculated to have risen by more than half. Over those same years, however, the infant-mortality rate fell by almost two-fifths. For "White," "Nonwhite," and "Black" children alike, the child-poverty rate and the infant-mortality rate moved in opposite directions over the course of the decade.

If the "poverty rate" is a poor predictor of the health of American infants over time, it seems not much better at indicating the survival chances of babies at any point in time. Data from the 1980 Census permit comparison of child-poverty rates for a variety of ethnic groups in America with the National Center for Health Statistics' breakdown on infant mortality. The result appears to be something less than strong correlation. For the group described as "Chinese," for example, child poverty was measured to be nearly a third higher than for the "White" group, yet its infant-mortality rate was less than half as high. Those classified as "Other Asian or Pacific Islanders" had a measured child-poverty rate about a fifth higher than the national average, yet their infant-mortality rate was almost 40 percent *lower* than that for the nation as a whole.

Differences in infant mortality among America's ethnic groups appear to be explained much more effectively by a different (though not entirely unrelated) factor: their illegitimacy ratios. There was a striking correspondence in 1980 between the proportion of births reported to unmarried mothers and babies' survival chances in the first year of life. "Chinese" babies may have been more likely than "White" babies to be born into families measured as poor, but they were far less likely to be born illegitimate.

Changes in American Childhood

The correlation between illegitimacy and infant mortality—arguably the most important indicator of the material well-being of the very young—should make us reflect upon some of the changes in the condition of childhood in America over the past generation.

Other things being equal, one would have expected the past generation to have witnessed a progressive improvement in the material circumstances of American children. Three factors would suggest such a judgment. First, the United States has enjoyed a substantial increase in both per capita income and disposable per capita income since 1960. Second, the decline in fertility over the past generation has meant that a smaller fraction of children are born to fathers fifty or older—ages at which a decline or even total interruption of earnings becomes more likely. Third, the general increase in the health of the American population has dramatically reduced the chances that one or both parents will die during their offspring's childhood. In 1986, the percentage of children under 18 whose fathers had died was less than half of what it had been in 1930; the risk of being a full orphan was less than a twentieth of what it had been 56 years earlier.

Improvements in survival chances for parents, however, have not translated into improved survival chances for traditional family units. In 1960, more than 90 percent of families with children were headed by a married couple; by 1986, that figure had dropped to 74 percent. Whereas the number of families in

200

America with one or more children under 18 increased by a quarter between 1960 and 1986, the number of female-headed families with one or more children under 18 tripled. In 1960, moreover, two-fifths of female heads of household with children were widows; by 1986, widows accounted for less than 7 per cent of such female heads of household. Divorcees, separated women, and unwed mothers accounted for the rest.

A Rapid Rise

The rise of illegitimacy has been particularly rapid. In 1986, the number of births identified as being to unmarried mothers was nearly four times greater than in 1960, even though half a million more babies were born in 1960 than in 1986. By 1986, more than 23 per cent of all American births were identified as illegitimate—nearly four and a half times the fraction in 1960. With the spread of illegitimacy, the nature of the phenomenon has also changed. Illegitimate children, for example, are no longer predominantly black. To be sure, the fraction of children born illegitimate is much higher among American blacks than among American whites. But the rise in the number of illegitimate births has been much faster for whites than for nonwhites since 1960. In 1981, for the first time on record, more illegitimate children were born to whites than to blacks. By 1983, whites accounted for an absolute majority of the illegitimate births in America.

Illegitimacy, moreover, is no longer primarily associated with teenaged mothers. As recently as 1973, more than half of the illegitimate children in America were born to teenagers; by 1986, the fraction had dropped to less than a third. In 1986, in fact, almost as many illegitimate children were born to women 25 or older as to girls 19 and under. Illegitimacy has been increasing most rapidly among women in their twenties and thirties— women too old for us to ascribe such behavior to mistakes of youth or inexperience.

The rise in illegitimate births over the past generation has broadly coincided with an increase in the incidence of "welfare" recipiency. By 1984, more than a sixth of America's families were receiving one or more means-tested government benefits. In 1986, about one American child in nine was a recipient of Aid to Families with Dependent Children (AFDC). The AFDC program has been transformed by the spread of illegitimacy among its ranks, and diverted far from its original purposes. In 1937 and 1938, shortly after the inception of the program, nearly half of the children on AFDC were paternal orphans; for nearly three-quarters of AFDC children, the father was either dead or incapacitated. By 1982, less than 5 per cent of all children on AFDC established their eligibility by such claims. By 1986, just under half of all AFDC children were identified as illegitimate (compare that fraction with the 3 per cent figure from the program's early years). In 1986, over 3.6 million illegitimate children were on AFDC; this would be more than three-fifths of all children living in households headed by a never-married mother. It seems fairly clear, then, that the AFDC program, as it currently operates, is to a great degree a vehicle for financing illegitimacy. One may debate causes and effects in this arrangement, and argue whether things would be worse for children if this program did not exist—but one cannot contest this fact.

Staggering Consequences

If increasing numbers of our children are born or raised outside of marriage. . .there will be staggering consequences for us all: greater poverty, more crime, a less educated workforce, mounting demands for government spending, higher taxes, worsening deficits and other crises we have only begun to anticipate.

Gary L. Bauer, *The Washington Post National Weekly Edition,* January 5, 1987.

If illegitimate children could expect to be as healthy as children born to married couples, the correspondence between public assistance and illegitimacy might be seen merely as a matter of financial or moral interest. But there is considerable reason to believe that illegitimate children *cannot* expect to be as healthy as children born into wedlock. In 1981, according to the National Center for Health Statistics, illegitimate black babies were more than 40 per cent more likely to have "low birth weight" (roughly, less than five and a half pounds) than legitimate black babies; for whites, the risk of low birth weight was more than 50 per cent higher for illegitimate babies than for legitimate ones. The difference is consequential. A major study of 1980 data by the Centers for Disease Control estimated that the infant-mortality rate for low-birth-weight babies was about twenty times higher than for children whose birth weight was five and a half pounds or more. Other figures from the National Center for Health Statistics reinforce the impression that illegitimacy is a risk to the health of infants.

For both black and white American babies, the risk of low birth weight is higher the later prenatal medical care begins. (Prenatal care itself does not wholly account for this difference; the decision to seek early prenatal care is indicative of other parental attitudes and actions.) Black babies who receive no prenatal care are two and a half times as likely to be born low-birth-weight as those whose prenatal care begins in the first or second month of pregnancy; for white babies, the risk increases by a factor of almost three. According to the latest data available (1985), unmarried black mothers were two and a half times as likely as married black mothers to go into delivery without any pre natal care; white babies were over five times as likely to have received no prenatal care if the mother was unmarried. . . .

Health may be the best synecdoche for overall social well-being; for children, low infant-mortality rates may be the best synecdoche for health. By that reckoning, if we are truly concerned with the well-being of our children, we can only view the continuing spread of illegitimacy with the deepest dismay.

Parental Responsibility

The data and computations given above cast a troubling light on the social programs that have been constructed to address the needs of the youngest and the most vulnerable among the deserving poor. On the one hand, it is apparent that social-welfare programs may provide children with food, medical services, and other benefits that they might not otherwise be able to obtain. On the other hand, it now seems to be the case that these same programs subsidize or finance practices on the part of parents that are distinctly perilous to children. (From this perspective, it is immaterial whether such social programs have themselves created pernicious behavior or merely accommodated it.) It is to be hoped that recognition of the connections between social-welfare programs, illegitimacy, and child health will lead to public policies that are more genuinely protective of the well-being of our children. One might also wish that, after a generation and more of trying to avoid the issue, the realization that illegitimacy is a direct hazard to the well-being of the young will help direct public discussion of the child-welfare problem back where it should have been all along: toward the attitudes, practices, and responsibilities of our nation's parents.

"A comprehensive child health policy, long overdue on a compassionate basis, is now—more than ever—in the self-interest of all of our people."

A National Child Health-Care Policy Can Improve Children's Health

Birt Harvey

America's health-care system for children is inconsistent and undependable, Birt Harvey argues in the following viewpoint. Because the quality of care and the availability of services varies from state to state, Harvey maintains, children receive inadequate care. He supports a plan in which all American children would have equal access to health care. Harvey is the president of the American Academy of Pediatrics and a senior fellow at the Institute for Health Policy Studies at the University of California in San Francisco.

As you read, consider the following questions:

1. What factors, in Harvey's opinion, determine which children receive health care?
2. Why does the author believe America's system of child health care is inefficient?
3. How would Harvey fund a national child health-care plan?

Birt Harvey, "Toward a National Child Health Policy," *Journal of the American Medical Association,* July 11, 1990, vol. 264, no. 2, pp. 252-253. Copyright © 1990 American Medical Association. Reprinted with permission.

A *3-year-old and a 5-year-old both have pneumonia. They live with their mother, who earns $5000 per year working part time.* In New Jersey, care for the 3-year-old is available through Medicaid. This is not true of the 5-year-old sibling.

An infant develops acute leukemia. His family has insufficient insurance or other financial sources to pay for his care. In Arkansas this child would receive care through Children's Special Care Services, the state's crippled children's program. In Colorado no state-supported medical care would be available.

Three 4-year-olds who live in equal economic circumstances have major organ failure: one kidney, one liver, and one heart. Anywhere in the United States, the child with kidney failure would receive care through Medicare. This is not true of the other two children.

The operating factors in these examples—how much money the parents earn, how old the child is, where the family lives, and which organ is failing—are examples of what determines which children in this country have access to health care and which children do not; many do not. In all of the developed countries of the world except for the United States and South Africa, such factors are irrelevant because all children have health insurance as part of a national child health policy.

Prevention

Is our system of preventing illness or injury among children more equitable than our system of financing therapy?

Children under 14 years of age who live in one state are twice as likely to die of injuries related to motor vehicles as children who live in another state. In Wyoming, the last state to mandate child restraints in cars, any child over 2 years of age could ride unrestrained until June 1989. In Tennessee, the first state to mandate child restraints, all children and adolescents must use them. Marked variation among state child-restraint laws is a continuing problem. With the exception of Canada and the United States, all developed countries that have any child-restraint laws have a national policy regarding them. . . .

Inequitable though it may be, is our system of administering child health care nonetheless efficient?

The federal government has over 35 health programs in 16 different agencies that serve children. Most of these programs are categorical, based on disease, age, family means, or geography. Some children in desperate need of health care fall into no covered category. Other children require services from multiple programs, complicating the burden of those who care for them, e.g., the abused child in foster care. Programs scattered through the Department of Health and Human Services include the Administration for Children, Youth, and Families; the Office of

205

Adolescent Pregnancy Program; the Office of Family Planning; the Office of Maternal and Child Health; the Early Periodic Screening, Diagnosis, and Treatment Program; the Adolescent and School Health Division; and the Birth Defects and Developmental Disabilities Division. In addition, the departments of Education, Agriculture, and Justice all have programs involving child health.

State organization tends to mirror federal organization: in one large state, 160 child health programs with 25 separate eligibility criteria are located in 37 units in 7 departments.

The Cost Factor

Is our child health system at least cost-effective? Consider the odds for cost-effectiveness in a system like this:

Even though every dollar spent on prenatal care saves $3.38 in newborn intensive care and even though insured women are three times as likely to receive appropriate, timely prenatal care, 14 million women of childbearing age have no maternity care coverage, and many others have only limited coverage.

Even though every dollar spent on measles, mumps, rubella immunization saves $13.40 and every dollar spent on pertussis immunization saves $11.10, both immunization rates are declining, primarily because government funding and insurance coverage have failed to keep up with increased vaccine prices.

A Glaring Irony

Our maternal and child health policy is plagued by a glaring irony: The United States has the most sophisticated medical care in the world, yet, of all the industrialized countries, we offer the most inequitable access to our services. Millions of pregnant women and children cannot take advantage of our highly advanced prenatal and pediatric care. These women must have access to information and services if we are to begin to eliminate the inexcusable scourge of infant mortality.

Bill Bradley, *Los Angeles Times,* June 21, 1989.

Even though children with insurance receive more care and have better health outcomes than do those without insurance, 12 to 14 million children under age 21 years are uninsured. Even the insured child is more likely to be covered for services better tailored to adult subscribers—hospitalization and surgery —than for services more appropriate for children: prevention and outpatient care. . . .

We have, then, an inequitable, inefficient, wasteful system of child health care. If a system is defined as a combination of parts forming a unitary whole, we may have no system at all, flawed or not. Surely, we have no national policy, no governing principle, plan, or course of action for assuring the health of our children.

The Right to a Nurturing Environment

The governing principle of a national child health policy should be that all children are entitled to grow and develop to their maximum potential in a safe, healthful, and nurturing environment.

An administrative structure organized to deal with children's health in an integrated, comprehensive manner at the federal level, with state and local counterparts, is needed to implement such a policy. Considerable effort and a willingness to surrender jurisdiction are required to bring programs currently in various federal departments into the Department of Health and Human Services under an Assistant Secretary for Child Health. Within the White House, which now has no designated office to address children's issues, an advocate for child health should be included in the Office of Domestic Affairs. In Congress, a single committee in each house might be given jurisdiction over child health and welfare issues, now divided among many committees, if only statesmanship could prevail over turf considerations. Parallel approaches reflecting federal structures could then be initiated at the state level.

Child health objectives should be organized into a comprehensive, measurable, integrated, and feasible set of goals within a national policy. Such goals could be evaluated and prioritized in an ongoing manner so that periodic revision of resource allocation could be guided by progress toward individual goals. A major goal would be financial access to care for all children, the cornerstone of a national child health policy. Incrementalism— gradual expansion of Medicaid eligibility and expansion of employer-mandated insurance—is not likely to solve our child health problems. Medicaid, as initially envisioned, was a bold attempt to gain access to health care for the poor, but limited benefits, state variability, low reimbursement rates, and inadequate systems for providing care indicate the need for a new approach. Because of high administrative costs and lack of cost control, small employers are resistant to coverage for both employees and their dependents.

Funding Health Plans

Consequently, the American Academy of Pediatrics has developed a plan to provide financial access to care for all children through age 21 years and for pregnant women. Mandated benefits would be provided either through employer-based insurance or through private insurance contracted for by states. State funding would come from three sources: continuation of currently budgeted state and federal Medicaid expenditures, insurance premiums, and—for those employers who choose not to cover pregnant women and children—an employer payroll tax. The plan includes methods to assure adequate provider reimbursement. . . .

States should contribute to the implementation of a national child health policy by addressing nonfinancial barriers to access, by serving as advocates for child health, by collecting data to determine progress toward objectives, and by assuring the quality of care.

The health of each child should be valued as if the future of this country depends on it, which it does. Our children will contribute to the national good by becoming healthy, self-supporting, productive adults; they will be needed to support, in an increasingly competitive world, the generations that precede and follow them. A comprehensive child health policy, long overdue on a compassionate basis, is now—more than ever—in the self-interest of all of our people.

Ranking Priorities in Children's Health Care

This activity will allow you to explore the priorities you think are important to improve the health of America's children. While your answers may differ from those of other readers, these disagreements mirror the reality of an important, complex issue such as children's health care.

Peoples' opinions about child health care may vary according to their relationship to children. For example, parents may have different priorities than the childless, and a parent with a child dying of AIDS may have different priorities than a government official who must allocate resources to millions of children in need of health care.

The authors in this chapter offer several suggestions on how to improve the health of America's children. Some people believe the nation's child health care system should be reformed to improve the overall health care of children. Others believe that resources should be targeted at those children who are the most seriously ill—those born with AIDS or those born drug-addicted, for example. Other possible priorities are listed below.

209

Part I

Working individually, rank the child health care concerns below. Decide what you believe to be the most important priorities for America's children and be ready to defend your answers. Use number 1 to designate the most important concern, number 2 for the second most important concern, and so on.

_____ providing free prenatal care to all women

_____ providing free eyeglasses for children who need them

_____ increasing the penalties for pregnant women who use drugs

_____ finding a cure for AIDS

_____ funding drug rehabilitation programs for pregnant women

_____ supplying all children with free toothbrushes

_____ providing free vaccinations to poor children

_____ creating a nationalized health care system for children

_____ educating teenagers about contraception

_____ teaching elementary children about proper hygiene

Part II

Step 1. After each student has completed his or her individual ranking, the class should break into groups of four to six students. Students should compare their rankings with others in the group, giving reasons for their choices. Then the group should make a new list that reflects the concerns of the entire group.

Step 2. In a discussion with the entire class, compare your answers. Then discuss the following questions:

1. Did your individual rankings change after comparing your answers with the answers of others in the group?
2. Why did your reasons differ from those of others in the group?
3. Consider and explain how your opinions might change if you were:
   a. a pregnant drug addict
   b. a father whose hemophiliac son has AIDS
   c. a government health official

Periodical Bibliography

The following articles have been selected to supplement the diverse views presented in this chapter.

George M. Anderson — "Dying Young: Infant Mortality in the United States," *America*, December 26, 1987.

Bryce J. Christensen — "Healthy Families in a Sick Society," *The Family in America*, July 1987. Available from The Rockford Institute, 934 N. Main St., Rockford, IL 61103-7061.

Geoffrey Cowley — "Does Doctor Know Best?" *Newsweek*, September 24, 1990.

Ann Marie Cunningham — "I Don't Want My Son to Be Forgotten," *Ladies' Home Journal*, August 1990.

Mark Curriden — "Holding Mom Accountable," *ABA Journal*, March 1990. Available from the American Bar Association, 750 N. Lake Shore Dr., Chicago, IL 60611.

Peter Dworkin — "The AIDS Threat to Teenagers," *U.S. News & World Report*, October 23, 1989.

Nicholas Eberstadt — "Out of Wedlock and into Danger," *The Human Life Review*, Winter 1990.

Good Housekeeping — "Good Housekeeping Child Care '90," special section, September 1990.

Barbara Kantrowitz — "A Vital Aid for Preemies," *Newsweek*, August 20, 1990.

David L. Kirp — "The Politics of Pediatric AIDS," *The Nation*, May 14, 1990.

McCall's — "A Parent's Guide to Children's Health," special section, November 1989.

Sonia L. Nazario — "High Infant Mortality Is a Persistent Blotch on Health Care in U.S.," *The Wall Street Journal*, October 19, 1990.

The Progressive — "Pregnancy Police," special section, December 1990.

Janny Scott — "Nightmare of Deadly Lullabies," *Los Angeles Times*, August 5, 1990.

Harvey C. Sigelbaum — "A Rational Approach to National Health," *USA Today*, March 1990.

Daniel Stern — "Diary of a Baby," *U.S. News & World Report*, August 20, 1990.

Dick Thompson — "Should Every Baby Be Saved?" *Time*, June 11, 1990.

Are Working Parents Harming America's Children?

Chapter Preface

The American family has changed dramatically since the 1970s. More families are headed by two working parents or by single working mothers, and more children attend day care while their parents work. As congresswoman Patricia Schroeder states, "Today's family faces increasing pressures in order to balance work and family responsibilities." With these pressures come concerns about how the changing family affects children.

Some experts argue that working parents are neglecting their children. They predict that these children will become troubled adults. "Children who go unheeded are children who are going to turn on the world that neglected them," states Harvard psychiatrist Robert Coles. Some contend that a return to the more traditional family is needed. "After witnessing two decades of unprecedented attacks upon the family, the citizens of our nation are slowly understanding that the stability and continuation of our free society depend upon intact families," writes Gary L. Bauer, undersecretary of education in the Reagan administration. Bauer and others maintain that children do not thrive in day care and in nontraditional households.

But not all Americans believe that the U.S. can—or should—return to the traditional family. After all, fewer than 10 percent of Americans live in a traditional, male-headed, one-career household. Many American parents have found that they need two incomes to make ends meet. "We can no longer afford to hold on to the antiquated notion—no matter how appealing—of two separate worlds. Work and family have become inextricably woven together," states Patricia Schroeder. In addition, some experts believe that both working and single mothers provide good role models for children and that children can benefit socially and academically from day care. For example, an extensive study by child development expert Alison Clarke-Stewart found day-care children significantly more intellectually advanced than children reared at home.

Recent changes have presented American families with new opportunities and new problems. The authors in the following chapter debate how these changes have affected children and what policies can best help today's families.

"There is no adequate substitute for the bonding and attachment that take place between a child and his mother."

The Rise of Women in the Work Force Has Harmed Children

Phyllis Schlafly

Phyllis Schlafly, an outspoken supporter of traditional family values, publishes *The Phyllis Schlafly Report,* a monthly newsletter of political and social opinion. In the following viewpoint, Schlafly argues that children are harmed when their mothers work full time. Children whose mothers work are less secure and more aggressive and withdrawn, Schlafly contends. She believes that Americans should support social and government policies that help women stay at home.

As you read, consider the following questions:

1. What does the author believe happens to a child whose mother is available, responsive, and helpful?
2. Why does Schlafly support "sequential careers"?
3. What four groups does the author believe comprise the day-care coalition?

Phyllis Schlafly, "A Child's Place Is in the Home," *The Phyllis Schlafly Report,* April 1989. Reprinted with permission.

More and more research is piling up to indicate that a young child's place is in the home and there is no adequate substitute for the bonding and attachment that take place between a child and his mother. A secure attachment in infancy provides the basis for self-reliance, self-regulation, and ultimately the capacity for independence combined with the ability to develop mature adult relationships.

"The primary goal of parenting should be to give a child a life-long sense of security—a secure base from which he can explore the world, and to which he can return, knowing he will be welcomed, nourished, comforted and reassured," according to child psychologist John Bowlby of London's Tavistock Clinic. Bowlby is one of many psychologists who emphasize the importance of what is called the "attachment theory." The child's ability to establish intimate emotional bonds throughout life, as well as his mental health and effective functioning, depends on the strength and quality of his attachment to his parents, particularly his physical and emotional contact with his mother.

Childhood Attachment

Research by Mary Ainsworth at the University of Virginia, Mary Main at the University of California, and Alan Sroufe at the University of Minnesota has consistently shown that the pattern of attachment developed in infancy and early childhood is profoundly influenced by the mother's ready availability, her sensitivity to her child's signals, and her responsiveness to his need for comfort and protection.

When a child is confident that his mother is available, responsive and helpful, he develops a pattern of secure attachment. Extensive research shows how patterns of attachment that have been developed by 12 months of age are not only highly indicative of how the child will act in nursery school, but how he will act as an adolescent, as a young adult, and as a parent.

While the scientific and medical evidence shows the importance of a mother's consistent and ready availability, it does not show the need of a perfect mother. Pediatrician and psychoanalyst Donald Winnicott, who was as influential in England as Dr. Benjamin Spock was in America, showed that the conditions for secure attachment are fulfilled with what he called "good-enough mothering" and "holding" the child.

Winnicott said that adequate "holding" of a baby is indispensable to emotional development and essential for developing the child's capacity for empathy. The child should experience his mother as a "good and happy" person, and should also know that his mother sees her infant as a "good and happy" person. Later, the child internalizes and draws on these images to comfort himself when the mother is not present. These same images are a reservoir from which the child can draw as he comforts others in his adult life.

Pennsylvania State University psychologist Jay Belsky (a former advocate of daycare) has concluded that recent research reveals that infant daycare is "a risk factor for the development of insecure infant-parent attachment, noncompliance and aggression." Fifty percent of the daycare children he studied developed insecure attachments to their mothers and a wide range of negative behaviors.

BY DUFFY FOR THE DES MOINES REGISTER

Reprinted with special permission of North America Syndicate, Inc.

Of course all children's behavior problems cannot be blamed on daycare. Belsky describes what he calls the "ecology" of daycare, by which he means the child's total environment including the mother's and father's emotional attitudes and skills, the family's socioeconomic circumstances, and the behavior of the mother upon reunion with the child.

Recent research by other scholars confirms that the greatest risks in non-maternal care come from the failure of mother-infant attachment which results from frequent and prolonged separations. Daycare infants are more likely to cry, more likely to be troublemakers, more likely to withdraw and be loners, more easily influenced by their peers, less cooperative with adults, and less likely to pursue tasks to completion. While it would be wrong to conclude that daycare harms all children, it clearly adds a significant level of extra distress and conflict to the all-important infant-mother-father relationship.

Mommy Tracks

An article in the *Harvard Business Review* of January-February 1989, written by a credentialed career woman, Felice Schwartz, argues that corporations should offer their management-level female executives a "Mommy track" instead of foolishly expecting them to perform like men with 100 percent commitment to their careers. This heretical proposal has upset the feminists like the little boy's assertion that the emperor has no clothes. Congresswoman Pat Schroeder denounced it as "tragic" and other feminist spokesmen are keeping their word processors hot by writing angry letters.

Ms. Schwartz comes from a feminist perspective. She admits that some women are "career primary" and says they should have every opportunity to rise to the top, in competition with men. But this decision, she points out, "requires that they remain single or at least childless or, if they do have children, that they be satisfied to have others raise them."

Ms. Schwartz argues that the majority of women are "career-and-family women" who could be induced to stay on the job if the company would offer part-time work, flexible hours, job-sharing, and a Mommy track with lower pay and reduced rates of advancement. She says that "most career-and-family women are entirely willing to make that trade-off." She says this would be smart business for corporations because it would enable them to keep talented mothers on the job and eventually realize their investment in them.

Sequential Careers

Meanwhile, the *American Medical News* published an article called "Medicine + Motherhood" featuring authentic accounts of women doctors who successfully and happily had "sequential careers." The article gave example after example of women who raised their children first and then went to medical school, or had their babies immediately after graduation or residency training, dropped out for 10 to 20 years, and then started a medical career.

No, they didn't earn as much money as some full-time career-primary doctors. But most sequential physicians earn more than $50,000 and some more than $70,000.

The article described the lifetime satisfaction enjoyed by these sequential women. They made comments such as, "I have had the best of both worlds of parenthood and a medical career. . . . The time I spent with my wonderful daughters is worth every minute of the 10-year delay. . . . I would advise my daughters to have children early and pursue a professional career later."

Now that even *The New York Times* and *The Washington Post* have conceded that we are in the "post-feminist" era, it's time to shed some of feminism's silliness and bias against motherhood and recognize that, despite all the media propaganda and peer pressure on young women to become career-primary just like men, that's not what the majority of women want, especially if they are past 30.

Whether women want to be career-primary and childless, or mothers and then career women sequentially, or part-time mother /part-time careerist, is a personal choice. It's a choice that should be allowed by our laws and business practices, not be restricted by laws that require a mindless gender-neutrality.

Unfortunately, the federal Pregnancy Discrimination Act of 1978, and the proposals for federally mandated parental leave and daycare for employed mothers, are incentives to push new mothers back into the workforce a few weeks after delivering a baby, where they rejoin the fast-track of competition against career-primary men and women. Mothers deserve other options, and a frank debate about the Mommy track could start making them available.

"There is no evidence to suggest that the dual-career lifestyle. . .is stressful for children. "

The Rise of Women in the Work Force Has Not Harmed Children

Cynthia Fuchs Epstein

Cynthia Fuchs Epstein, a professor of sociology at the Graduate Center of the City University of New York and a resident scholar at the Russell Sage Foundation, is the author of *Women in Law* and *Deceptive Distinctions: Sex, Gender and the Social Order*. In the following viewpoint, Epstein asserts that there is no evidence that children are harmed when their mothers work. She believes that mothers with careers are often more involved in their children's lives than are women who choose to remain at home.

As you read, consider the following questions:

1. What two assumptions does the author believe society makes about children and working parents?
2. What does Epstein cite as one result of the increase in divorce and remarriage?
3. In the author's opinion, how will women change their view of motherhood as they become more attached to the labor force?

Cynthia Fuchs Epstein, "Toward a Family Policy: Changes in Mothers' Lives," in *The Changing American Family and Public Policy,* Andrew J. Cherlin, ed., Washington, DC: The Urban Institute Press, 1988. Copyright © 1988 The Urban Institute. Reprinted with permission. All rights reserved.

[One] consequence of the movement of women into the labor force is the concern about the effects of maternal employment on children. Most studies of this issue, it should be noted, ignore the effect of paternal employment on children. This is not surprising because the assumptions are (1) that if women are not minding the home, no one is, and (2) that it does not matter whether fathers spend much or little time in the home as long as they are consistent breadwinners and have a regular attachment to the family. Whether these underlying assumptions are justified or not, a brief review of some studies indicates the inconsistency of findings and calls attention to the problems of viewing them without attention to context.

Research Theories

M. Woods states that full-time work by mothers is better for children than part-time work; Lois Hoffman claims the opposite; and, according to Mary Howell, there are "almost no constant differences" between children of employed and nonemployed mothers. Hoffman has noted that, as children develop through adolescence, positive outcomes accompany maternal employment. For example, girls are felt to develop a greater sense of independence, are less likely to accept traditional sex roles, are less fearful and more outgoing and ambitious, and have higher self-esteem.

Other findings do not indicate agreement on these points. Willem Van Vliet, for example, has found less traditional sex roles and attitudes among the daughters of employed mothers but also found them to be less independent and to have lower feelings of self-esteem and control. Hoffman raises the question of whether older children run more risk of delinquency if they are less supervised at home after school, but the evidence is scant. In contrast, Robert O. Hansson and colleagues note that although being home alone offers the child an opportunity for promiscuity and mischief, the experience of being home alone often leads the child to an increased sense of self-discipline and responsibility. D. Gold and D. Andres believe that employed mothers are less restrictive with their children and that children in these families often have more contact with their fathers (which they feel adds to the child's positive sense of nontraditional roles).

Effect on Achievement

Quite a bit has been written on the effect that maternal employment may have on a child's achievement. Until fairly recently, it was believed that a mother's employment had a small but consistently negative effect on the child's reading and mathematical achievement, and that this effect was cumulative and proportional to the mother's time spent working. However, Barbara Heyns and Sophia Catsambis argue that this research is based on faulty methodology, and they pose an alternative analysis of the data. They conclude:

> There do seem to be patterns of employment that are consistently related to children's achievement, irrespective of background factors. In particular, when other family characteristics are controlled, children whose mothers work briefly during only one period, or who decrease their commitment to work over time, are one to two percentage points behind children whose mothers never worked. For women who are eager to increase their hours or loath to leave the labor force, these results clearly suggest that their children will not be adversely affected. The cumulative negative effect of mother's employment hypothesized by Milne et al. seems to be a figment of a psychologist's nightmare.

William Michelson summarizes the literature on the effects of maternal employment in this way: "While there are many concerns and claims about how children may encounter negative outcomes as a consequence of maternal employment, the literature as a whole does not support these or very many of the hypothesized positive outcomes." As Denise Skinner put it:

> There is no evidence to suggest that the dual-career lifestyle, in and of itself, is stressful for children. What may be more significant for the children is the degree of stress experienced by the parents which may indirectly affect the children.

Few researchers interview children, and few data indicate the attitudes of children in different social contexts. For example, it is probable that children who expect their mothers to work do not regard their time away from the home as unusual, and therefore do not feel deprived. William J. Goode hypothesized that, as more mothers work, resistance of children will decrease. Of course, in the past as in the present, women in poor families worked and children (and other family members) did not regard it unusual or detrimental. It was seen, rather, as a normal contribution to the family.

Historical Patterns of Child Care

Although much of the discussion about women's employment today centers on the problems this creates for children, many other latent concerns have to do with women's growing independence and the disruption of the middle class life pattern that has set the norm for family life more generally. We might well ask to what extent our attitudes toward child care, and the consequences for children of mothers' employment, are class bound and time bound.

Through history many patterns of child care have reflected the living patterns of Americans. Children were certainly tended more by kin and other members of the community when small-town life was characteristic of the American way of life and in places where people were rooted in community and not affected by the mobility inflicted by expanding corporations that expected its managers to move. Models of child care tend to be predicated on the middle-class mobile families rather than working-class settled families whose preference is for work lodged in their communities. Of course, Americans, more than other people, have tended to be mobile, creating several different patterns of child care. For those who were rooted in community-based work, kin shared child care. For those who were mobile, child care became more focused on individual mothers. There are some notable exceptions to this. Among mobile black families, child care was often shared by grandparents and other family members who took in children whose parents needed to travel far from home to obtain employment.

Positive Differences

Mary Howell, a pediatrician and psychologist, has made a thorough study of the effects of mothers employed outside the home on older children. In a ten-year review of the literature, Dr. Howell concluded that when such factors as widowhood and poverty were eliminated, "the more closely children of working mothers are studied, the more they appear just like the children of mothers who are not employed." Actually the main differences between the two populations appear to be positive ones. Children with two employed parents are less likely than children who have only an employed father to make sex-stereotyped assumptions about appropriate male/female roles and are likely to be more independent.

Barbara J. Berg, *The Crisis of the Working Mother: Resolving the Conflict Between Family and Work*, 1986.

The social changes resulting from mother's employment are difficult to disentangle from other social changes, and few researchers attempt to do so. In the discussions on child care, few ask the question, What are the optimum social arrangements for child care? Not only have there been changes in the work force behavior of mothers, but also lower fertility has meant that children have fewer siblings. Many children also have fewer other relatives around, such as grandparents, uncles, aunts, and cousins. In addition, they also have fewer informal relationships with people such as shopkeepers, occasional home workers, farm workers, the policeman on the corner, the family doctor, and so on. Fewer diffuse ties probably make for more intense mother-child ties.

Yet nontraditional ties have increased as a result of divorce and remarriage. Many young people now acquire half sisters and half brothers, stepfathers and stepmothers, and even step-grandparents. Ironically, the increase in divorce has altered the roles of some grandparents in that they are reassuming the functional role that was more widespread a few generations ago. Furthermore, both mothers and children have acquired diffuse ties created by their involvement with formal organizations (such as with social workers). Thus, more non-kin people perform kin-like services. Many people object to certain of these ties without understanding their consequences. Certainly, the new diffuse relationships are considerably different from the ones of the past. New step-family ties are not institutionalized and there are no established norms regarding "proper" behavior in them. Some of the more formal ties are centered in bureaucratized settings without linkages into the community.

Another question has to do with the zero-sum perspective that assumes a mother's well-being is achieved at some cost to the child's well-being. Here, the common referent is to the mother's interest in and commitment to a demanding but satisfying job. Of course, there is a zero-sum dimension to the total number of hours in a day and a week, but mothers who can share child care with fathers, other relatives, friends, paid caretakers and teachers in school and after-school programs may even improve their children's well-being.

Are women who are interested in their careers less interested in their children than full-time mothers? There is no evidence to support this view. In fact, there is a great deal of anecdotal evidence that middle-class, career-oriented mothers are even more invested in the intellectual and psychic development of their children and pay more attention to their supervision (even if some of it is delegated). The mother need not be on board, so to speak, for the child to know she has arranged for music and sports lessons, for medical checkups and birthday parties. In fact, the same mothers who focus a great deal of attention on children are often placed in the double bind of being faulted for too much concern and too much input into their children's development. The no-win situation with regard to child care is not unlike what women face in the occupational world where they are "damned if they do and damned if they don't" commit themselves to work. . . .

Women's View of Motherhood

One could argue that as women become more attached to the labor force, given the inadequacy of child care provisions, they may become less interested in mothering and less resigned to its inevitability. It seems doubtful that many women will decide against motherhood altogether; instead, motherhood may assume a more measured place in women's lives, and most women will expect to combine motherhood and employment in their lives. They are less fearful of negative effects on children, a view supported by research that shows the consequences for children are not harmful. Mothering remains a powerful source of affirmation for women who have yet to assume the privileges and options of men in creating their future. It provides one domain in which a woman may exercise authority no matter what her class.

"The deepest truth about paid child-rearing is that it is rarely more than a weak stand-in for parental care."

Day Care Harms Children

Karl Zinsmeister

Karl Zinsmeister is an adjunct research associate at the American Enterprise Institute, a think tank in Washington, D.C. He lives at 430 South Geneva, Ithaca, NY 14850. In the following viewpoint, Zinsmeister contends that day care harms children. Children in day care are uncooperative, lack confidence, and do poorly in school, he believes. Zinsmeister maintains that nothing can replace the care and love of a parent.

As you read, consider the following questions:

1. What does the author believe parents are buying when they buy day care?
2. How do many infants interpret repeated daily separations from their mothers, according to Zinsmeister?
3. Why does the author believe a day-care worker cannot be relied upon to give a child everything he or she needs?

Karl Zinsmeister, "Are We Demanding More than Day Care Can Deliver?" *The Washington Post National Weekly Edition,* October 3-9, 1988. Reprinted with permission.

On the left and right alike, there is growing conviction that modern parents need more help from society in bringing up the next generation of Americans. Yet for all its new urgency, the national day-care debate often ignores a central question: What effect does it have on our children?

Research indicates that as much as half of one's adult character may be formed by the age of 4. How will increasing use of paid child care affect that development? A growing and worrisome body of evidence suggests that when infants and toddlers go into full-time day care, long-term emotional, intellectual and cultural damage can result.

A Profound Change

The mass surrender of child-rearing responsibilities to nonrelatives and state-regulated institutions marks a profound change in human history. It represents the final victory of the Industrial Revolution: the industrialization of the family. In essence, we are attempting to make child-rearing—the original social imperative—into a branch of the modern service economy. But when someone buys day care, they are buying much more than a service that permits them to work. They are buying an environment that determines much of what their children—what this society—will become.

As yet our experiment in proxy parenting on a mass scale is still very young; the first large cohorts of children growing up in day care are just now beginning to mature. So is the second generation of more sophisticated studies.

The definitive review of research conducted during the '70s, which pronounced day care to have a generally neutral effect on child development, was co-authored by child psychologist Jay Belsky. But in September 1986 he published an article expressing concern over a "slow, steady trickle" of accumulating negative evidence.

Weak Bonds

For one thing, a number of different investigators have found that when babies younger than a year old are placed in day care, many of them—perhaps as many as half—develop weak and insecure bonds with their parents, bonds that are thought to be crucial to healthy later development. Moreover, this effect is apparent in all social strata: in both poor and middle-class children, in good or bad programs and even among youngsters with extremely expensive at-home caretakers.

One study in Chicago examined 110 children of affluent, intact families. Half were cared for full-time by parents; half had stable, high-quality caretakers in their homes because both parents worked. The hired care began at eight months or earlier. The

substitute-care infants turned out to have significantly less secure relationships with their mothers, as measured by a standard scored psychological test. The researchers concluded that
many infants interpret repeated daily separations from their
working mothers as rejection, which they cope with by with-
drawing. Related studies elsewhere have found similar alien-
ation problems.

Reprinted by permission: Tribune Media Services.

Other follow-up studies of children as old as 10 have shown
that those with a record of early non-parental care tend to ex-
hibit more serious aggression, less cooperation, less patience,
more misbehavior and a pattern of social conflict or withdrawal.
A study of 5- to 8-year-olds who had spent part of their first
years at a highly regarded day-care center at the University of
North Carolina found them more likely to hit, push, kick,
threaten, swear and argue than children who were not in day
care or who started later. Research on middle-class third-graders
in the Dallas area found that children who had spent extensive
time in day care were more uncooperative, less popular and had
lower grades, poorer study skills and less self-esteem than their
counterparts who were cared for exclusively or predominantly
by a parent.

Of course, individual circumstances such as a child's temperament and family status can have a lot to do with how well he or she adapts to day care. The nature and quality of the program make a difference too; so does whether the care is full- or part-time. Age at enrollment also seems to be critical: What might be disorienting for a child under 3 can often be handled adequately by an older preschooler. In addition, large numbers of children apparently suffer no negative effects; and much remains that we don't know. But the findings already accumulated ought to give us pause in our uncritical plunge toward more child-raising by hire.

Moreover, one of the dark little secrets of day care—sure to come as a surprise to those listening only to activists and "children's defense" groups—is that even before the latest troubling evidence appeared, many leading child-development experts were expressing doubts.

Penelope Leach, the British psychologist and author of perhaps the most influential child-raising handbook in America at the moment, "Your Baby and Child," speaks out regularly against group care for the very young, insisting that babies need one-on-one tending.

Dr. Benjamin Spock has for years resisted infant day care. Despite a good deal of backtracking in successive editions of "Baby and Child Care" in response to criticism from feminists, he still states, "It is stressful to children to have to cope with groups, with strangers, with people outside the family. That has emotional effects, and, if the deprivation of security is at all marked, it will have intellectual effects, too." Until age 3, Spock now argues, a child at least needs individualized care from the same person.

Serious Reservations

Burton White, the former director of the Harvard Preschool Project and author of The First Three Years of Life says that "after more than 30 years of research on how children develop well, I would not think of putting an infant or toddler of my own into any substitute-care program on a full-time basis, especially a center-based program" during the first six months of a child's life. Moreover, he writes, "unless you have a very good reason, I urge you not to delegate the primary child-rearing task to anyone else during your child's first three years of life. . . . Babies form their first human attachment only once. Babies begin to learn language only once."

Selma Fraiberg, Lee Salk, Urie Bronfenbrenner and other authorities have also expressed serious reservations. The American Medical Association, the Centers for Disease Control and other groups have warned that day-care centers—where drooling, diapered, toy-sucking infants put their fingers in their mouths an average of once every three minutes—were becoming dangerous sources of infections. Many of the germs thus encountered would eventually have entered the child's system anyway at a later age. But given that a baby's immune system is not well developed until the third month, and not fully effective until about age two, early exposure can be risky. . . .

Uniting Families

Any pro-child day-care policy must seek to unite parents and children as much as possible in the early years. (It so happens that this is also what most parents want: Three out of four mothers with children under three still either do not work at all or work only part-time or seasonally.) Hired care must be viewed as a distinct second choice, not favored as it is under current policies.

Unbearable Stress

Over 37 years ago, a British psychiatrist explained to the World Health Organization that "What is believed to be essential for mental health is that the infant and young child should experience a warm, intimate, and continuous relationship with his mother in which both find satisfaction and enjoyment."

Enter daycare. Where children who are beautifully formed and physically healthy are all too often subjected to unbearable stresses, loneliness, and emotional trauma. Child development experts are becoming increasingly worried and vocal about the effects daycare may be having on a whole generation of American children. The revelation that serious disease epidemics are occurring in many daycare centers adds yet another frightening dimension to their concern.

David Kupelian, Mark Masters, and Gene Antonio, *New Dimensions*, November 1990.

Any sensible policy must acknowledge that much of the economic pressure parents feel today stems from changes in the tax burden on families. Middle-class families with children were largely exempt from taxation in the period following World War II.

If the current federal dependent exemption were adjusted to retain its 1948 value, each child would now bring his parents well over $6,000 in tax benefits. . . .

A pro-family day-care policy must avoid standardized models and attempt to increase parental choice in recognition of the wide range of family situations to be accommodated.

It must continue to work to improve the economic status of low-income and single parents, who have the fewest childbearing options. It must recognize that parents alone can judge what qualities they want in a care provider. The things really important to children—such as rapport, trustworthiness and love—are not amenable to state stipulation. Regulatory norms dictated in the name of "quality control" will simply reduce the range of services available (driving informal caregivers like neighbors out of business, for instance) and increase their price.

Parents using day care ought to be encouraged to shorten its duration as much as possible, by reducing work hours, using caretakers close to work or home or staggering work schedules. Employers ought to be encouraged to provide more part-time, flexible and sharable work. The many regulatory obstacles to home-based work ought to be removed.

A Weak Stand-in

The deepest truth about paid child-rearing is that it is rarely more than a weak stand-in for parental care. Someone is being asked to do for money what very few of us are able to do for any reason other than love. It will always be extremely difficult—no matter what laws or subsidies prevail—to find persons who feel such affinity for an unrelated child that they will repeatedly go out of their way to do the tiny, precious things that make children thrive rather than merely survive: giving a reason why rather than just saying no; rewarding a small triumph with a joyful expression; risking a tantrum to correct a small habit that could be overlooked but would be better resolved; showering unqualified devotion. A child and a parent are bound eternally, by blood and destiny. A day-care worker is doing a job. If he or she manages simply to be a kind friend, and reliable guardian, that is all anyone ought to expect. Giving the child the rest of what he so urgently needs—a self-image, a moral standard, life ambitions and a sense of permanent love—is too much to ask of anyone other than parents.

"Good day care. . .not only has no ill effects but can be beneficial. "

Day Care Does Not Harm Children

Tamar Lewin

Research shows that children are not harmed by day care and can benefit socially and intellectually from the interaction with other children, Tamar Lewin states in the following viewpoint. In her analysis of the national day-care chain Kinder-Care, Lewin maintains that children thrive from quality care, whether that care comes from parents or from day-care workers. She believes the standardized care provided by Kinder-Care and other day-care centers benefits both parents and children. Lewin is a national correspondent for *The New York Times.*

As you read, consider the following questions:

1. Why does the author believe many parents prefer day-care centers to family day care?
2. What do Kinder-Care teachers do to help parents maintain contact with their children, according to Lewin?
3. Why does the author think many child-care experts have rejected the findings of well-known child development expert Jay Belsky?

Tamar Lewin, "Small Tots, Big Biz," *The New York Times Magazine,* January 29, 1989.

In Maple Heights, Ohio, just off the highway that leads to downtown Cleveland, at the building with the big red bell tower in front, a steady stream of traffic comes through every weekday morning from 6:30 to 9. Mothers and fathers drive up, unbuckle the baby seats, lift their children out and take them inside to one or another of the long, open, bright rooms.

The infants go into Miss Diane's room, where each has a crib. The toddlers go to Miss Gloria, who helps them paste paper eyes, arms and legs onto a precut figure. The kindergarteners go to Miss Nancy, who exhorts them to "try really hard to stay on the dotted lines" when they trace shapes in their workbooks.

The names are different, but the scene is the same in Danbury, Conn., Jurupa, Calif., Watauga, Tex., Minnetonka, Minn., and more than 1,200 other locations around the nation where parents leave their children at the Kinder-Care Learning Centers.

A New American Scene

The trademark red bell towers, topped by bells that do not ring, are printed on the smocks every Kinder-Care teacher wears, on the company newsletter, and on the quarterly activity calendar that goes to 115,000 Kinder-Care parents. And they are fast becoming a familiar part of the American scene.

Since 1969, when the real-estate developer Perry Mendel opened his first day-care center in Montgomery, Ala., Kinder-Care has enrolled more than a million children—and in the process, heralded the birth of a burgeoning new for-profit child-care industry. With 17,000 employees in 40 states and Canada, Kinder-Care, the largest day-care chain in the nation, has become big business, with quarterly operating revenues of nearly $75 million, and net profits of $6.25 million.

But the growth of Kinder-Care is far more than a business story: it represents not only the rapid evolution of the nation's attitudes toward child care but the professionalization of parenting.

Until the 1980's, most mothers stayed home during their children's preschool years, and those who did work usually chose to have their children cared for in the home of a relative or neighbor.

"People didn't think they were using day care if they dropped their child off with the lady down the street," says Ellen Galinsky, project director of work and family studies at the Bank Street College of Education. "There was this idea that day care was only for poor single mothers who had to work and had no choice but to leave their child with strangers. It was tainted with a welfare mentality. In 1977, after I published a book on child care, I found that many people had the image of it almost as a kind of concentration camp for children, with little hands sticking out around wire fences. But now that most mothers are working, we call it child care, and it's become mainstream."

Although family day care—provided in the care-giver's home —is still the most commonly used form of child care, especially for infants and poor children, the Census Bureau's data, for 1984-85, show that the percentage of working mothers of children under 5 who chose formal day-care programs had doubled to 25 percent, from 13 percent in 1977. It also showed that working mothers who had completed college were twice as likely to use a formal day-care program as those who did not graduate from high school.

PATTERNS OF CHILDCARE FOR CHILDREN UNDER FIVE

▨ Mother Is Not Employed
▢ Care by Relatives
▨ Informal Care by Non-Relatives
▤ Group Day-Care Center

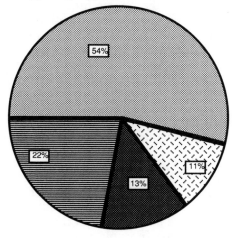

The Bureau of the Census, U.S. Department of Commerce, *Household Economic Studies,* May 1987.

"There has been a lot of research in recent years showing that children can benefit from early childhood education or enrichment programs," says Sheila Kamerman, a social-policy expert at the Columbia University School of Social Work. "So more and more middle-class parents now want to enroll their children in some kind of organized program when they get to be 2 or 3 years old."

Most of the parents who choose Kinder-Care say they have considered family day care, and rejected it, either on safety grounds, or because they like the idea of Kinder-Care's formal curriculum. "You look at the day-care homes, and there's only one lady with 10 or 15 kids, and you think she just can't have time for all of them," says Jackie McGough, whose 4-year-old daughter, April, is at Kinder-Care Learning Center No. 1, the original center in Montgomery. "Here, there are more grown-ups around, so it seems safer, and they teach them things and have a lot of toys and activities."

To many parents, Kinder-Care seems safer simply because it is so much better known than the mom-and-pop centers with which it competes. Even people without children have become familiar with Kinder-Care through a barrage of Drexel Burnham Lambert advertisements, touting how innovative financing can provide capital for a new industry.

For many people, the concept of a for-profit day-care chain— quickly nicknamed "Kentucky Fried Children"—was unsettling. But though a few experts still fear that for-profit child care may be marked more by concern for money than for children, most have come to agree that there is no inherent reason why a publicly traded corporation cannot care for children as well as, or better than, the lady next door or the local Y.M.C.A.

"There was a lot of uneasiness about us, just as there was a lot of uneasiness around the development of for-profit hospitals and nursing homes," says Ann Muscari, the vice president for corporate communications. "But the family just can't handle everything anymore, and it turns out that in child care or in nursing homes, for-profit service companies can sometimes maintain standards and quality controls that are hard for the voluntary sector to match."

Child-Oriented Environment

Kinder-Care's appeal stems partly from its child-oriented environment: the chairs, tables, sinks and toilets are kid-sized, the toys and equipment are abundant, and the attention to safety is meticulous, in everything from placing electric outlets four feet off the floor to the safety checklists that must be initialed each day by each center's safety coordinator and returned to headquarters. Accidents, such as a child falling off playground equipment, or a tooth knocked out, are written up in formal "incident reports." There's no guarantee that all of Kinder-Care's procedures are followed at every center, and state licensing authorities say that Kinder-Care has been cited for its share of safety violations.

Still, there is little that is slipshod or random about Kinder-Care—and little that is very homey either. The centers are relentlessly upbeat, with a full schedule of activities. Artwork and learning aids fill the walls, the doors and the ceilings. Even the rugs are less cozy than educational, with a bright mix of numbers and designs inspired by checkers, backgammon, Parcheesi and Chinese checkers.

Most Kinder-Care centers have a capacity of 100 to 150 children, and because of the open architecture the din can be overwhelming. Though the infants have a separate room, the rest of the children at most centers are in a large open space divided by cubbies. While the group at one end of the room is singing "Gotta Shake My Sillies Out," the group at the other end may be hearing the story of "Goldilocks and the Three Bears," while the group next to them is talking about the letter G—the sound of the week—and getting ready to glue gold glitter on large, pre-drawn G's.

Corporate Planning

Parent visits are always welcome. But the idea of parents setting policy or changing the program is alien to a corporation that develops its curriculum, safety guidelines, nutrition plans and even its pleas to raise money for the Muscular Dystrophy Association, Inc., at the large modern headquarters building in Montgomery, Ala.

Every month, the teachers receive a packet of curriculum materials from headquarters, suggesting activities for each age group. Some have been developed by Kinder-Care's own educational specialists and some are purchased from various educational publishing companies. On a day in November, Kinder-Care 4-year-olds across the nation were hearing "La Tortuga," a Spanish-English story about a turtle, finding the hidden turtles in the picture and following the fold-up pattern to make their own paper turtles. But, despite the standardized curriculum, the teachers' own enterprise determines many of the daily activities. Though they have to begin with the basic required curriculum, they can go further with it. Some children on this day might also be making Mexican hats, playing with maracas, or looking at real turtle shells.

"For teachers without much experience, the suggested activities can provide a lot of guidance," says Ms. Muscari. "But teachers with a lot of experience tend to use them mainly as a springboard for their own ideas. The only thing we care about, as a kind of truth in advertising, is that the things listed in the calendar for parents actually happen."

The day's activities for each age group are posted on a special parent board, explaining, for example, that the group did finger painting with chocolate pudding that day. For parents of babies in the infant rooms, the documentation is even more formalized. Every morning, they put stickers on a wall chart to show when they want their babies to have bottles, naps and play time. And every afternoon, they get a written report on exactly when their infant slept, ate or had a diaper change—and a note on the child's development.

At the Somerset, N.J., center, reports may be written in the voice of the child: "Mommy, I have been trying to say mommy but it did not come out yet but when it does, you will be the first to know," said one recent report.

"We have to put it in writing, because a lot of these babies are here for a long day, and the care-giver who was there at the end of the day might not be the same one who was working at the beginning of the day," explains Suzanne Kazi, a Kinder-Care district manager in New Jersey.

Kinder-Care works hard to help parents hold on to the feeling that they are the primary people in their babies' lives—a feeling that can be all too fragile when an infant has been in day care from the age of 6 weeks.

"I always tell the infant teachers, 'You think you saw the first step, but maybe the baby was just putting her foot out to keep from falling,'" says Dr. Laurene Smith, the vice president for educational research and development at Kinder-Care headquarters in Alabama. "You can tell the mother she seems so ready to walk, you bet she'll do it tonight. But don't take that first step away from mom. She needs it more than you do."

The Benefits of Day Care

Many experts believe day care at a young age can be beneficial. Amy Wilkins, a lobbyist with the Children's Defense Fund in Washington, can quote a number of authorities who claim that good day care is good for children and bad day care is bad for them.

Ms. Wilkins says studies show that children in day care learn cooperation skills better and sooner than children who are raised by their mothers. These same studies, Wilkins says, show that day-care kids are more advanced in their language skills. And particularly contrasted to smaller families with only one or two children, Wilkins says, day-care kids have a chance to interact with their peers at a younger age. So when they get to school, such necessities as sharing or making friends don't come as such a shock.

Bonnie Erbe, *The Christian Science Monitor*, September 11, 1989.

Because most American women, unlike their counterparts in many other industrialized nations, have no legal right to maternity leave, many women must be back at their jobs six weeks after giving birth, and most are back in the work force before their babies are a year old. The demand for infant care is growing rapidly.

At the Somerset, N.J., Kinder-Care, there are 150 children on the waiting list for the eight cribs in the infant room. "People are so worried about finding a place that we have someone on the waiting list who isn't even pregnant yet," says Tanjilla Ahmed, the director of the center.

Working Parents

Unlike preschools, Kinder-Care is specifically designed to meet the needs of working parents, with most centers open from 6:30 A.M. to 6:30 P.M. Most Kinder-Care children stay at their center for 10 to $11^1/_2$ hours a day. Hot meals, varying from cheese grits in the South to macaroni and cheese in the North, are served every day. School-age children attending Kinder-Care's Klubmates program are taken by a Kinder-Care van from the center to school in the morning and from school to the center in the afternoon.

The increasing number of women in the work force insures a continuing demand for services like Kinder-Care, but most working parents—and even the strongest Kinder-Care enthusiasts, like Ms. Kazi, the New Jersey district manager—still have ambivalence about the effect their working has on their children.

"I don't think there's a day that goes by when I drop my kids off that I don't wonder if I shouldn't be home with them," says Ms. Kazi, whose two children, Allison and Christopher, spend their days at the Somerset Kinder-Care. "We're the first generation where working moms are the norm, so I have nothing to tell me what that does to the kids. My sense is that Allison has much better verbal and social skills than kids who stay home all day, but that she also has more difficulty playing by herself. I've been thinking that it would be nice to provide some private space in the centers, so kids could have more of a chance to play by themselves."

Parents' mixed feelings about day care have been fueled by the much-publicized findings of Jay Belsky, a professor of human development at Pennsylvania State University. He found that infants under 1 year old who were in nonmaternal care for more than 20 hours a week were more likely to be insecurely attached to their mothers than others, and were more likely to become aggressive 5-year-olds. Most child-care experts, however, reject Professor Belsky's findings, because they say he did not differentiate between good and bad child care. Indeed, the consensus at recent conferences has been that good day care—that is, day care with adequate staffing by trained, responsive adults—not only has no ill effects but can be beneficial. . . .

Increasing Standardization

Professionalization—and standardization—is what Kinder-Care is all about, and what is happening to the child-care industry as a whole. With ever more women working, it is becoming harder all the time to make individualized, informal arrangements for child care. Increasingly, state regulatory bodies are expanding and upgrading their child-care licensing standards, and there is now serious talk about federal standards for child care.

For most American children, these are probably good developments, moves that will, within the next decade, establish minimum standards for care and eliminate some of the worst day-care facilities.

"Single-parent households often bestow. . .positive things on their children. "

Single-Parent Households Can Benefit Children

Sheila Weller

Children in single-parent households learn responsibility and independence, Sheila Weller states in the following viewpoint. Weller writes that children can thrive in single-parent homes, which can be more stable than homes in which the parents constantly argue. She believes that Americans should support government and social policies that help single parents. Weller is a contributor to *McCall's,* a monthly women's magazine.

As you read, consider the following questions:

1. According to the author, what percentage of American children will at one time reside in single-parent homes?
2. What does Weller cite as the benefits of living in a single-parent home?
3. Why does the author believe many Americans oppose policies that support single parents?

Sheila Weller, "One Woman's Family: The Plight of Single Mothers," *McCall's,* February 1989. Reprinted with permission.

Every weekday morning, just as the sun breaks through the skyscrapers of downtown Chicago, 31-year-old Barbara Martin finishes her ten-to-six shift as a cardiac nurse and drives to the suburban home she shares with her son, Jason, seven, and another divorced mother and child. There she softly rouses Jason from his sleep, gets him fed and dressed and walks him and the other child to the school bus stop while the other mother drives off, in the car she and Barbara share, to her job as an office manager.

Then Barbara goes home, where, in the luxury of silence, she straightens up the house, pops in a load of laundry, puts the sheets on the living room couch—which serves as her bed—and, if she can free her mind of what she calls "my worry of the day" ("What can I cut out of the budget for the next six weeks so I can give Jason a birthday party as nice as his schoolmates?" "Was the 'mild attention problem' his teacher mentioned last week because his dad promised to take him to a Bears game and didn't show up?"), she falls asleep.

When the alarm goes off at three, Barbara jumps up, throws on a sweat suit and goes to meet the school bus. Then she and Jason do food shopping and whatever other errands they can squeeze in. ("Jason could do the whole grocery list by himself—including comparison shopping," she says proudly. "This life of ours has made him very responsible.") After that, it's home for homework, dinner, one rationed hour of TV, bath.

Difficult Choices

As Barbara reads her son his bedtime story, she mentally reviews her situation, determined to somehow forge an opening between the rock and the hard place each choice comprises. "I'll be able to move us to our own apartment if I sign up for those extra shifts. Yet if I work extra shifts, who's going to be there for Jason? After-school day care—which, because he's still shaky after the divorce, I don't really want to stick him in, anyway—only goes until five. But even if Jason *did* adjust well to the day care, what would twelve hours of work twice a week do to *my* nerves? Anyway, if we stop living with roommates, I'll have to give up the high-paying night shift because I can't leave him all alone at night."

Barbara sighs and kisses her sleeping son's cheek. Then she makes his next day's lunch, showers, puts on a fresh uniform and, smiling to herself at something funny he said before he fell asleep, she leaves for work.

Not long ago we would read stories about single mothers like Barbara Martin and react in that awed, admiring—but slightly relieved—way we feel about people who are "different." Unfortunately, Barbara Martin isn't "different" anymore. In a statistical leap of 230 percent in 15 years, families led by single parents now make up more than one quarter of all U.S. families, and 60 percent of our country's children are likely to spend part of their childhood or adolescence in a family with just one parent (or, possibly, as in Barbara's son's case, in a makeshift family led by two single mothers). . . .

Satisfied Children

A national survey of 11-to-16-year-olds showed that despite the general discontents of that age, 76 percent of young teens in mother-only homes are "very satisfied" with their families. (Only 7 percent more teens in the usually three-times-richer mother/father families gave the same answer.)

"It's conflict between parents—not marital breakup—that hurts kids," says Martin Levin, Ph.D., professor of sociology at Emory University in Atlanta. "A happy single-parent home may be better for children than a quarrelsome dual-parent one."

Few Differences in Family Types

Single-mother families are as successful on a wide range of measures as two-parent families. On measures of emotional adjustment, IQ, scholastic achievement, and culturally accepted masculine behavior in boys, children fare equally well in both kinds of families. Except for the greater likelihood of poverty for children with single mothers, there are only two differences noted between the groups. One is that girls from single-mother households are more independent and more competent than girls from households with a father present. Second, some children from single-mother families show lower self-esteem, but researchers report that the cause is prejudiced social opinion, not family structure.

Research describes the single-mother family as warm and close, a way of relating created by consensual decision making and by the participation of all family members in tasks and rewards.

Thelma Jean Goodrich, Cheryl Rampage, and Barbara Ellman, *The Family Therapy Networker*, September/October 1989.

Neil Rosenblum, Ph.D., a clinical child psychologist who works with children and divorcing parents in the Pittsburgh area, agrees. "So many children, when asked if they're unhappy that their parents got a divorce, say, 'No! They don't fight anymore!' The kids finally get some peace. Along with that, they get something else—or, rather, their mother gets it and it rubs off on them—and that is *autonomy*. I have clients who say, 'Hey! My husband used to say, "You can't go out to that lecture—you have to stay home and make me supper."' Now she has a better sense of control."

Single-parent households often bestow two other positive things on their children. One is heightened responsibility. "My son and daughter know how to cook, to clean, to wash and iron clothes," says a divorced office supervisor in St. Louis. "They're always amazed, when they visit my sister and her husband's family, how much their cousins don't know how to do."

The other positive, which several of these women have alluded to, is the image of a strong, competent mom. Says Rosenblum: "When a mother says, 'It may not be easy at first but, darn it, we're gonna cut that grass ourselves and pay these bills ourselves!'—and the child sees, from an early age, that his mother *can* do many of the same things that are left to other kids' dads. . . well, it's good for everybody."

Some Risks

Still, being raised in a single-parent family does have its risks. Behavior problems are about 8 percent higher in such homes. And a study by researchers at the University of Illinois reveals that the more time boys spend in single-parent homes—especially if the father pays no child support and left the home early—the less schooling they are likely to complete. (Girls aren't affected because the value, to them, of having a working mother as a role model all but erases the negative effects of their father's absence.)

One San Francisco insurance company manager who raised her son alone from birth remembers a "well-meaning" psychologist saying to her, when her son was in preschool: "You know, your son is a very bright child, but he's not going to make it unless you get him a father within two years." That mother says, "I went home and cried for two hours! A father is not something you can buy at Woolworth's!" When that same son graduated with honors from high school "all of us parents cried," she says with a trace of a smile. "But *my* tears were wetter."

With her numbers so large now, the single mother is finally beginning to see a little more hope. . . . Congresswoman Marge Roukema (Republican of New Jersey)—who sponsored the landmark 1982-83 legislation under which support could be taken out of the salaries of the nonsupport-paying husbands—would like to see new, loophole-free measures extended beyond welfare mothers so that "women of all economic walks of life could get the support money that is legally and morally their right. But," she adds, "it will be a real uphill fight.". . .

Why is there so much resistance to these proposals? Pat Schroeder says: "I think we have several currents of thought running in our society that get in the way of our seeing the problem, and looking for the solution. One is the idea, 'You shouldn't have a family unless you can afford it' and by afford it, we mean that the woman should stay home. With *that* thinking, only a small percentage of our population could afford to have children at all! And, two, if a woman becomes a single parent, there's the thinking, 'Well, that's *her* problem. She didn't plan ahead.'

"We go out of our way to listen to businessmen talk about how difficult certain things are for them—the policymakers nod and say, 'Right. . .right. . . .' Yet when a woman comes in and says, 'You know, I really need to be able to deduct my child care,' there's the big challenging voice: 'What are you coming to us with *that* for?'

"Finally, there's the feeling that single-parent families are not worthy of the help because they're 'different.' Well, I applaud the diversity of families in this country, which, let's remember, gets its *strength* from diversity. I think a family should be defined as 'wherever you go at night and they can't throw you out.' That haven—that place of protection and nurturance and loyalty: *That's* the foundation we're all building from, whether there are two parents or one."

"Traditional families are happier and more successful than single-parent or 'melded' homes."

Single-Parent Households Harm Children

Bryce Christensen

Single-parent households and other types of nontraditional families do not benefit children, Bryce Christensen contends in the following viewpoint. All attempts at creating nontraditional families have failed, Christensen maintains, proving that such families are ineffective. He believes that Americans should work to keep the traditional family intact. Christensen is the editor of *The Family in America,* a monthly publication of The Rockford Institute, a research institute in Rockford, Illinois.

As you read, consider the following questions:

1. What examples of unsuccessful nontraditional families does the author give?
2. What did Harvard sociologist Pitirim Sorokin predict about the future of families, according to the author?
3. Why does Christensen believe the traditional family benefits children?

Bryce Christensen, "Why the Family?" *The Family in America,* March 1987. Reprinted with permission of The Rockford Institute.

American marriage and birthrates stand at all-time lows, while divorce and illegitimacy have reached record highs. Nearly one-fourth of all American children under 18 now live with only one parent, compared with only 1 in 10 in 1960. "Public schools, hospitals, asylums, prisons, now stand in *place* of the family at many points," observes the Yale historian John Demos. Some commentators are beginning to wonder if we even *need* the family in the modern world. Some even cheer the decline of the family as an institution which has "subjugated women" and fostered "authoritarian personalities."

But the family has not yet joined the passenger pigeon and the Studebaker in the graveyard of history. In 1984, five million Americans did choose to get married, and we may reasonably hope that at least half will never seek a divorce. In 1984, 2.6 million legitimate children were born to two-parent homes. As of 1987, over 30 million Americans (including a disproportionate number of the nation's children) still live in "traditional" families, in which Dad goes to work while Mom stays home with the children. Even in homes where unprecedented economic pressures now require two incomes, millions of parents still manage to preserve a strong family life. The descriptive anthropologist interested in the intact, healthy family would not lack for specimens in contemporary America.

And after all of the heated accusations *against* the family have been reduced to their factual inaccuracies and ideological distortions, a great deal remains to be said in *favor* of mankind's oldest institution. Nearly 100 years before Christ, Cicero praised the family as "the first society" and "the seed-bed of the state." Three centuries earlier, Aristotle wrote of "the family [as] the association established by nature for the supply of men's everyday wants." The very antiquity of the family should give us pause before we set it aside. . . .

The Failed Alternatives

But neither its antiquity nor its ubiquity will convince everyone that the family ought to be retained in modern America. After all, don't Americans make progress by trying the new and the different? Whether we like to admit it or not, all previous experimental alternatives to the family have failed miserably, usually with painful consequences for all involved. Modern Israel made a concerted effort within its *Kibbutzim* to take child care away from the individual family and to turn the task over to specialists. Eventually, *Kibbutzim* authorities gave up the initiative because of strong protests and allowed individual families to return to a largely traditional pattern. As Boris Stern reported 20 years ago in *The Kibbutz That Was*: "The role of women in the *Kibbutz* has practically completed a cycle of revolutionary changes. Now, instead of working side by side with their men in the fields. . .the women have return[ed] to their old domain of looking after children and performing other household services."

Marriages & Divorces: 1960 to 1984

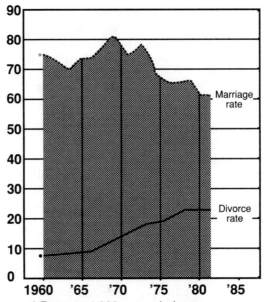

* Rate per 1,000 unmarried women.
• Rate per 1,000 married women.

National Center for Health Statistics, 1987.

Just as unsuccessful were attempts in the United States during the late 1960's and early 1970's to replace the traditional family with "open marriages" and countercultural communes. The authors of a tremendously popular book on "open marriage" in the 1970's eventually came "to admit that their open marriage concept ha[d] led to divorce in every couple they personally knew who followed the guidelines prescribed in their book." Historian Joseph Conlin offers no more favorable assessment of life in the New Age communes of the 1960's and 1970's, calling them "garbage dumps" and "hells": "children smeared in their own filth for days, hysterical under the LSD given to pacify them. . . venereal infection, pneumonia, influenza, and the unprimitive affliction of hepatitis reached disastrous proportions."

Nor have more recent feminist attempts to find fulfillment outside the family lived up to their promise. In her book, *The Cost of Loving*, Megan Marshall found that many young women who lived out the feminist agenda in the 1970's now wish they had married and borne children instead. "Every day I wake up alone and ask myself, What kind of acid did I take to choose a life like this?" said one postfeminist woman interviewed by Marshall. Even the leading feminist, Betty Friedan, now says, "I think we must at last admit and begin openly to discuss feminist denial of the importance of family, of women's own needs to give and get love and nurture, tender loving care."

Studies have also exploded the feminist myth of the strong, self-sufficient "female-headed family": "In 1983 over 40 percent of all female-headed families were below the poverty level ($10,178 for a family of four), and many more of these families were living marginally close to it." Work done by Lenore Weitzman has also shown that the "no-fault" divorce laws passed in the 1970's have had the unintended consequence of impoverishing millions of women and children, as millions of men found it only too easy to abandon their wives and children. According to Weitzman, "Divorced women and the minor children in their households experience a 73 percent decline in their standards of living in the first year after divorce.". . .

Changes in Family Structure

Events are sadly fulfilling the gloomy prediction of Harvard sociologist Pitirim Sorokin back in 1941. Sorokin anticipated a future in which "divorces and separations will continue to increase" and "children will be separated earlier and earlier from parents." These changes in family structure would be accompanied by "suicide, mental disease, and crime. . . . Weariness will spread over larger and larger numbers of the population." True, some children do survive the trauma of divorce remarkably unscathed, and millions of conscientious mothers still find ways to meet their children's needs even if economic pressures force them to work outside the home. But it seems unlikely that many children will ever count their parents' divorce as a blessing or that any outstanding American statesman will ever declare: "All that I am or ever hope to be, I owe to my angel day-care supervisor."

In contrast to the failed experiments of "no-fault" divorce and no-parent child-rearing, the traditional family deserves defense because it works. Social philosopher Michael Novak calls the family "the only department of health, education, and welfare that works." "We have all counted upon the family for 1,000 years, during many eras when no other institution worked, not the state, not the church, not the educational institutions, nothing," observes Novak. "The only thing that worked and made survival possible was the family."

According to Blanche Bernstein's 1982 book *The Politics of Welfare*, less than 1 percent of those receiving public assistance in New York City live in intact families. And far from *exposing* children to abuse, the intact family actually shields children from mistreatment: Studies show that child abuse occurs far more frequently in one-parent and "melded" homes than in intact families. Rita Kramer argues that "only in a stable family with strong and affectionate parents does a child grow up with the sense of being protected in a world that makes sense. Such a beginning provides the basis for the flexibility of response that will help him learn and overcome difficulties in later life.". . .

We [have] a set of core convictions: that marriage and family life are good and are rooted in both the natural and the supernatural order; that divorce and illegitimacy are tragic and destructive; that, in general, parents can administer to their own children's emotional and spiritual needs better than can credentialed strangers; that most traditional families are happier and more successful than single-parent or "melded" homes.

Distinguishing Between Fact and Opinion

This activity is designed to help develop the basic reading and thinking skill of distinguishing between fact and opinion. Consider the following statement: "Nearly one-fourth of all American children under eighteen now live with only one parent." This statement is a fact which could be verified by checking an almanac or another source of government demographic statistics. But the statement, "Traditional families are happier and more successful than single-parent homes" is clearly an opinion. Not everyone would agree that all traditional families are happy, or that all single-parent families are unhappy.

When investigating controversial issues it is important that one be able to distinguish between statements of fact and statements of opinion. It is also important to recognize that not all statements of fact are true. They may appear to be true, but some are based on inaccurate or false information. For this activity, however, we are concerned with understanding the difference between those statements which appear to be factual and those which appear to be based primarily on opinion.

Most of the following statements are taken from the viewpoints in this chapter. Consider each statement carefully. *Mark O for any statement you believe is an opinion or interpretation of facts. Mark F for any statement you believe is a fact. Mark I for any statement you believe is impossible to judge.*

If you are doing this activity as a member of a class or group, compare your answers with those of other class or group members. Be able to defend your answers. You may discover that others come to different conclusions than you do. Listening to the reasons others present for their answers may give you valuable insights in distinguishing between fact and opinion.

> O = *opinion*
> F = *fact*
> I = *impossible to judge*

1. More than thirty million Americans live in traditional homes.

2. Good day care can be beneficial.

3. Paid child-rearing is rarely more than a weak stand-in for parental care.

4. Through history many patterns of child care have reflected the living patterns of Americans.

5. Lower fertility has meant that children have fewer siblings.

6. Despite all the peer pressure on young women to become career-primary just like men, that's not what the majority of women want.

7. Single-mother families are as successful as two-parent families.

8. The number of children living with stepparents has increased as a result of divorce and remarriage.

9. Families led by single parents make up more than one-quarter of all U.S. families.

10. Children of working mothers are just as emotionally secure as children of mothers who are not employed.

11. Studies have exploded the feminist myth of the strong, self-sufficient female-headed family.

12. Cicero praised the family as "the first society" and "the seed-bed of the state."

13. Employed mothers are less restrictive with their children.

14. The single-parent family is warm and close.

15. There is a growing conviction that modern parents need more help from society in bringing up the next generation of Americans.

16. Kinder-Care has enrolled more than a million children.

17. Day care adds a significant level of stress and conflict to the all-important infant-mother-father relationship.

18. The mass surrender of child-rearing responsibilities marks a profound change in human history.

19. Fewer than 10 percent of Americans live in traditional, male-headed, one-income households.

20. Women who lived out the feminist agenda in the 1970s now wish they had married and borne children instead.

Periodical Bibliography

The following articles have been selected to supplement the diverse views presented in this chapter.

Deborah Edler Brown and Michele Donley	"The Great Experiment," *Time*, special issue, Fall 1990.
Leslie Dreyfous	"Mom's First Day Back on the Job," *Los Angeles Times*, November 22, 1990.
Dianne Feeley	"Child Care: Unfinished Agenda," *Against the Current*, May/June 1990. Available from 7012 Michigan Ave., Detroit, MI 48210.
Thelma Jean Goodrich, Cheryl Rampage, and Barbara Ellman	"The Single Mother," *The Family Therapy Networker*, October 1989.
Susan Hartman	"Single Mothers: Making It Their Way," *The New York Times*, January 12, 1989.
Dyan Machan	"The Mommy and Daddy Track," *Forbes*, April 16, 1990.
Connaught C. Marshner	"What Social Conservatives Realize," *National Review*, September 2, 1988.
Daniel Patrick Moynihan	"Families Falling Apart," *Society*, July/August 1990.
Nancy Pearcey	"The American Mother: Balancing Career and Family," *Current*, November 1990.
New Dimensions	Special section on day care, November 1990.
New Perspectives Quarterly	"Prodigal Parents: Family vs. the Eighty-Hour Work Week," Winter 1990.
Newsweek	"The New Teens: What Makes Them Different," special edition, Summer/Fall 1990.
Carl Rowan	"Day Care Need Is Here to Stay, So Let's Deal with It," *Liberal Opinion*, October 1, 1990. Available from PO Box 468, Vinton, IA 52349.
Phyllis Schlafly	"The Family: Preserving America's Future," *The Phyllis Schlafly Report*, February 1988. Available from The Eagle Trust Fund, Box 618, Alton, IL 62002.
Jill Smolowe	"Last Call for Motherhood," *Time*, special issue, Fall 1990.
The World & I	"Parenting: Today's Complex Challenges," special feature, September 1989.
The World & I	"Symposium: The Family—A Search for Norms," special section, November 1990.

Organizations to Contact

The editors have compiled the following list of organizations that are concerned with the issues debated in this book. All of them have publications or information available for interested readers. The descriptions are derived from materials provided by the organizations. This list was compiled upon the date of publication. Names and phone numbers of organizations are subject to change.

Child Care Action Campaign (CCAC)
330 Seventh Ave., 18th Floor
New York, NY 10001
(212) 239-0138

CCAC supports working parents and children in day care. It publishes a bimonthly *The Child Care Action News*.

Children's Defense Fund (CDF)
122 C St. NW
Washington, DC 20001
(202) 628-8787

The CDF works to promote the interests of children, especially the needs of poor, minority, and handicapped children. The Fund supports government funding of education policies and health care policies that benefit children. In addition to its monthly newsletter, *CDF Reports*, the Fund publishes many books, articles, and pamphlets promoting children's interests.

The Children's Foundation
725 15th St. NW, Suite 505
Washington, DC 20005
(202) 347-3300

The Children's Foundation is a national nonprofit organization established in 1969 to promote policies that benefit children and families. The Foundation works to increase federal assistance to children and to provide affordable health and day care for children. Its publications include the quarterly *Family Day Care Bulletin* and directories and papers on child care.

Clearinghouse on Child Abuse and Neglect Information
The Circle, Inc.
8201 Greensboro Dr., Suite 600
McLean, VA 22101
(703) 821-2086

The goal of the Clearinghouse is to educate the public about child abuse and neglect. It maintains a database of documents, audiovisual materials, service programs, statutes, research projects, and other sources of information on child abuse.

Eagle Forum
PO Box 618
Alton, IL 62002
(618) 462-5415

Eagle Forum is dedicated to preserving traditional family values. It believes mothers should stay home with their children, and it favors policies that support the traditional family and reduce government intervention in family issues. The Forum publishes the monthly *Phyllis Schlafly Report*.

Elementary School Center (ESC)
2 E. 103rd St.
New York, NY 10029
(212) 289-5929

ESC is a national research center committed to elementary and middle-level schools and their students, families, and personnel. ESC believes that schools can become centers of social change to benefit children. It publishes the newsletter *Focus* and provides information to the public.

Focus on the Family
Pomona, CA 91799
(714) 620-8500

Focus on the Family believes the family is the most important social unit. It believes that poverty, teen pregnancy, and drug abuse are linked to the dissolution of families in the U.S. This group maintains that reestablishing the traditional two-parent family will end many social problems. In addition to conducting research and education programs, Focus on the Family publishes *Focus on the Family Citizen*, *Clubhouse*, *Breakaway*, *Family Policy*, and *Research Developments*.

The Heritage Foundation
214 Massachusetts Ave. NE
Washington, DC 20002
(202) 546-4400

The Heritage Foundation is a public-policy research institute that supports limited government and the free-market system. The Foundation opposes government-funded day care and believes the private sector, not government, should be relied upon to ease social problems such as childhood poverty, poor education, and inadequate health care. The Foundation publishes the quarterly journal *Policy Review* as well as hundreds of monographs, books, and papers on public policy issues.

National Center for Education in Maternal and Child Health
38th and R Streets NW
Washington, DC 20057
(202) 625-8400

The Center is a private organization that provides information and educational services to agencies, professionals, and members of the public interested in the health of mothers and children. The organization provides resource guides listing publications and other sources of information. In addition to its annual *Abstracts of Active Projects*, the Center publishes many directories, bibliographies, bulletins, and monographs.

National Center for Missing & Exploited Children
2101 Wilson Blvd., Suite 550
Arlington, VA 22201
(703) 235-3900

The Center is a nonprofit organization that serves as a clearinghouse for information on missing and exploited children. The Center publishes pamphlets such as *Just in Case . . . Parental Guidelines in Case Your Child Might Someday Be Missing*, that provide information on how to prevent child abuse and abduction and what to do if abuse should occur.

National Committee for Citizens in Education (NCCE)
10840 Little Patuxent Parkway, Suite 301
Columbia, MD 21044-3199
(301) 997-9300

NCCE is a nonprofit organization dedicated to improving the quality of public schools through increased public involvement. The Committee believes that public schools are the best way to educate America's children, and it works to make parents and the general public more involved in education. NCCE publishes handbooks, the newspaper *Network*, and other resources on educational issues.

National Committee for Prevention of Child Abuse
332 Michigan Ave., Suite 1600
Chicago, IL 60604-4357
(312) 663-3520

The Committee seeks to increase public awareness of the incidence, origins, nature, and effects of child abuse. It promotes discussion on policies, activities, and research that can help prevent child abuse, and serves as a liaison between other child welfare organizations. Publications by the Committee include *Monthly Memorandum* and monographs, research reports, and pamphlets.

National Council on Family Relations
3989 Central Ave. NE, Suite 550
Minneapolis, MN 55421
(612) 781-9331

The Council is a nonprofit organization of professionals who research family issues such as education, social work, psychology, sociology, home economics, anthropology, and health care. It publishes the quarterly journals *Journal of Marriage and the Family* and *Family Relations*.

Pediatric AIDS Coalition (PAC)
1331 Pennsylvania Ave. NW, Suite 721-N
Washington, DC 20004
(800) 336-5475

PAC is an organization of health groups that works to advance AIDS research, treatment, and education, with a primary focus on children with AIDS. PAC provides reports, brochures, and information packets to the public.

Planned Parenthood Federation of America
810 Seventh Ave.
New York, NY 10019
(212) 541-7800

Planned Parenthood is a national organization that promotes family planning by educating the public in methods of contraception. Its many activities include sponsoring research in contraception and reproduction, developing education programs, and providing counseling. Planned Parenthood publishes an annual report as well as pamphlets such as *Teen Sex: It's OK to Say No, Facts About Birth Control,* and *How to Talk to Your Child About AIDS.*

Rockford Institute
934 N. Main St.
Rockford, IL 61103-7061
(815) 964-5053

The Institute works to return America to Judeo-Christian values and supports traditional roles for men and women. It maintains that mothers who work or place their children in day care harm their children. The Institute publishes the newsletter *Main Street Memorandum* and the monthly periodical *The Family in America.*

Single Mothers by Choice
PO Box 1642
Gracie Square Station
New York, NY 10028
(212) 988-0993

Single Mothers by Choice is a national nonprofit organization that provides support and information to single women who are or are considering becoming mothers. The organization also conducts research and works with the media to promote the issues facing single mothers. Single Mothers by Choice publishes a quarterly newsletter and provides a resource information packet and a literature packet of articles about single motherhood.

U.S. Department of Health and Human Services
Office of Human Development Services
Administration for Children, Youth, and Families
200 Independence Ave. SW
Washington, DC 20201
(202) 245-0347

The Administration for Children, Youth, and Families manages many government programs that affect children and families. Write for information and a list of publications.

Victims of Child Abuse Laws (VOCAL)
PO Box 17306
Colorado Springs, CO 80935
(800) 84-VOCAL

This support group offers advice and help for parents and others who feel they have unjustly suffered under existing child abuse laws. VOCAL works to reform these laws and to promote the prosecution of filers of false child abuse reports. It works to educate the community by providing relevant information on child abuse and victimization issues.

Bibliography of Books

Mortimer J. Adler	*Reforming Education.* New York: Macmillan Publishing Company, 1988.
Stanley Aronowitz and Henry A. Giroux	*Education Under Siege: The Conservative, Liberal, and Radical Debate over Schooling.* South Hadley, MA: Bergin & Garvey, 1985.
Prentice Baptiste Jr., Hersholt C. Waxman, Judith Walker de Felix, and James E. Anderson, eds.	*Leadership, Equity, and School Effectiveness.* Newbury Park, CA: Sage Publications, 1989.
Ann Bastian, Norm Fruchter, et al.	*Choosing Equality: The Case for Democratic Schooling.* Philadelphia: Temple University Press, 1986.
William Bennett	*Our Children and Our Country.* New York: Simon & Schuster, 1988.
Barbara J. Berg	*The Crisis of the Working Mother: Resolving the Conflict Between Family and Work.* New York: Summit Books, 1986.
Douglas J. Besharov, ed.	*Family Violence: Research and Public Policy.* Washington, DC: American Enterprise Institute, 1990.
Roger Betsworth	*Social Ethics: An Examination of American Moral Tradition.* Louisville, KY: Westminster/John Knox Press, 1990.
Frank G. Bolton, Larry Morris, and Ann E. MacEachron	*Males at Risk: The Other Side of Child Sexual Abuse.* Newbury Park, CA: Sage Publications, 1989.
T. Berry Brazelton	*Working and Caring.* Reading, MA: Addison-Wesley Publishing Company, 1985.
Andree Aelion Brooks	*Children of Fast-Track Parents.* New York: Viking Penguin, 1989.
Kevin Browne, Cliff Davies, and Peter Stratton, eds.	*Early Prediction and Prevention of Child Abuse.* New York: John Wiley & Sons, 1988.
Rachel Calam and Cristina Franchi	*Child Abuse and Its Consequences.* New York: Cambridge University Press, 1987.
Andrew J. Cherlin, ed.	*The Changing American Family and Public Policy.* Washington, DC: The Urban Institute Press, 1988.
Bryce Christensen	*Day Care: Child Psychology and Adult Economics.* Rockford, IL: Rockford Institute, 1989.
John E. Chubb and Terry M. Moe	*Politics, Markets, and America's Schools.* Washington, DC: The Brookings Institution, 1990.
John Crewdson	*By Silence Betrayed: Sexual Abuse of Children in America.* Boston: Little, Brown & Company, 1988.
Leon Dash	*When Children Want Children: The Urban Crisis of Teenage Childbearing.* New York: William Morrow, 1989.
Sanford M. Dornbusch and Myra H. Strober	*Feminism, Children, and the New Families.* New York: The Guilford Press, 1988.

Marian Wright Edelman	*Families in Peril: An Agenda for Social Change.* Cambridge, MA: Harvard University Press, 1987.
Marian Wright Edelman	*Portrait of Inequality: Black and White Children in America.* Washington, DC: Children's Defense Fund, 1980.
David Ellwood	*Poor Support: Poverty in the American Family.* New York: Basic Books, 1988.
Kathleen Coulborn Faller	*Understanding Child Sexual Maltreatment.* Newbury Park, CA: Sage Publications, 1990.
David Finkelhor, Gerald T. Hotaling, and Kersti Yllo	*Stopping Family Violence.* Newbury Park, CA: Sage Publications, 1988.
David Finkelhor and Linda Meyer Williams with Nanci Burns	*Nursery Crimes: Sexual Abuse in Day Care.* Newbury Park, CA: Sage Publications, 1988.
Richard J. Gelles and Claire Pedrick Cornell	*Intimate Violence in Families.* Newbury Park, CA: Sage Publications, 1990.
Neil Gilbert, Jill Duerr Berrick, Nicole Le Prohn, and Nina Nyman	*Protecting Young Children from Sexual Abuse: Does Preschool Training Work?* Lexington, MA: Lexington Books, 1988.
Beverly Gomes-Schwartz, Jonathan M. Horowitz, and Albert P. Cardarelli	*Child Sexual Abuse: The Initital Effects.* Newbury Park, CA: Sage Publications, 1990.
Paula S. Fass	*Outside In: Minorities and the Transformation of American Education.* New York: Oxford University Press, 1989.
Amy Gutman	*Democratic Education.* Princeton, NJ: Princeton University Press, 1987.
Timothy J. Iverson and Marilyn Segal	*Child Abuse and Neglect: An Information and Reference Guide.* New York: Garland Publishing, 1990.
Michael B. Katz	*Reconstructing American Education.* Cambridge, MA: Harvard University Press, 1987.
David T. Kearns and Denis P. Doyle	*Winning the Brain Race: A Bold Plan to Make Our Schools Competitive.* San Francisco: ICS Press, 1988.
David W. Kirkpatrick	*Choice in Schooling: A Case for Tuition Vouchers.* Chicago: Loyola University Press, 1990.
Loretta M. Kopelman and John C. Moskop	*Children and Health Care: Moral and Social Issues.* Norwell, MA: Kluwer Academic Publishers, 1989.
Jonathan Kozol	*Rachel and Her Children: Homeless Families in America.* New York: Crown Publishers, 1988.
Jean La Fontaine	*Child Sexual Abuse.* Cambridge, MA: Basil Blackwell, 1990.
Marsha Levine and Roberta Trachtman, eds.	*American Business and the Public School.* New York: Teachers College Press, Columbia University, 1988.
Sar A. Levitan, Richard S. Belous, and Frank Gallo	*What's Happening to the American Family?* Baltimore: The Johns Hopkins University Press, 1988.

James Lewis Jr.	*Achieving Excellence in Our Schools . . . by Taking Lessons from America's Best-Run Companies.* Westbury, NY: J.L. Wilkerson Publishing Company, 1986.
Myron Lieberman	*Privatization and Educational Choice.* New York: St. Martin's Press, 1989.
Frank J. Macciarola and Alan Gartner, eds.	*Caring for America's Children.* New York: Academy of Political Science, 1989.
Kathleen McCoy	*Solo Parenting: Your Essential Guide.* New York: New American Library, 1987.
Peter Maher, ed.	*Child Abuse: The Educational Perspective.* Oxford: Basil Blackwell, 1987.
Jo Ann Miller and Susan Weissman	*The Parents' Guide to Daycare.* New York: Bantam Books, 1986.
Bob Mullen	*Are Mothers Really Necessary?* London: Boxtree Limited, 1987.
Charles Murray	*Losing Ground: American Social Policy, 1950-1980.* New York: Basic Books, 1984.
Ann Muscari and Wenda Wardell Morrone	*Child Care That Works: How Families Can Share Their Lives with Child Care and Thrive.* New York: Doubleday, 1989.
Joe Nathan, ed.	*Public Schools by Choice: Expanding Opportunities for Parents, Students, and Teachers.* St. Paul, MN: The Institute for Learning and Teaching, 1989.
Michael Novak	*The New Consensus on Family and Welfare: A Community of Self-Reliance.* Washington, DC: American Enterprise Institute, 1987.
Lisbeth Schorr with Daniel Schorr	*Within Our Reach: Breaking the Cycle of Disadvantage.* New York: Anchor/Doubleday, 1988.
Lucy Scott and Meredith Joan Angwin	*Time Out for Motherhood.* New York: St. Martin's Press, 1986.
Leonard Shengold	*Soul Murder: The Effects of Childhood Abuse and Deprivation.* New Haven, CT: Yale University Press, 1989.
Anita Shreve	*Remaking Motherhood: How Working Mothers Are Shaping Our Children's Future.* New York: Viking, 1987.
Ruth Sidel	*Women and Children Last: The Plight of Poor Women in Affluent America.* New York: Penguin Books, 1986.
Diana T. Slaughter, ed.	*Black Children and Poverty: A Developmental Perspective.* San Francisco: Jossey-Bass, 1988.
Joel Spring	*The American School, 1642-1985.* White Plains, NY: Longman, 1986.
George Thorman	*Day Care . . . An Emerging Crisis.* Springfield, IL: Charles C. Thomas, 1989.
Gail Elizabeth Wyatt and Gloria Johnson Powell, eds.	*Lasting Effects of Child Sexual Abuse.* Newbury Park, CA: Sage Publications, 1988.
Michael W. Yogman and T. Berry Brazelton	*In Support of Families.* Cambridge, MA: Harvard University Press, 1986.
William Julius Wilson	*The Truly Disadvantaged: The Inner City, the Underclass, and Public Policy.* Chicago: University of Chicago Press, 1987.

Index

259

263

Please remember that this is a library book,
and that it belongs only temporarily to each
person who uses it. Be considerate. Do
not write in this, or any, library book.

DATE DUE

MY 14 '91			
DE 07 '91			
5-9-96			
JUL 05			
5/24/97			
DC 3 1 '05			
NO 08 '06			